LITERATURE AND FILM
AS MODERN MYTH

LITERATURE AND FILM
AS MODERN MYTHOLOGY

William K. Ferrell

Westport, Connecticut
London

Library of Congress Cataloging-in-Publication Data

Ferrell, William K., 1930–
    Literature and film as modern mythology / William K. Ferrell.
        p.   cm.
    Filmography: p.
    Includes bibliographical references and index.
    ISBN 0–275–96757–3 (alk. paper).—ISBN 0–275–96813–8 (pbk. :
alk. paper)
    1. Myth in motion pictures.   2. Mythology in motion pictures.
3. Myth in literature.   4. Mythology in literature.   I. Title.
PN1995.3.F47   2000
791.43'615—dc21   99–36018

British Library Cataloguing in Publication Data is available.

Library of Congress Catalog Card Number: 99–36018
ISBN: 0–275–96757–3
        0–275–96813–8 (pbk.)

First published in 2000

Praeger Publishers, 88 Post Road West, Westport, CT 06881
An imprint of Greenwood Publishing Group, Inc.
www.praeger.com

Printed in the United States of America

The paper used in this book complies with the
Permanent Paper Standard issued by the National
Information Standards Organization (Z39.48–1984).

10 9 8 7 6 5 4 3 2 1

Contents

PART I
THE JOURNEY BEGINS

Chapter 1

In the Beginning

Myth comes from the French language, which took the word from the Latin root *mythus*, derived from the Greek word *muthos*, and is defined in all three languages as a narrative, a fable, or a myth (Partridge 424). *Webster's New Collegiate Dictionary* defines myth as "1: A traditional story of ostensibly historical events that serves to unfold part of the world view of a people or explain a practice, belief, or natural phenomenon. 2: parable, allegory. 3 a: a person or thing having only an imaginary or unverifiable existence, b: an ill-founded belief held uncritically especially by an interested group. 4: the whole body of myths" (755).

Mythology books, depending on the background, belief system, or approach of the writer, will vary the definition using one or more of the following perspectives: myths are (1) a fanciful and entertaining verbalization of tribal superstition; (2) the literal translation of a ritual or the creative story enabling a ritual; (3) the transcendental creation of a primordial archetype by the subconscious mind; or (4) a poetic/metaphoric explanation of an objective reality. This diversity in application stems from the variety of disciplines that study myth. Anthropologists, paleontologists, mythologists, historians, theologians, archaeologists, psychologists, and literary scholars all have an interest in the study of myths.

One fact upon which all agree on is that ancient Sumerians developed written language around 3000 B.C.E. and left some of their myths, which date from at least 2500 B.C.E. These myths are known as the Enuma Elish, or "The Epic of Gilgamesh." It is also known that long before the time of written language, in dark caves and around tribal fires, primitive people plotted and celebrated their hopes and fears in their oral stories, pictures, and symbols. One such inference may be made from a cave painting found at Lascaux, France, and dated around 30,000 years ago, in which there is a representation of a bison disemboweled by a rhinoceros. Between the two animals lies the stick figure of a man, all of the elements necessary for a narrative plot (Brockway 29). At some point between 30,000 and 3000 B.C.E., humans, in response to their spiritual nature, added a metaphysical dimension to the stories they created. It is at that point that narrative became meaningful in an abstract sense—an attempt to unite the spiritual dimension with the physical.

Humans are physical beings and, as we all know, spiritual beings. Humans know they exist and are able consciously to assess their world simultaneously in past, present, and future tense. In performing this action, one must make contact with the world of abstraction, universally known as the metaphysical—those things we know to exist but cannot actually see, hear, touch, taste, or smell. They can be known only through our innate ability to think intuitively. It is our intuition, a conceptual ability to obtain knowledge without a rationally conscious action, that causes us to know there is something that exists that is not physically present. It is this innate cognitive ability that makes us spiritual beings.

Generally, when one thinks of spirituality, the first thing coming to mind is religion. Instead, think of religion as only one way in which one conscious human being may use his or her intuitive ability. However, before a spiritual dimension can be defined, a means must be developed within the conscious mind that will communicate it in a manner by which it may be understood. In simple language, a device must be created that will translate the abstraction into a comprehensible form. Religion, using metaphors, parables, and "divinely inspired scripture," is one way; science has another way—the discovery of theories and laws in physics and chemistry regarding the behavior of matter; somewhere between the two comes the literary form of a metaphoric myth. In form, a myth is a story one person conceptualizes in order to reveal a specific relationship to a reality he or she knows exists but cannot define or locate objectively. From early human history into the nineteenth century, mythology, or metaphoric explanations, functioned as a source for both scientific and religious explanations in most cultures. The myth form function is to communicate an understanding about the world.

At a point in history, humans realized that effects have causes. They understood that in order for a plant to grow, it must have water. Therefore, water causes plants to grow. This simple understanding allowed early humans to develop an agrarian culture, moving away from nomadic hunting and gathering and into communal societies. But when an effect was experienced and the cause was beyond understanding, humans sought an explanation by using their intuitive ability to devise a cause. In order to place the explanation in comprehensible form, they conceived a story that would explain the cause, at least for the moment. As knowledge increased and was more accurately understood, the story became modified or perhaps even discarded as it was replaced by new knowledge.

The origin of the universe is an example of this process. There are many metaphorical explanations for the origin prior to modern scientific discoveries, which at the time of their creation presented a rational cause-and-effect syndrome. Today, most scientists accept the big bang as a rational scientific explanation for the universe. However, although humans are able to explain scientifically how the universe began, they cannot seem to agree on a *why*. It is the *why* that continues to perplex humanity. And, interestingly enough, science seems unable to deal with the question—which is why religion and its parent, or to some its illegitimate child, myth, continue to exist and thrive within all cultures. With all of our knowledge, there are just some things in life that continue to confound us. For example, why do some of us, living in a modern setting, continue to cause harm to others deliberately? Is there a universal code of morality? We continually hear from our politicians the term *family values*. What are those? If they exist, from whence did they come? Who decides what values are the right ones, and upon what authority? How does one balance individuality and human relationships? How much is a life worth? Is there a way life *ought* to be lived?

These, then, are just some of the many and complex questions that writers of myth continue to discuss. Myths are not merely fanciful stories told to entertain children at bedtime. They are stories that attempt to provide an understanding of the real world at the time they are conceived. Today, just as the Greek poet Hesiod and the writers of the ancient poetic Hindu text the *Rig-Veda*, once did, contemporary authors attempt to craft stories that will provide insight into how we should live. They either provide us a positive model or models to follow, a "knight in shining armor," or the negative, showing us what can happen if we do not follow the right path. What is interesting to note is that many of the same circumstances Hesiod wrote about in his poetry are still with us. We have never solved the problem of evil nor are we able to define clearly those "values" we all should possess. Modern writers may approach the problem romantically, realistically, or naturalistically, but they do approach it, time and time again, and just like those ancient stories, the ones we find most enlightening become a part of our lore, our mythology. Others fall by the wayside and are never heard from again. What remains will be "discovered" by future generations and will be the means by which our society is historically evaluated.

It is not really very complicated. We will take some of the popular stories of our time—stories told, first in literary form and again told, only this time to be acted out using pictures and sound. The stories are new, but the form is ancient. Each story is connected to other stories going back in time as far as one can go. Just as life is a continuum, so are the problems and solutions of life. However, before we get into the stories themselves, we need a little background on myths. Keep in mind that in each myth, form and content coexist. The form or plot will follow to a varying degree the same form the ancients used. An example might be to look at what happens to the western hero, a popular icon of America's past. In the 1930s, 1940s, and 1950s, a popular myth form was the gunfighter with a good heart. This was the man—John Wayne (*Stagecoach*, 1939), Alan Ladd (*Shane*, 1953), Yul Brynner (*The Magnificent Seven*, 1960), Gary Cooper (*High Noon*, 1952), or someone else—who used his courage and skill with a gun to save innocent citizens from the clutches of a clearly defined and evil antagonist. The hero does not act for personal gain, but follows a code—an abstract belief there does exist a "right way." In most stories he both overcomes the villain and in the process restores the rule of law. Shift forward twenty years and we have Rambo (*First Blood*, 1982), a Green Beret, left over from the war in Vietnam, who enters a community that appears quiet and peaceful. Rambo runs afoul of the law and is brutally beaten. He escapes and in the violent aftermath that follows destroys most of the town. In the earlier story, the villain was a man who has chosen evil over good and must be destroyed. In the later version, Rambo is a victim of a duly elected authority and in triumphing unfortunately destroys the innocent along with the guilty. To take the form a bit further into the future, consider Clint Eastwood's film *Unforgiven* (1992). All of these stories are reflections of the culture that created them. Somewhere between 1950 and 1980, the protagonist and antagonists change, although the hero form did not. In each case, a stranger enters into a community and rights a wrong. Each story tells us about the values of the culture at that moment in time in which the story was written. In the 1950s the antagonist was simply a man with an evil nature who exerts illegal power over innocent victims. In the 1980s, that antagonism is more likely to be a misuse of authority and, too, the protagonist does not always act because it is the right thing to do. The hero's motives are much more personal rather than a belief in an abstract concept of what is right and wrong. In many contemporary novels and films, it is the authority that has abused its power and must be destroyed. Interestingly, the audience is not informed what power will fill the vacuum left by the destruction of the abusive authority. In modern stories, there is a subtle rejection that a real pattern for living—a sense of how one ought to live—exists; or if a pattern does exist, it is beyond the scope of people to know it.

Hesiod's epic poetic narratives of Hercules and Prometheus tell us about the values of the Greek culture in the Hellenic period. Ernest Hemingway and John Steinbeck tell us about life's values and what it takes to be a hero in the 1930s, 1940s and 1950s. During this generation, it falls to authors such as Stephen King, Joseph Heller, Toni Morrison, and John Grisham to create the narratives that follow the mythological form and convey the values this generation considers important. By comparing the various versions, we can see what each culture advocates and, to some extent by comparing it to what is happening in the world, know why.

Every culture has its heroes and its villains, and those heroes become the living model for the myths the culture will inevitably produce, while its villains will tell us what that society sees as evil.

They [myths] form a fully organized pattern of ideas and behaviors which imposes itself more or less forcefully on the individuals inscribed in a society. Myth is above all obligatory in nature; it does not exist unless there is a sort of necessity to reach agreement on the themes that are its raw material and on the way these themes are patterned. (Bonnefoy 7)

Fundamentally, myths serve a specific purpose: to connect the physical, the known, with the abstract, the spiritual, the unknown. To conceive there is a pattern that tells us how one should live and why one should live in that manner presupposes that a pattern exists. Since we do not have that pattern in concrete form yet we know it does exist, it must exist as an abstraction. Whether you choose religion or science as the source, our intuition tells us it exists, and it is only through human intuition that we can know it.

The anthropologist, in studying primitive peoples, was the first scientist to identify the importance that myth has to a culture. One theory that explains what we can learn from these stories comes from Polish-British anthropologist Bronislaw Malinowski (1884–1942). In *Magic, Science, and Religion*, based on field studies in the Trobriand Islands, he stated that man "in myth, learns a new and strange art, the art of expressing, and that means organizing his most deeply rooted instincts, his hopes and fears" (98). The key words are *art*, *instincts*, and particularly *organizing*. Whatever is instinctive (intuitive) originates from a natural or intrinsic source, which for humans means it springs from within our own consciousness. In addition, a myth provides an understanding of the importance of conscious organizing as "an intimate connection exists between the word, the mythos, the sacred tales of a tribe on the one hand, and their ritual acts, their moral deeds, their social organization, and even their practical activities, on the other" (96). The most meaningful stories become animated as ritual and are passed from one generation to another through an oral tradition that will eventually evolve into written form. During this evolutionary process, the meaning of the ritual becomes a part of the individual groups' genetic makeup. What becomes reality is that myths, in their most basic form, are simply extensions of our human consciousness, being expressed as hopes and fears through the medium of art—what it means to be human.

It would seem logical that these early cultures, by bringing to the light their deepest and most profound thoughts, are fulfilling a need for themselves and their progeny. These ancient people's lives were governed not by some high political, social, or economic system; rather, their primary concern was survival. Yet each culture developed a cadre of artists to create their narratives. These artists, labeled *wizard, witch doctor, medicine man,* or *shaman,* possessed intellectual abilities that separated them from the rest. They possessed the ability to interpret intuitively how people should live and to some extent why. It was their job to interpret the metaphysical world and place the information into a comprehensible form, the myth stories.

We should not assume that all the stories from the myriad of cultures that have been preserved are profound, but it is not too difficult to separate those that are truly meaningful and thus assume archetypal status. Holman's *A Handbook to Literature* defines *archetype* as a literary form that "applies to an image, a descriptive detail, a plot pattern, or a character type that occurs frequently in literature, myth, religion, or folklore and is therefore believed to evoke profound emotions in the reader because it awakens a primordial image in his unconscious memory and thus calls into play illogical but strong responses" (40–41). Archetypal stories connect to each other and connect to us through the same instinctive nature that we, through our collective unconsciousness, share with those who originated them. "What psychology designates as archetype is really a particular, frequently occurring, formal aspect of instinct, and is just as much an *a priori* factor as the latter" (Jung *EJ* 236). Simply, we do not think about connecting to an archetype; we just do it.

By studying archetypal myths, we can learn what was important in both the culture and in individual lives—what they cared most about and what they feared. We know from the most ancient cave pictures and signs on cave walls. As oral language developed, the stories were organized into a more specific form, some being accompanied by ritual, as confirmed by pottery designs, beads, and other archaeological remnants. Following the acquisition of writing skills, the written narratives we know as myths were placed into a literary form, a linear narrative. Once the form was preserved in stone, papyrus, or clay; we can actually touch the original, giving us direct contact with the people from whom the stories emanate. (The order in which ancient cultures developed their mythology is the same order in which a modern child acquires knowledge.)

The study of these myths has taken some interesting twists over the years. Western myths prior to total domination by Christian culture during the Middle Ages were considered examples of pagan (non-Christian) religious beliefs. "From the point of view of any orthodoxy, myth might be defined simply as 'other people's religion,' to which an equivalent definition of religion would be 'misunderstood mythology' " (Campbell *IR* 55). (A "misunderstood religion" is identified by attaching the term *fable* to one story and *parable* to another when both follow the same basic form.) As Christianity advanced during the Middle Ages, those "other people's" religious myths not connected to the Judeo-Christian tradition were largely ignored as being irrelevant. Later, during the Western Renaissance, scientific enlightenment caused the Judeo-Christian beliefs to suffer somewhat the same problem they had bestowed on "pagan" religious stories. They too began to be questioned, only this time by scientists and philosophers. When that happened, the great myths of Greece, Rome, Sumeria, and the Celts were further denigrated, falling to the status of children's entertainment. To some extent, they are still considered children's literature, particularly by Hollywood and the cartoon industry. For example, critics note how Disney's 1996 animated version of *Hercules* is an overly exaggerated account of the original myth. However, by relying on his myth identity, Hercules continues to connect to audiences of all ages. Today, Hercules has his own television show, and, to be politically correct in our culture, the show about a male hero is balanced by his female counterpart, *Xena*.

During the late nineteenth and into the twentieth century, mainly through the study of myths by anthropologists and sociologists, a scholarly appreciation was given to those stories that connect all human culture together. This new era of study began in 1890 when Sir James George Frazer (1854–1941), a British classicist, published the first two volumes of what became a thirteen-volume study of primitive myths, *The Golden Bough*. The final volume was added in 1936. This study, which was developed in its entirety from literary sources, became the basis for a wide range of study into the subject. The overall thesis was to show the natural evolution of myths within a culture and how similar myths were developed within cultures that presumably were beyond direct contact. Frazer's work opened a dialogue that was developed through the works of America's Joseph Campbell (1904–87), a pure mythologist; Claude Lévi-Strauss (1908–), a French anthropologist and linguist; Bronislaw Malinowski (1884–1942), a Polish-English anthropologist noted for his field studies with a Polynesian group; German professor Ernst Cassirer (1874–1945), philosopher and historian; and Swiss psychologist Carl Jung (1885–1961), who is credited with establishing the archetype theory emanating from our collective unconscious. Each of these men approached the study of myth from a slightly different perspective. Their importance as a group comes from the impact they had in demonstrating the scope to which the study of mythology can be applied. Mythology is no longer a study of children's literature. It is now a viable means to understand human consciousness and the development of human culture.

It is now accepted that each culture, in its time, will develop its own version of these archetypal myths. For cultures today, the myths are certainly sophisticated and literate, having been produced by our most creative artists. While all art may connect in some manner to a mythological heritage, the medium that most closely relates to the general populace is found in literature.

In defining myth from a literary perspective, myths are stories that place into metaphoric form the profound thoughts of a culture. As poetic metaphor, myths harbor a deeper sense of truth not usually found in legends or folktales, which generally originate from a natural action, integrating in many stories, a sense of the supernatural with the natural. By stemming from a natural action or event, legends possess a historical base, while a myth assumes a more metaphysical orientation. In some cases, a mythological hero may be used as the example for an extraordinary act by a person within the culture. As a result of the action, a connection may be made conferring on the person attributes previously belonging to the myth.

For example, Western cultures have a tendency to give mythical status to members who perform legendary tasks. The romantic stories about the exploits of the real Texas Rangers, a small group of very efficient law enforcement officers during the late 1800s, grew into the legend of the Lone Ranger. A mythological connection does exist: the Lone Ranger becomes a masked "knight" who rides throughout the West saving the innocent from the clutches of evil villains. In this form, the character becomes associated with King Arthur's knights of the round table and the age of chivalry. The difference between the Lone Ranger legend and a cultural myth is that a metaphysical truth is not a concern or a criterion for the Lone Ranger's exploits. He is not searching for a holy grail and a meaning for human existence. For a story to reach mythical proportions, a myth must exist not as fact but as a metaphor for truth. For Malinowski, this means the story achieves myth status "when rite, ceremony, or a social or moral rule demands justification, a warrant of antiquity, reality, and sanctity" (107). When an act, a tradition, or a rule of conduct requires sanction by the culture and it, for whatever reason, remains outside the scope of legislation, the manner in which that rule is communicated is in a literary form—a novel, short story, poem, or motion picture—which in essence is a modern myth. The act, tradition, or rule of conduct is, in the judgment of the author, a fundamental truth. There is one abstract idea manifest by an appearance of the Lone Ranger. His successful actions do confirm that ultimately good will triumph over evil, a belief as old as the Bible and a very important American cultural truth.

An archetypal myth is, at the time of its creation, a truth—a truth not in a literal sense but in a metaphorical one. In essence, a myth is a story told and retold that conveys a sense of identity, who the group is in relation to other groups, explains how and why they came into being as a group, and defines and codifies their way of life. On a broader spectrum, according to Mircea Eliade, "myths narrate not only the origin of the world and all things in it, but also the primordial events which shaped man into what he is today—mortal, differentiated by sex, organized into a society, forced to work in order to live, and obliged to work in accordance with certain rules"

(Eliot 25). Rules, as codified by myth, apply from two perspectives. First, the group is subject to the laws of physics and nature; second, because humans possess a conscious will and are able to transcend nature, they require a set of oughts—a moral or ethical code.

Myths are not historical records or scientific explanations. They go to the spiritual core of a culture. The stories we know as archetypal myths are a product of an intuitive and creative mentality, providing a metaphysical insight into both the conscious and subconscious minds of the people and the cultures that create them. Lévi-Strauss explained that by studying myths, we "do not learn how men think in myths, but how myths think in men, unbeknown to them" (Hawkes 41). It would seem that myths come from an inner consciousness and "thus, the only true service of a proper artist [for our study, novelists and filmmakers] today will have to be to individuals, reattuning them to forgotten archetypes (Campbell *IR* 145). By comparing and contrasting our versions with previous forms, we can actually measure whether we are progressing forward or backward, or remaining static.

This book examines several modern versions of archetypal myths, first as a recurrent literary art form and then, a visual translation of the artist's narrative. The literature of mythology, in a formal sense as epic poetry and ancient drama, is studied as its own genre. However, since the word *myth* (with a small *m*) simply means a "traditional story," we will consider it to be the mode or device (in modern terms, the media) that presents the ideas a culture generates to express what it considers important. In simple terms, the myth is a vehicle—a device with a practical purpose. To justify, sanctify, and clarify those rules of conduct, we need to attain a better life both individually and for society in general. We study the myths of the Greek or Norse civilizations or the mysterious myths of the Orient in order to understand better the cultures and the people who produced them. For humans then and now, myths define who they are and what they consider important, individually and collectively.

Myths, then, are important to understanding a culture, wherever and whenever it existed. However, to study myths without some knowledge of the culture is meaningful only in a metaphysical sense. When knowledge of an ancient culture, gained through such activities as anthropological digs, is compared with its mythology, scholars begin to understand not only what these people held as their beliefs and values, but also why they held those beliefs. As a civilization moves in time, myths inform us about how and why those beliefs might have changed. Each group uses a myth, in pictures and stories, to record not only their presence but also what they chose as their most deeply held values. The narratives we read and the films we view provide insights into our own culture.

This process works as each culture adopts the archetype and recreates the basic story, adding those aspects of its culture that it deems important.

For example, most of us are familiar with the quest for the holy grail, if not from the tales of King Arthur, then from Monty Python's version. Fundamentally, the story concerns the mythical search for the cup that Christ drank from during the Last Supper. This search for a miraculous object is the Christian form of a Greek myth, Jason and the Golden Fleece, or any one of a thousand similar stories documented by Joseph Campbell in his best-known work, *The Hero with a Thousand Faces*. In those stories, a stranger, prince or pauper, enters into a quest whereby he or she must survive a series of challenges before being able to attain the object that will save a community under siege from some evil force, be it plague or dragon, and, like our own knights, the Lone Ranger or Zorro, save innocent victims. By performing a benevolent act, a hero not only connects to the quest but also incorporates into his or her actions those social or ethnic features of the culture as it exists during the time in which the new version of the story is created. The search for the holy grail provides a base for a study of *One Flew over the Cuckoo's Nest*.

Modern versions of recurrent mythological themes are found in libraries, bookstores, home bookshelves, and theaters and video stores. Literature, in the form of the novel, short story, poetry, drama, and motion picture, provides the cave wall on which the current storytellers represent and present the ideas of their most deeply rooted instincts, hopes, and fears. Ernst Cassirer, in "An Essay on Man," speculated that "the narratives being constructed during the late 19th and early 20th century are the stories from which future generations will construct *our* mythology. These then are our stories reflecting a narrative of *our* primeval reality. . . . A dramatic world— a world of actions, of forces, of conflicting powers" (77). Cassirer continued, "The real substratum of myth is not a substratum of thought but of feeling" (81). He surmised that art gave to people a "unity of intuition," connecting us to a spiritual or metaphysical consciousness, while science connects us to a more rational "unity of thought." The word *intuition* has a much deeper meaning for Cassirer than Americans may ordinarily infer. Intuition in this sense refers to a genetic component embedded within the brain of each individual that connects to the outside world as an unconscious reaction in the recognition of archetypes. It is only through religion, art, and/or myth that a culture or society expresses its spiritual or abstract being.

The stories that each organized culture creates can be categorized by plot similarities and recurrent themes. *Theme* is the focus or connection the story has to the beliefs of the people for whom the story was written. *Plot* means that the stories provide responses to similar conflicts that have concerned cultures throughout history and continue to concern us today. The two major mythopoeiac genres are stories relating to natural phenomena and those concerning a human quest for the ideal way to live. One natural phenomenon with which myths deal are stories relating to the origin of the earth and its abundant life. Early cosmological stories of creation are very closely allied to religion and "explain," in adherence to a culture's beliefs, how the culture's world and specific branch of humanity came into existence. These poetic narratives are a metaphorical explanation for their cosmological origins. This is an attempt by the culture to explain rationally what appears, at the time the myth is created, to be irrational—to comprehend a circumstance, event, or action for which, at a specific time and place, there is not a knowable natural explanation.

A most familiar story in our culture is Adam and Eve in the Garden of Eden, found in the Judeo-Christian Bible. The Babylonians tell a similar story: Tiamat, goddess of chaos, is defeated in battle by her son Marduk, who then establishes order, separating chaos into the earth and sky. The Greeks believed a war between the Titans, led by Uranus and Cronus, and the gods, led by Zeus, explains how their world began. Most cultures, East and West, have similar stories. What these stories have in common is how the world and humanity, possibly in a similar form as the evolution of communities and society, originate from chaos and war. It was their creator who establishes order for the earth and for their culture. Eastern cultures reject the idea of a violent origin believingly that Brahma, a spirit, exists eternally, independent of space and time. Brahma exists as sound—a reverberation (om) in harmony with the universe. Out of this sound, echoing through the emptiness of space, came wind and water, which combined to create mother earth (Purusha), who spawns all life.

All of the stories have a basis in truth. As modern physicists tell us, the earth was formed of matter that was at one time "without form and void" (Gen. 1:2). These ancients, both East and West, seemed to know intuitively this to be true.

Today science has supplied rational and natural answers that neither reject nor confirm a preternatural or supernatural origin. Whether we accept the answers as closure is a matter of choice. However, science has delivered answers that are justifiable using an orthodox method of proof. That means that the questions concerning creation are no longer considered unknowable; they have been logically answered. Almost everyone accepts the big bang theory and evolution of life. These theories are not metaphorical narratives. They are based on scientific calculation and method of proof and, as such, provide a rational answer to the questions concerning earth's natural history. Science does not engage in questions relevant to the existence of a spiritual dimension—a supernatural force or forces as a first cause. The effect on modern literature has been to remove any serious cosmological theme from modern myths.

A second major genre of mythopoeia explains and substantiates how life ought to be lived. This aspect of metaphoric narrative is a continuing source for literary plots and themes. Early cultures approach an individual's life as a journey or quest. They see a human not as a separate entity existing outside the environment but rather as an extension of nature. We are told, for example, that Adam is formed from the dust of mother earth and to that same dust he will return, eternally connecting humanity to the physical universe. In fact, all of earth's life forms are extensions of the physical world. An awareness of the physical motion of nature, the phases of the moon, the equinoctial movement of the sun, and the seasonal cycles in nature combine to convey a logical source for life as a journey or quest. It follows inductively that if nature conforms to a cycle of birth, dormancy (exile), death, and resurrection or rebirth, humans, as an integral part of nature, will follow the same order. Primitive humans, with the same logic they used in seeking their cosmological origins or connecting water and plant growth, believed that there must be a preternatural or supernatural force exercising some degree of control over life. Early cultures concluded there must be something out there—some kind of force acting to connect life and life's events together. The Melanesians have a word for this concept, *mana*.

Philip Wheelwright, in "Notes on Mythopoeia," explained "that mana may be, not just a fanciful (mythical) superstition of ignorant primitives, but something absolutely primal which (paraphrasing J. S. Mill) I may define functionally as *the permanent possibility of genuinely mythic experience*" (62). It would seem, according to Wheelwright, that we all possess this innate sense of equilibrium with nature as a "law of participation." Noted historian Arnold Toynbee expressed the same idea: "A human being is not simply a social animal: he is also a personality seeking a directing relation with an ultimate spiritual reality" (90). And psychologist C. G. Jung, in "The Relations between the Ego and the Unconscious," described *mana* as that part of our collective unconscious that connects us to a spiritual source (*EJ* 123). *Mana*, or intuition, is embedded within our unconscious mind and causes us to seek a metaphysical meaning for life.

In this sense, myth may be defined as the intuitive process by which humans attempt to understand the relationship between experience, conveyed to the brain through the senses, and conceptualization, the means of recording and making the experience meaningful. Recent studies on how the brain functions have led to some rather startling theories. Robert Ornstein, possibly America's best-known theorist regarding brain function, has reached a tentative conclusion: "It's not superfluous to consider that there is a right-[brain]hemisphere component of the religious and spiritual attempts at understanding" (103). An article in the *Arizona Republic* (29 Oct. 1997) reporting on a meeting of the Society for Neuroscience in New Orleans ventured that "the human brain may be hard-wired to hear the voice of heaven, in what researchers [from the University of California at San Diego] said was the first effort to directly address the neural basis of religious expression" (Hotz A6). The effect of such a belief establishes a direct connection between people and myth much more deeply than previously thought. It provides a "deepened framework for the meaning of life, and the meaning of one's life (Ornstein 165). It, in essence, establishes a physical basis for spiritual cognition. The effect is to place individuals as participants in life and simultaneously, because of consciousness, as able to view it somewhat objectively. An individual is both the first-person narrator of his or her life and at the same time is able to view it as a third-person observer. One part, the physical, is in synthesis with nature, and another part, the *mana*, our spiritual consciousness, is both intrigued and unfulfilled. What this confirms is an understanding that

the mythic mode of consciousness is a vision of reality [the spiritual dimension], and therefore also of men's place in reality [the physical dimension], in which the perceived presence and activity [those events that seem to defy explanation] of certain gods, super-human creatures, or cosmic forces, is accepted by a community as an adequate and satisfying perception of all the main events of the world as it is ordinarily experienced. (Falck 116)

This simply identifies a myth—or, a flurry of activity within the brain's right hemisphere—whether it be ancient or contemporary as simultaneously narrative and theme, concrete and abstract, real and metaphysical. As we accept the myth as the purveyor of truth about those unexplainable aspects of nature, it is a rather simple transformation to accept it as a base for truth about everything. What makes this a universal concept is that the basic theme or truth expressed by the myth remains the same no matter who tells the story or when the story is told. "Its substance [meaning] does not lie in its style, its original music, or its syntax, but in the story which it tells" (Lévi-Strauss *SA* 210). With consciousness comes a need, a motivation to seek understanding not only of one's self but of all the perceptions we receive in our consciousness awareness. It is important to recognize that the early versions of these stories are told not to advance knowledge but to satisfy a human need, to explain the nature of their existence, and to provide a conscious reason or purpose in that existence. Emanating from that purpose, an understanding is derived about how life ought to be lived. The culture and the artist, in creating a myth, look on their story not as objective reality but as a metaphoric reality or truth encoded in images drawn from the dream or spirit world.

The recognized cycles of physical human existence are universal. Humans journey through birth, puberty, initiation (adolescence), courtship, marriage, pregnancy, paternity, occupation, old age, and death. To call the stages of this journey a quest implies a goal—a search for something beyond the physical. It seems logical to assume there must be an end product. How we identify and relate to that product emerges from that spirituality (*mana*) embedded deeply within us. The presence of a metaphysical goal provides a basis for two physical rituals: one for preparation, the initiation factor, and, once a goal is attained, celebration as a birth or rebirth. Either circumstance provides a cause-and-effect relationship in nature and ritual.

Although ancient cultures originated stories and corresponding ceremonies for these stages, modern society continues many of the rituals in one form or another. This confirms that the existence of *mana* is as relevant for us today as it was for any primitive group. In fact, in our fast-moving technical world, the relevance of spirituality may be more important to our culture than it was to primitive ones. Ironically, because of increased scientific knowledge, industrialization, and urbanization, our perspective toward our relationship with nature and *mana* is not as close as in previous eras.

Because early civilizations believed nature and natures' forces (wind/air, water, the sun/fire, and earth) were provided by their creator (God) in establishing their culture, rule naturally becomes theocratic. Theocracies are able to coalesce the physical and spiritual dimensions as the creator or his earthly agents establish the rules for living. When God acts as the cause *and* effect, the meaning and way of life for which people search is easily defined. In Western culture the Ten Commandments provide an example of this evolution. These laws were theocratically established as directly given by God to Moses, who gave them to his people. The Ten Commandments are divided into two separate categories: four dealing with the human relationship to God (one God and form for worship) and six focusing on social relationships (Thou shalt not kill, covet, bear false witness, etc.) (Exod. 20:1–17). The religious authority—in this case Moses—administers all the rules, including those relating to social and ethical values. Those who violate one of the commandments are not only criminals but also sinners. Modern religious organizations take a somewhat different approach. In his most recent book *The Right Mind* (1997), Ornstein, in addition to establishing a physical base for *mana*, makes a connection between contemporary spiritual movements and nature:

Much of what the genuine spiritual traditions—Christian, Muslim, esoteric—really teach is more like a skill, or a knack, knowing where we are in life, knowing what our role is, when to do what, when to be angry, when to allow our emotions full flow, when to suppress, when to use different parts of the mind. A sense of where we are and what to do, an interest in a higher context, wisdom, or a framework for one's life basic to these traditions. (166)

While individual sects and denominations continue the tradition, the fact remains that just as science and religion separated regarding cosmology, political and social laws have also separated from religious doctrine. While the Constitution and laws of the United States incorporate into law some form of the six social commandments, the founders, particularly Thomas

Jefferson, chose to separate the first four that deal specifically with how people should worship.

Today we rely to a greater extent on natural and human forces to govern and sustain our physical lives, while simultaneously, as Wheelwright, Jung, Malinowski, Campbell, Toynbee, and Ornstein suggest, we possess a spiritual, albeit a moral, nature. It then becomes imperative that a practical means be developed to unify these two forces in humanity. Twentieth-century America is not a theocracy, and the government cannot impose itself as a moral authority, for we know, from many years of experience, that morality cannot be legislated. Therefore, a means of unification outside government or religion, since religious groups differ greatly in how they view morality, becomes a necessity. It is upon this imperative, art, in the form of literature and film, becomes a social force. This spiritual force (*mana*) within all humans demands that we create connection (stories), providing a bridge of truth between the physical and spiritual worlds. "It will not be surprising if a great deal of modern literature seems to be less concerned with experience itself and more concerned with the nature of experience . . . the defining objective of literature continues to be realism: its function is to express what it truly feels like to be alive" (Falck 160). To express this in more basic terms, a metaphysical concern identified within the society motivates an artist to create a story, poem, painting, sculpture, or musical composition that communicates the principle in comprehensible language. Ancient cultures, relying on the storyteller or shaman, constructed a ritual or ceremony that placed the myth in a visible or animated form. In today's world, the ritual or ceremony becomes a novel or film that by design informs the reader or viewer how one ought to live or how one ought not to live. For ancient cultures, this ritual or tradition began as myth; for Western cultures, during the eighteenth and nineteenth centuries, it became the novel; and for twentieth-century Americans, it became literature and film.

Why literature or film? From the Christianization of Rome (313) until the Renaissance (1500), the moral base in Western culture came from the stories, parables, and directions contained in the Bible. In the sixteenth century, an explosion of scientific knowledge, beginning with Copernicus's discovery that the earth was just one of several planets orbiting the sun, the Bible became challenged as a final authority. At that point, the novel, which began in the seventeenth century with Miguel de Cervantes' *Don Quixote* and reached its pinnacle in the English and Russian novels of the nineteenth century, slowly replaced the Bible as a guidebook. "As religion progressively ceases to provide the social 'cement,' affective values and basic mythologies by which a socially turbulent class society can be welded together, 'English' [literature] is constructed as a subject to carry this ideological burden from the Victorian period onwards" (Eagleton 24). Literature, in the form of novels and plays, became the mass media conveying social values and mores in language and action that any literate person could comprehend. In the continuing advance of technology throughout the twentieth century, film is joining literature in the quest to define and express life's rules. In reading fictional narrative and viewing films, children and adults become witnesses to a wide range of behaviors and cannot help but be affected by what they see, hear, or read. The types of behavior they perceive will range from the ideal, heroic, and good to the abominable and evil. This is not to imply, as some modern critics such as Michael Medved (*Hollywood vs. America*) suggest, that there is an indirect yet substantive cause-and-effect relationship in behavior and motion picture viewing. It is simply to acknowledge that behavior can be confirmed or rejected by what is seen on the movie screen or read in current literature, just as nineteenth-century citizens were affected by authors like Charles Dickens and Mark Twain. Readers of novels could learn what actions were acceptable by their society and those that were not. The novel "was an arena in which the most fundamental questions of human existence—what it meant to be a person, to engage in a significant relationship with others, to live from the vital centre of the most essential values—were thrown into vivid relief and made the object of the most intensive scrutiny" (Eagleton 31). Mark Twain, in his novels *The Adventures of Huckleberry Finn* and *Tom Sawyer*, tells us about coming of age in nineteenth-century mid-America just as J. D. Salinger (*Catcher in the Rye*) and John Knowles (*A Separate Peace*) do for the 1950s and 1960s. In the 1980s, we have Alice Walker's *The Color Purple* (film by Steven Spielberg) set in southern black culture and Stephen King's novella *The Body* (film *Stand by Me*, by Rob Reiner) about middle-class white children. All of these stories, by following the same basic form, convey what the culture holds as important. Readers are able to empathize and learn from the characters and at the same moment be entertained. All of these stories, whenever or wherever they are read, influence both adults and adolescents. For young people, they provide insight and substantiation for their feelings; for adults, a means of understanding another perspective. By examining the stories, we can learn about the culture at a moment in time.

Films and novels continue to provide, just as the stories of ancient Greece did for their children, a pattern for living. By focusing on the natural rites of passage from one stage of life to another, with all its relevant hopes, fears, aspirations, and values, an effective story will connect to our spiritual consciousness (*mana*). Simply stated, modern humans derive their way of life in much the same manner as a primitive society did. "Myth," represented in this century by novels and films, "fulfill[s] an indispensable function: it expresses, enhances, and codifies belief; it safeguards and enforces morality; it vouches for the efficiency of ritual and contains practical rules for the guidance of man" (Malinowski 101). For "art is necessary (1) as a counter to dogmatic belief, and (2) as a counter to the culture's prevailing technological mentality. In a more ontological or spiritual world, both of these needs would be less insistent" (Falck 169). Myth, in the form of novels and films, forms a natural opposition to the mechanization and secularization of contemporary society. More important, they allow us to view reality in a form we can understand. In addition to opening our own minds, novels and films open lines of communication through dialogue and discussion because they connect to our spiritual side by their restructuring of the mythological base. It has been theorized that one reason the Irish and British have produced some of the world's most talented authors is that the climate forces people to remain indoors and talk. Novels, and especially films, provide a source for open discussion among people of every stratum of society.

As we move into the twenty-first century, our nation becomes more and more secularized and less dependent on religious teachings. One testimony to the lasting effectiveness of myth is found in the ironic situation that secularization does not extinguish ritual; it merely alters the process. For example, religious rituals, such as weddings and initiation rites, were in our not-to-distant past formal church or synagogue ceremonies. Each is an important phase of our life cycle, and thus remains a very important part of our myth memory (*mana*). However, just as society's laws separated from the church, many of the formal rituals have become more social. Religion may have provided a base from which the recurrent rituals began, but now there is a widening gap in how society and religion depict and perform them. At one time in American society, it was accepted practice to be married in a church, or at the very least, with a minister presiding. Several Christian denominations would not recognize a marriage unless it was performed by clergy. Now it is common for couples, if they bother to marry at all, to head to Las Vegas, which advertises a drive-in window for solemnizing the marriage vows, or to a commercial wedding chapel, or to a judge or county Recorder, or in some cases to write and recite their own vows while leaping into space on a bungee cord. There is no question that weddings, as in the case of same-sex marriages, will continue to undergo more and more secularization. It is reasonable to surmise that if the marriage ritual was no longer important, there would not be so much argument about same-sex marriages. The fact remains, however, that marriage is becoming much more of a social and legal ritual than a religious one. Nevertheless, whatever manner or method, it remains a ritual, a continuance of a rite as old as society.

THE PROCESS

Novels and films provide insight into how authors and film directors choose to relate modern versions of age-old archetypes. They reflect how these artists express "our hopes and fears, our values and aspirations." By studying, analyzing, and criticizing, we gain a better understanding of who we are and how we got to be that way, and also learn about the media we use in recording it. These examples show how narratives are structured and, to some extent, how motion pictures are made.

We must become critical interpreters of both form and content in films and novels. The focus here is on a mythological or archetypal interpretation of the art forms: narrative literature and motion pictures. All literature—plays, short stories, novels, and motion pictures—is one genre of art. In simple terms, consider a novel or a motion picture as being a representation in concrete or objective form presenting, as content, an abstract truth, idea, or concept. The approach here is to focus on the central idea or theme. An artist uses structural forms to produce his or her content, ideas, and themes. If the content is not well communicated, a weak idea or, more probably, an ineffective use of one or more structural forms will be the problem. The medium—literature or motion picture—is an object made up of many constituent parts working together to present an idea. Beyond the form, the idea, in order to connect as *mana*, must present an archetypal truth, for it is in an expression of truth that we are able to perceive actual reality. "Beyond all ideological distortions and falsifications which may infect our work, poetry or literature [or motion pictures] remains the most reliable access to reality that we can have" (Falck 169). This means that a good novel or motion picture is a metaphor, a signifier, representing an idea, a concept, or a central truth that may be perceived intuitively as reality. Reality in this sense exists as *mana*, that metaphysical dimension beyond sensory perceptions. In life, what we view through our senses is in constant motion and real only to the degree that our physical perceptions and intellectual knowledge allow. A novel or film, on the other hand, presents a static view of reality—one that can be analyzed and discussed and will always remain just as it is in time and place. When the artist's concept connects us to a metaphysical truth, the novel or film reaches toward an ultimate reality. It may be forces of good and evil, a universal moral code, or simply a concept of a supernatural deity. Paradoxically, the greater the connection is to *mana*, the closer the artist brings us to an actual physical reality.

To be fairly and critically judged, a novel and film must be analyzed on two levels: the structural and the thematic and the mythological or archetypal. In prose fiction and motion pictures, there are basic structural techniques involving language and organization, covered in detail in Chapter 2. In general terms, whether in literature or film, the process begins when a writer, using language, creates a manuscript or a screenplay. The author uses basic structural forms (sentences, paragraphs, dialogue, etc.) to create diction (words, syntax) in order to construct details (description, action), which together produce the story. In movie making, in addition to the story's literary origins, there are a multitude of structural aspects—far more than are available to a novelist. These technical advantages include not only the obvious ones of pictures and sound, but also all of the camera technologies, lighting, theatrical performance, soundtracks, dubbing, editing, and special effects that may be generated in a laboratory before, during, and after the actors finish. All of these technical and structural aspects will be recognized and discussed; however, the critical analyses with which we will be most involved will focus on thematic content. Our intent is not to ignore structural criticism but to examine it as the means for developing content, theme, and a relevant archetypal connection in each story. Structural forms and relevant meaning are irrevocably interwoven; a full analysis requires a knowledge of both.

There is a difference between entertainment or commercial value and depth of meaning. Many novels and motion pictures are created each year specifically for their commercial value. This structurally does not constitute a negative. Novels and screenplays use the same literary devices to produce a story whatever thematic value is present. For the novel or play to connect archetypally, it must contain a theme that possesses a recurrent mythical truth—a *mana identity*. If a story places greater emphasis on plot and action to the detriment of its thematic content, the novel or play may receive great popular success but will probably not last very long beyond its initial presentation. When an effective connection to myth occurs and the literary and technological devices are performed in a superior manner, the novel or play or film reaches toward classic acceptance. A well-known film example of this concept is the *Star Wars* trilogy. George Lucas, writer, producer, and director of the films, engaged mythologist Joseph Campbell as an adviser to create a modern myth that would connect to audiences of all ages. The first film, *Star Wars*, attracted huge audiences at its original presentation in 1977 and was followed by two successful sequels, *The Empire Strikes Back* (1980) and *The Return of the Jedi* (1983). Twenty years later, in 1997, the trilogy was successfully returned to theaters across the United States. Time has not diminished the popularity of this classic as the story connects through its eternal archetype. Many directors, before and after Lucas, use the same basic plot; however, none has connected with both the public and critics as did *Star Wars*. Lucas made an archetypal connection to a wide audience *and* created new standards for special effects. His ability to combine unique yet believable characterizations, a mythical journey, and superb computerized graphics made the story meaningful and entertaining. The film was nominated for Best Picture and Best Original Screenplay, winning six Academy Awards for its technological excellence. Interestingly, the film to win the Best Picture Oscar for 1977 was Woody Allen's classic portrayal of modern city life, *Annie Hall*. Both stories appeal archetypally, both were produced with great technical skill, and both may be considered classic. However, the one closer to reality won. Neither Lucas's nor Allen's film originated as a novel, although both were later successfully published in narrative form.

It is to those stories labeled classic that we turn when we seek a novel or film with depth. For escape or entertainment, we look to novels or films that cater to popular culture. In fact, the majority of films produced cater to popular culture, as today's plethora of special-effects dominated movies attest, and therefore are primarily commercial in intent. Although these special-effect films have adopted many of Lucas's technological innovations, none, except perhaps Steven Spielberg's *Jurassic Park* (novel by Michael Crichton), attempted to recreate a mythological archetype. Crichton's novel, in similar form to Mary Shelley's *Frankenstein*, involves the ancient conflict between humans and nature—a kind of warning that scientists should be very careful when they begin to "fool with Mother Nature." Unfortunately, the film chooses to emphasize special-effects technology and either omits or dilutes most of Crichton's thematic content.

Movies that focus on symbolism and depth of story are known as art films. They appeal to a much smaller audience because of their strong symbolic content and generally do not do well at the box office. In fact, most major cities have only one theater specializing in the showing of art films. An example is a nominee for Best Picture in 1996, *Breaking the Waves*. The film did not receive wide distribution in this country even though the Academy Award Committee felt it deserved the same recognition as the winner, *The English Patient*. Even after these films receive nominations, they do not usually become box office successes. This seems to suggest most movie patrons go to the theater to be entertained and escape.

For those who want more, there are productions that entertain and connect on an intellectual level. Novel/film combinations such as *Mutiny on the Bounty* (1935), *Gone with the Wind* (1939), *The Grapes of Wrath* (1940), *All the King's Men* (1946), *From Here to Eternity* (1953), *Ben-Hur* (1959), *To Kill a Mockingbird* (1962), *The Godfather* (1972), *Dances with Wolves* (1990), *Schindler's List* (novel: *Schindler's Ark*, 1993), and 1996's Best Picture winner, *The English Patient*, are archetypal representations that have had great success as literature and were either winners of or nominees for Best Picture. For "the true field of the movies is not *art* but *myth* . . . a myth is a fiction, and this is its bare link with art, but a myth is specifically a free, unharnessed fiction, a basic, prototypic pattern capable of many variations and distortions, many betrayals and disguises, even though it remains *imaginative* truth" (Tyler 47).

A novel or film that challenges the mind requires a high degree of concentration and analysis. The novels and their companion films examined in this book have established themselves as meaningful stories, having been recognized by their peers as more than entertainment entities. Each uses a recurrent theme or archetype that in its telling connects to ancient myth and simultaneously critically assesses aspects of culture. It does not mean that they all qualify as classics. It *does* mean that the authors and directors included in the narrative *mana*, projecting a truth beyond the plot, character, and action. It reveals how a contemporary artist adapted an ancient and recurring myth/ritual to the values and aspirations of our culture at this point in time.

Aniela Jaffe, a psychoanalyst and biographer of psychologist C. G. Jung, in describing art and its relevant meaning, wrote that art is the "embodiment of the spiritual matured to the point of revelation" (Jung *MS* 250). The key words here are *spirit* and *revelation*. In exploring the art of fiction and that fiction being a source of film, we will examine exactly what part of our spirit each medium is revealing. Jaffe continues, "The forms of this embodiment may be arranged between two poles: (1) great abstraction; (2) great realism" (251). *Abstraction* refers to the use of metaphor and symbol to connect with the reader or viewer on a level beyond the senses. It appeals to our collective unconscious: "The symbol is an object of the known world hinting at something unknown; it is the known expressing the life and sense of the inexpressible" (264). One function of myth is to resolve an unexplained reality reasonably. It is using an objective reality (the symbol or metaphor) to suggest that an unknown (the abstract) may be knowable and, as such, its own form of reality. An idea that we comprehend but cannot produce in sensory fashion, is an abstraction. One rather simplified explanation of this concept comes from Supreme Court Justice Louis Brandeis while he was struggling to define obscenity: "I don't know how to define it, but I know it when I see it." He knew in his own mind (the abstract idea and for him a truth) what it was but could not define it in concrete language. In order to convey a meaning, a symbol, the word *obscene* is used to signify the abstraction. Each person, when hearing the word, will understand its meaning, subject to his or her own experience and knowledge. In fiction, a word, an object, a character, an event, or, in some cases, the entire story may become a symbol, an objective or a subjective reality whose structure can be sensorially perceived, in order to connect to an abstract idea. We cannot see, hear, taste, smell, or touch the abstraction, but we know it is there. When the abstraction connects to our inherent spiritual nature, it connects to us as *mana*, that a priori mythological force in all of us. It is the symbol *and* its meaning that conveys the significance. A symbol becomes subjective only when the author or director manipulates it in such a manner as to alter its normal or natural being.

To illustrate how a novel or film may express itself through concrete action or characters and simultaneously suggest a meaning far beyond the action, consider the novel *Being There* by Jerzy Kosinski. The novel's protagonist, a semiretarded middle-aged man, is unavoidably forced to vacate his home because his benefactor has died and there is no longer anyone to care for him. The character's job at his home has been to take care of a garden surrounded by a high wall. What we have is a man, deficient in any human skills except gardening, abruptly removed from his garden environment and forced to find his way in an unknown and, for him, dangerous world. As you read this brief synopsis, it may have suggested a similar story: the story from Genesis of Adam's being cast out of the Garden of Eden to fend for himself in a dangerous world. The mere fact that one story suggested the other, without formally stating a connection, makes it a symbol. Did the author intend the reader to make the connection? It would be surprising if he did not, but it really does not make any difference. If the reader makes a substantive connection of the two stories, it is present whether the author overtly intended it or not. How we, as readers of the novel or viewers of the film, will interpret the abstract meaning conveyed through the connection to biblical myth is certainly a point for discussion. We can objectively identify the specific connections and apply our own cultural values to the story. What point is Kosinski making about our culture by utilizing and connecting to the biblical myth of Adam? The abstract meaning emerges from a discussion of the many nuances Kosinski includes in the novel's narrative form, and by comparison, how the motion picture portrays not only the story but any alterations made for the filming. The film, perhaps in deference to a wider audience, chooses to make the connection overtly. At the end of the film, we see the protagonist walking across a lake, thereby leaving no doubt in the viewer's mind about the symbol.

How effectively an author uses metaphor and symbol to amplify his or her meaning determines the quality of the creation to a great extent. In fact, one common attribute of every good author is a unique ability to interweave metaphors and symbols without lessening the reality of the story. The symbols do not interfere with the action; they strengthen it. Ernest Hemingway in his Nobel Prize–winning work *The Old Man and the Sea* used a giant marlin to symbolize man's conflict with the environment. An old man, alone in a small boat, fights time (three days holding onto a line with his bare hands), rain and wind, hunger and thirst, and the sea in order to land a huge marlin, only in the end to lose his "great fish" to a school of ravenous sharks. The challenges presented by the environment won physically, but the old man walks away with pride because he never gives in or up to everything the environment can throw at him. His loss did not change him, and the reader could empathetically feel his pride in the outcome. In the 1958 film, starring Spencer Tracy as the old man, this heroic attitude comes through just as effectively as it does in the novel. Without being consciously aware of the depth or breadth of the heroic archetype, we know, whether we read the novel or view the film, that real heroism is not determined by winning or losing but in how you play the game—an American value. Hemingway, in addition to the archetype, adds his own recurrent theme: how well the protagonist would adhere to "man's code," which connects Hemingway directly with the rules of knighthood established by King Arthur. For Hemingway, this means living one's life according to the rules of honor that Western culture has evolved—not only in determining "manhood," but in proving it. The combination of simplicity in the structure of the story with its subtle use of symbols makes this a modern classic because the story not only signifies the author's theme but pits one man, representing everyman, struggling against the sea, a universal symbol for life. The story connects to Jonah and the Whale, to Noah and the Flood, to Christ's three days in the tomb, and even in a very subtle way to all of Christianity in the sacrifice of the great fish, a traditional symbol for Christ. This makes the story the more ironic because Hemingway professed to be an atheist.

The presence of *mana* does not require one to believe in God. What is necessary in modern literature is that "man is free to decide whether 'God' shall be 'spirit' or a natural phenomenon . . . whether 'God' shall act as a beneficent or a destructive force" (Jung *EJ* 245). For Hemingway, "God" is manliness expressed as courage in the face of death. The story's religious overtones enhance the concept that there are certain archetypal themes deeply embedded within us, even when outwardly we tend to reject the basic belief.

A second area with which we must be concerned is how the culture of the time and place is reflected in the story. The time in which each story is written influences how the story is told. "A myth is always, in its individual telling, located in time: it always refers [connects] to events alleged to have happened a long time ago. Yet, in operation, the specific *pattern* or structure of events described is bound to be timeless; embracing, and linking in an explanatory mode the present with both the past and future, while it is told" (Hawkes 42). Each author is a product of his or her time, and even if the story's setting is in the past or future, the author's thinking is relative to the time it is written. Silvano Arieti, writing in *Creativity, the Magic Synthesis*, states: "Thus a creative product has to be considered from two points of view: that is, as a unity, in itself, and as a part of a culture, either a specific culture, or the general cultural patrimony of mankind" (5). The work may be representative of a specific culture and simultaneously represent a universal in its application. Ken Kesey's *One Flew over the Cuckoo's Nest* features a messianic quest as its central truth. Within that quest is the narrator's personal story. The Chief is a very large Native American man suffering from paranoid schizophrenia. During the course of the story, we learn what happened to the Chief's family and how he came to be a patient in a mental hospital. The author, a native Oregonian, is obviously influenced by the manner in which white industrialists manipulate and "steal" tribal lands from Native Americans in the Northwest and chooses to make it a part of the novel. It is integrated into the story in such a way that we do not focus on it, but we know the narrator has been wronged, so that we cheer when he escapes. This is a regional cultural influence in the telling of the story. It does not dominate the story, functioning as a subplot, but its integration enhances a rebirth and restoration theme (which, by the way, is omitted from the film).

We will consider each title, film and novel, as a single entity, looking at subcategories of quest/ritual myth. Chapters 3, 4, and 5 examine stories of heroism. Chapters 6 through 8 focus on the rite of passage from youth to adult, stories of a quest to find one's own identity, so vital in Western culture. Chapters 9 through 12 delve into the quest to find a universal moral code in an immoral world. One combination deals with the search for morality in the wake of a destructive war. There are two dealing with the problems of politics in a free society. And just to prove the world is not all bad, Chapter 10 takes us into the literary world of fantasy, adding to the moral quest a search for immortality. Each story connects to ancient myth, which in turn connects to an archetypal truth and, if it is successful, ultimate reality. To that eternal truth, each author and director adds, in form and content, his or her subjective meanings. By *form*, I mean that it is presented utilizing the technology available for that medium. Content refers to its archetypal theme. Interwoven within content are acts and events representative of the time and place in which it is produced, thereby reflecting a cultural perspective. This is an important aspect, for it is the evaluation of cultural influence that will provide insight into the culture at that particular moment in time. It reflects changes in attitude and behavior when compared to its founding archetype. It is on that concept that analysis and critical judgment will be made. For example, does the author or director accurately represent the culture?

The question will surely arise as to whether any critical judgment is acceptable because we are merely expressing an opinion. We will base the accuracy of all interpretations on logic and reasonable justification. Can the reader or viewer justify his or her conclusions using an acceptable inductive reasoning process? To place this within a context, we will briefly review Northrop Frye's theory of criticism. Frye proposes a schema for critically analyzing literary abstraction based on the idea that fictional narrative is connected to a recurrent plot and archetype as a source for the story and connects to the natural cycles of nature and life to which all humans are subject. Frye's theory is explained in detail in his 1957 book, *Anatomy of Criticism*.

Frye notes that although literature (and I add film) is an art form, we should still be able to analyze it scientifically and critically. Criticism, by the way, begins when the writer or director finishes. A writer or a filmmaker, until the moment of publication or presentation, can continue to revise and edit the product; the object thus remains attached to its creator. When the moment of truth finally comes and the product is presented to the public, the critic and the public become judges. The work of art must now stand or fall on its own merit. Instead of the producer, director, or writer's identifying the points of strength and weakness, it is now the responsibility of the critic or the public to identify them. This process has a universal parallel in nature. A child is attached to parents until that moment in time when society demands he or she stand on his or her own. At that point, the young adult must place himself or herself among all the others who have reached that point and be judged on his or her merit as a responsible adult.

The public as critic assumes the responsibility of determining if the product—novel or film—succeeded in presenting its central idea, the archetype, as fully and effectively as possible. In order to do this, we will, for each film and book, identify the mode and the archetype that the particular work of art represents. The word *archetype* is derived from the psychology of Carl G. Jung. He stated that each individual possesses a "collective unconscious," that part of our psyche that is passed from one generation to the next, allowing us to connect to certain symbolic concepts. It is a predisposition inherent in each individual to connect to certain basic ideas and symbols found in the natural world. In a general sense, this corresponds to Wheelwright's concept of *mana*, or predilection to create a bond between the spiritual (the unconscious) and the physical (conscious) world. A familiar literary example of this archetype is the hero. Hero myths or messianic archetypes follow a universal pattern so eloquently detailed in Joseph Campbell's *Hero with a Thousand Faces*. Campbell demonstrates how every culture has stories of a hero's humble birth, an early proof of superhuman strength, a rapid rise to prominence or power, a triumphant struggle against the forces of evil, and finally, admission of a fatal flaw, which leads to his or her fall from grace or a sacrificial death in the performance of a heroic act. Our southwestern culture is replete with stories of the mysterious stranger, arriving unannounced, into a community that is suffering from some natural or imposed evil force, and is freed by the actions of the stranger who is motivated by purely humane reasons. In Judeo-Christian cultures, it relates to a dispelling of evil forces and a return to paradise. This recurrent myth is known as either the "hero and the dragon" or a "messianic myth."

To imply that myths have a connection to our collective unconscious is a simple context. As products of the natural world, we are both products of and subject to the same forces that govern or control nature. Nature produces the seasons from which we connect those cycles of our journey: birth, exile, redemption, death, and rebirth.

The conception of a heaven above, a hell beneath, and a cyclical cosmos or order of nature in between forms the ground plan. . . . The top half of the natural cycle is the world of romance and the analogy of innocence; the lower half is the world of "realism" and the analogy of experience. There are thus four main types of mythical movements; within romance, within experience, down, and up. The downward movement is the tragic movement, the wheel of fortune falling from innocence toward hamartia, and from hamartia to catastrophe. The upward movement is the comic movement, from threatening complications to a happy ending and a general assumption of postdated innocence in which everyone lives happily ever after. (Frye *AL* 162–63)

The four seasons provide a natural means of connecting us to life's cycles, both consciously and subconsciously. Each season corresponds to movement from one stage of life to another and evokes its own feeling. Spring and summer are the seasons of comedy, romance, birth, and rebirth; the autumn and winter are more suggestive of tragedy, redemption, and satire. Any subject can be treated as a comedy and romance, evoking the birth of the hero, creation, revival, and resurrection with the triumph of good over evil. Or the same subject may be treated as autumn and winter, with realism, tragedy, and satire, stories of the fall, of violent death, sacrifice, isolation, and defeat. Consider novels and films about war. During the 1940s and 1950s, comedy and romance dominated war stories in both literature and film. Productions such a *Guadalcanal Diary* (1943) and *Battle Cry* (1955) extolled the heroic qualities of America's military during World War II, while picturing the Germans and Japanese as the evil enemy. A more familiar romantic story is Stephen Crane's nineteenth-century novel, *The Red Badge of Courage* (film 1951) about a young man who goes from coward to hero during the American Civil War. For autumn and winter we can look to two recent stories about the Vietnam War. Both *Full Metal Jacket* (1987) and *Born on the Fourth of July* (1989) are noted for their stark realism and tragedy. For satire, *Catch-22* (1970) tells us about the army air force in World War II, and *M*A*S*H* (1970) tells of the Korean War. Each reflects the attitudes of the culture at the time. The novels of World War II are prowar; those about Vietnam and Korea, antiwar.

What we have is a familiar subject being presented in a variety of literary modes, yet each is representative of how the culture is relating to that particular subject at a specific point in time in which the story is created. Like the myths of any culture, it accurately represents the people of its time, or it would be summarily rejected and pass into oblivion. During the 1940s and early 1950s a story critical of America's World War II effort was unthinkable. For Vietnam, almost all stories were highly critical of the war. Only one novel and film supported the war, John Wayne's *The Green Berets*, from a novel by Roger Moore, which ultimately became an embarrassment to both Wayne and the culture. For cultural acceptance, "myth fulfills an indispensable function: it expresses, enhances, and codifies belief, it safeguards and enforces morality; it vouches for the efficiency of ritual and contains practical rules for the guidance of man" (Malinowski 101). Because our nature includes spring and summer, those romantic stories connect. Because fall and winter are also within our nature, we can equally connect with those stories that tend to depress us. In essence, a good novel or film connects us to a reality that exists at a specific point in time as reconstructed by an author.

Connecting our beliefs and values to seasons has its roots far back into recorded history. There are several accounts of the connections that earlier cultures made about the seasons to explain not only cause and effect, but extending far beyond into the very foundations of philosophy and religion. In England, the builders of Stonehenge arranged the gateway of their circle of boulders, an ancient Druid religious site, precisely facing the summer solstice, the height of the growing season. To the Greek culture, the coming of spring was celebrated by the Dionysian Festival, a national commemoration of rebirth, which, by including a poetry contest, opened the way for the literature of drama. For Romans, this annual spring festival became the Christian Easter after the Roman emperor Constantine adopted Christianity. These rituals celebrate that ultimately we, just like plants and hibernating animals at the end of winter, are individually reborn. The creative artists of literature and film, using a printed page and a movie screen as their canvas, recreate those feelings in the type of story told, and we as an audience connect to the story in a very natural manner.

Eastern religions such as Buddhism and Taoism perform rituals seeking harmony with the forces of nature, becoming physically and spiritually "one with the universe." The *om* sound, related to meditation, harks back to the idea of Brahma's existing only as motion creating vibration or sound. Finding spiritual peace is not therefore a seasonal experience. In deference to Western theology seeking a self-identity, the Eastern believer tends toward submersion into the All.

Will twenty-fifth-century anthropologists, mythologists, or literary and film scholars use our myths in evaluating our culture? We may presume that just as the myths of ancient Greece and the Middle East express their cultures, contemporary fiction and film will represent our beliefs, aspirations, and values. We can expect that the novels, short stories, and motion pictures of this century will appear in anthropology books of the twenty-fifth-century as the myths of the "primitive people" of twentieth-century America, stories that inform the reader how we observed the phases of life's natural cycle and our ritual observance of the same basic mythological truths that we inherited from our ancient progenitors. They demonstrate how we deal with our life cycle: birth and rebirth, fall, exile, redemption, and restoration, how we decide what constitutes heroism or adulthood; how we determine what was good or evil in our culture; what we consider paradise. How we respond to those questions that involve our hopes and fears, our aspirations and values, is fundamental to understanding what kind of people we are. It will be found in our myths, our literature and motion pictures, for they, drawing on many of the same myths that appeared in antiquity, reflect the beliefs, values, and aspirations of ordinary people. Those novels and films that stand the test of time and continue to be read and viewed for generations will be the ones to record our presence and establish our identity.

For example, those World War II stories previously mentioned provide a single common belief that runs through them all, the strength of ordinary people to look optimistically beyond war to a time when democracy and freedom would again prevail—the optimistic belief that spring (rebirth and restoration) will follow the winter (exile and death) and good will eventually triumph over evil. Recall the dialogue between Humphrey Bogart and Ingrid Bergman in *Casablanca* (1942) when Rick (Bogart) is sending Ilsa (Bergman) away with her husband in spite of their love for each other. Rick, representing Americans everywhere, explains how little their lives and love mean in a world threatened by fascist domination. Or, recall Montgomery Clift in *From Here to Eternity* (1953); though severely wounded in a knife fight, he explains to his girlfriend that he must rejoin his army unit because their lives as individuals are unimportant now that the Japanese have dared to attack the United States. Each of the stories, along with dozens of others, conveys the culture's belief that Americans have a "manifest destiny" to restore Eden. They provide our conception of heroism and identify a very important cultural principle of Americans. Not all of the stories have happy endings, for that is not a requirement for romance or comedy. What the heroes and heroines have in those stories is an inner strength that conveys the archetype—a belief that ultimately good will triumph over evil. The characters exercise control over the elements around them and make the world a better place. The stories tell the future world *what* Americans saw as their quest, individually and collectively, *why* they felt as they did, and *how* they made it happen. The stories demonstrate optimism and a deeply held belief that human nature is basically good. A continuing ritual, it has been a part of American culture for more than three hundred years, and its purpose is to lead in the journey toward a perfect world.

Between those years and now, there seems to have occurred a change in how Americans view the world—a change that conveys a slightly altered primeval reality. We seem to have lost some of the optimism and become cynical about ourselves and the future. It is the novels and films reflecting this changing world of actions, forces, and conflicting powers, that we will explore.

Chapter 2

Reading the Novel and the Film

THE WRITTEN NARRATIVE: HOW LITERATURE COMMUNICATES

The broadest division of fictional literature is **genre**, a distinct type or category into which literary works may be grouped according to the context or subject matter. The four major literary genres are poetry, fiction, nonfiction, and drama. This concept of genre applies to both literature and film as libraries and book and video stores tend to group novels and films according to their subject matter. Originally this term was used to separate comedy and tragedy. Theoretically **tragedy** occurs when the protagonist loses the struggle; **comedy** occurs whenever the protagonist succeeds in his or her conflict. As a practical matter, any area into which a number of stories can be grouped can be considered a genre. For example, comedy and tragedy are usually subdivided into types of tragedy and types of comedy. These generic subdivisions will include such categories as romance, adventure, science fiction, mystery, horror, humor, and drama. Subdivisions occur because an author manipulates the structural forms—the seven basic elements of literature—to create a specific type of literature. These forms are, for the most part, universally accepted as to meaning and application.

Plot applies to both the action and the arrangement of the episodes or sequence of events. All of the action and events that occur in the story must connect. By *connection*, there must be a sense of causality in that one event leads to another and all connect by their relation to a central plan of action.

Plot refers specifically to the sequence of event, episode, or incident in the story; causality forms a base for all aspects of the narrative. This connecting force includes everything from a specific character's motivation to the effect of environmental circumstance, which may or may not be a recognizably contrived circumstance. Because a story is a created entity and every action in the story must connect, there is a level of contrivance in all literature and film. When an action becomes too contrived, that is, it taxes one's imagination to accept it as believable, it conforms to an ancient Greek theatrical device called **deus ex machina**, or an act of God intervened. In ancient Greek theater, a large crane was used to manipulate the actions from above by allowing one of the gods to descend and interact with the characters. Obviously a crane transporting a god is not a part of modern literature or film; however, there are devices an author or director may use to create an intervention. Nevertheless, if an act of contrivance becomes too overt, by coincidence, fate, or karma, the story can lose its significance. In literary language this contributes to the very important aspect of **veri-similitude** (from the Latin *veri similis*: "like the truth"). In literature and film it is most important that the characters, the actions they perform, and the setting in which they perform the actions be truly believable within the scope created by the author.

Characters are individuals created by the author to act out the story. There are several types of characters. The **protagonist** is the focus, as orig-inator or principal recipient, of the action; the **antagonist(s)** may be one character or many who stand in opposition to the protagonist. Antagonism may extend to nature in the case of environmental forces, as in *The Old Man and the Sea*. In addition, there are **exposition** characters, necessary to provide information the reader or viewer requires in following the action. **Transitional characters** are those whose function is to move the plot in time or place. **Major** and **minor characters** are arbitrarily determined by their direct effect on the plot. And finally, **flat** characters are one di-mensional, providing the reader with limited knowledge about either their physical or psychological makeup or both, and **round** characters are mul-tidimensional. The more we know about the character, the rounder they become, which generally implies a greater function. A character's function or influence on the plot is the most important factor.

A **conflict** or **struggle** occurs when the protagonist encounters obstacles while attempting to accomplish something or to prevent something from being accomplished. Each obstacle becomes a function of the plot. There are the familiar definitions: man versus himself, man, society, the environ-ment, or the supernatural. This broad definition tends to generalize the concept. In approaching the story through its archetype, we will need to be more specific. In the case of McMurphy in *Cuckoo's Nest*, it is not just man versus man, but a messianic hero trying to free the inmates of a mental hospital from the forces of evil. These forces are represented by both character and circumstance. McMurphy encounters many obstacles, first, in conflict with a single character, the ward nurse, and then, by the entire system, the machine-like manner in which the hospital functions. If McMurphy is able to overcome and defeat the obstacles, the story becomes a comedy by definition; if he fails, it is a tragedy.

A **setting** is always the time and place of the story. The place is the space in which the story takes place. Time includes not only the date of the setting but also whether the story takes place in continuous **real time** or in **flashback**. A flashback may be presented chronologically, that is, maintaining the original order of events, or in nonchronological form, by merely connecting thoughts or memories in no particular order, discounting the relevance of time. The entire story of *One Flew over the Cuckoo's Nest* is narrated as a flashback, following chronological order. *The English Patient* takes a much different approach. Chronological time means nothing because this story is told by an omniscient narrator, interweaving memory with real time, making the element of time less important. It is the relation between memory, which contains no time element, and current action that conveys the story. In each case, the time-space relationship influences what the reader perceives. A place may be as small as a hospital ward in *One Flew over the Cuckoo's Nest* or cover half of the U.S. in *Shoeless Joe/Field of Dreams*. What is important regarding setting is not the size or scope but rather the amount of influence it imposes on the story's characters or theme. For example, in *The Last Picture Show*, it is the setting—a somewhat desolate and deteriorating Texas town—more than any single character that provides the antagonism. How necessary is the setting, both time and place, to the story? Could the character's action have occurred elsewhere with the same effect? To what extent is the character being controlled or manipulated by the environment?

Theme refers to the central or controlling idea of the work. From a reader's perspective, a theme in its simplest form may be that meaning of a story the reader can relate to his or her life. On a broader level, a reader or viewer may infer a metaphysical or metaphorical meaning in accordance with or even beyond what the author may have intended. This is particularly true of stories removed from their originating time and place. If the **archetype** theory exists, and in this book it does, today's meaning of a story may not have been a nineteenth-century author's conscious intent. In addition, a good novel may be approached from a variety of perspectives, which will shade a theme toward a relationship with life the author did not or could not know. Generally, there will be one dominant theme emerging from the story, but as each reader filters that theme through his or her own experience and knowledge, variations become the rule and not the exception. An author communicates thematically, but the reader translates the meaning into his or her own objective reality. It is through the sharing of these variations that a broader meaning to the story and, most important a clearer understanding of a theme is developed. This is what makes Jung's archetypal concept meaningful. The story may connect to each of us in a slightly different manner, but what ultimately separates the good from the mundane is that a good story actually does connect. When an archetypal connection is made, the story potentially appeals to a mass audience.

In addition, there are three elements over which an author has much more control than a film counterpart. It is through his or her manipulation of these elements that the story will generally succeed or fail.

First, and perhaps most important to a written narrative, is **point of view**. This is the **voice, persona,** or **narrator** who tells the story. Students are usually taught that a story may be **first person,** an identifiable narrator, or **third person,** an anonymous narrator. However, these are simply headings for several types of each available to an author. A first-person narrator may be from a **major** or **minor character, interior monologue, dramatic monologue, letter narration, diary narration, subjective narrator, detached autobiography, memoir,** or **observer narration.** An **anonymous narrator** may be categorized by how many characters with whom the speaker has **omniscience**—the number of characters and to what extent the narrator sees into the mind of a character. Or the anonymous narrator may be a fly on the wall and be a totally **objective observer,** unable to know the thoughts of any character. A unique form of either first or third person is **stream of consciousness,** where the voice relates seemingly unrelated thoughts that connect thematically. To use this form requires great control and generally relies on metaphors and symbols to convey meaning. **Point of view** also presents a major difference in literature and film. A written narrative always has an identifiable narrator, that is, a human voice telling the story. A reader must evaluate a narrator's reliability and relative objectivity or subjectivity in relating the events of the story. The persona telling the story contributes to the level of verisimilitude conveyed to the reader. For example, the narrator of *Cuckoo's Nest* is a schizophrenic-paranoid American Indian who wavers between hallucination and reality throughout the novel. However, as the novel progresses, his hallucinations become fewer and fewer, until, by the end of the flashback, he appears rational enough to leave the hospital. The longer he narrates, the more believable he becomes. Because the story is a flashback, we can accept the verity of his narration because we know he has been cured. On the other hand, the narrator of Larry McMurtry's *The Last Picture Show* sounds very much like a town gossip. Some of his narration seems to glory in the frailties of the characters and their misadventures. As a reader, we may want to take his words with a grain of salt—enjoying the satire, but always recognizing it as exaggeration. In film, the point of view is ultimately the camera lens.

Tone and **style** refer to the diction and detail of the story. **Diction** is the author's choice of words—the types and syntax of sentences. The **details** are the amount of dialogue, arrangement, and order of incident and information, and the number and location of descriptive passages. Other concepts applicable to diction and detail are the author's use of *imagery* and/or *tropes* (figurative language), use of *formal, informal, colloquial, obscene, concrete, abstract*, or other type of language or combination of these. The structure of diction and detail create a tone. This includes the attitude the author is expressing through his or her choice of words in descriptive narrative as well as the words used in dialogue. As a point to observe, verbs and their modifiers are the primary part of speech inducing tone. Tone, in some novels, may be the dominating element. **Satire** is frequently used to establish a particular perspective by ridiculing the subject or treating it in an absurd manner. However, satire can vary in its intensity. Larry McMurtry's narrator in *The Last Picture Show* used a mildly exaggerated form of satire in the somewhat absurd behavior of his teenage characters, while Robert Hornberger (Hooker) chose a more acerbic tone in *M*A*S*H*. George Orwell conveys his condemnation of the communistic form of government in *Animal Farm* by transferring his human characters into animal form, a totally absurd idea. Some other labels for tone include *formal, informal, solemn, somber, serious, ironic, patronizing, intimate, sardonic,* and *facetious*. The other side of tone is the emotional response the reader receives, generally categorized as **mood**. The author establishes a tone, which evokes a mood or feeling in the reader. Most frequently these are not the same.

These three literary elements—tone, style, and point of view—can be controlled and manipulated and provide an advantage the author of a literary work has over the film version. It is very difficult for a film to take a viewer into a character's thinking; it requires a level of contrivance, as in a disembodied voice, which lowers believability. Omniscience may in fact be the major difference between the written form and the motion picture. A reader is able to form a personal visual perception by being able to see through the eyes and mind of a character. Film to any formal degree is unable to accomplish this. The greatest of actors are certainly able to convey feeling, but they cannot convey a precise or specific thought visually. An actor can display anger but not the reasoning process that went through his or her mind evoking the anger. It may have been a series of memories of past associations with the character, the event, or a combination of the two. One artist who demonstrates the degree to which this can be taken is James Joyce in *Portrait of the Artist* or *Ulysses*. In both novels, Joyce uses a stream-of-consciousness point of view that upon a first reading is extremely confusing. The protagonist is allowing us to see the full range of memory and feeling an event may evoke. Joyce relies on symbols to connect the described memories to the action. Omniscience can take us there; acting, no matter how brilliant, cannot.

A thought to remember concerning word choice comes from a quotation attributed to Mark Twain: "The difference between the right word and the wrong word is similar to the difference between a light bulb and a bolt of lightning." When the right word appears within the right syntax, the readers feel the effect within their own being.

The cohesion of the elements in relation to the abstract quality of the narrative will determine the quality of the presentation. Just as in music or painting or any of the other fine arts, what determines quality, beyond a high proficiency with mechanics, is the harmony and unity the author can develop in the elements while simultaneously presenting a strong theme. The structural forms listed above are the basic devices used to identify specific weaknesses or strengths in a work of literature. The archetypal idea, which frames the theme and meaning of the work, can only be qualified by identifying which of the elements the author could have or should have improved. It is well to remember that a critic begins when the author finishes his or her creation.

HOW FILM COMMUNICATES

There was a time when it could be truly said that reading is fundamental. At ages four to six, children were exposed to the written word, and the only pictures were book illustrations or the occasional movie such as *Pinocchio* or *Snow White and the Seven Dwarfs*. Since the mid-1950s, children have been exposed to film almost from the moment they enter the world. Instead of being fundamental, reading has become, to some extent in the minds of many, an adjunct to their sensory world. A response such as, "It was a good movie, but the book was so much better," is no longer a common response. There are probably many explanations for such reactions, none of which is really relevant to our subject here. Our interest is not in determining which medium is superior. Each form of presentation has strengths and weaknesses in presenting an archetype. Our goal is to assess which form is a more accurate and comprehensible portrayal of our culture at a specific time and place.

This will be determined in the manner we approach each medium. When we read a novel, we tend visually to imagine the characters and action as described in the narrative. In other words, we are mentally creating our own picture version of the story. Since each of us creates a personal picture version, each will be different in detail, clarity, and depth. Each version becomes dependent on the level of knowledge and experience each of us has in relation to the story. For example, a black teenage girl reading Alice Walker's *The Color Purple* will imagine a particular set of images based on her own experience. These images will be different if the teenager lives in New Jersey rather than Mississippi. It will also differ if the teenager is male or white or Buddhist or whatever mixture he or she might be. It would even be different if he or she has read other novels by Walker. Each person has a lifetime of personal experience, both real and learned, that will influence the images he or she perceives. This is true for everyone who reads a novel and sees a motion picture.

This personal history adds degrees of complexity when viewing a film after having read the novel. A viewer enters the film with a multitude of biases based on an expectation generated by his or her imaginary perceptions and, in addition, how and to what degree he or she likes, or in the case of a classroom assignment, dislikes the novel. It is assumed very few people will force themselves to read a novel they dislike.

A third element has to be considered. In literary analysis, it is impossible to separate the author from the work. A good novel is, by any standard, a work of art. Therefore, the novelist has a reputation, perhaps a following that recognizes this author as having something meaningful to say. A culture holds its best writers, composers, painters, and architects in high regard, some attaining the status of national treasures. Based on cultural traditions, we expect a good novel to offer a psychological, social, or philosophical commentary that is worthy of consideration.

Generally we do not hold film directors to that same level of esteem. The question then becomes, Do films ever reach a level where they may be considered art? If not, then we could never have a film equal to a novel. Could a mediocre or bad novel or short story be turned into a classic film, deserving to be called art? How can we tell if it reaches such an elevated stature? The aesthetic standards for literature are generally accepted. There are some generally agreed-on standards we can apply to film. V. I. Pudovkin expresses the idea that the art in film production does not really occur in any one aspect. Rather, just as in literature, it occurs when the elements come together in a special manner in a finished product. "Between the natural event and its appearance upon the screen there is a marked difference. It is *exactly this difference that makes the film an art*" (86). Just as the author brings together all of the devices of literature in a harmonic manner that will express a meaningful theme, the film director brings together the elements of film at his or her disposal to accomplish the same end. Some devices are applicable in accordance with literature only, others are applicable only to the art of cinema, and some apply equally to both.

In considering film as art, we must recognize that each medium is dependent on the devices or conventions available at the time it is created. An author or a film director cannot go beyond what is available in the way of technology and understanding than is present at the time of creation. We have discussed some of those conventions with which an author must work. In order to understand the devices related to filmmaking, we need to identify process, function, and applicable terminology.

An approach to film analysis must begin with an area of study most associated with film criticism. **Semiology** as a term may be applied to both literature and film, but for communication accuracy, we will use it primarily as a film device. **Semiotics**, with regard to film analysis, is the study of the structural placement and integral function of major scenes in the development of the overall plot and theme. The creative process for film begins with a story idea (a novel or short story), which is translated into a screenplay. The screenplay or script places into written form the dialogue and a summary of location in space and time. The screenplay is then converted into a storyboard, a visual representation that places into structural form the scenes, in both content (location, characters, props, required action) and order (selection and placement of scenes), necessary to present the story. This concept differs from literary analysis primarily because from the very beginning, the story is being "reduced" to those components that can be translated into visual replications of the novel's action. At this point, the viewer will be an omnipresent participant in developing the production. The storyboard places into the planning the order and location for scenes, and identifies for the director, cinematographer, and sound engineer what the viewer will need to see and hear to comprehend the story.

An aesthetic judgment is made as to what scenes will be included in the visualization process and what scenes will be excluded. For example, consider a very dramatic, perhaps melodramatic, scene in the novel *Shoeless Joe*, from which the film *Field of Dreams* was made. Ray Kinsella, the protagonist of the film, is the Iowa farmer who hears the magical voice telling him, "If you build it, he will come." Early in the novel, in order to focus the reader's attention on Ray's mystic nature, we are given the following passage:

It was near noon on a gentle Sunday when I walked out to that garden. The soil was soft and my shoes disappeared as I plodded until I was near the center. There I knelt, the soil cool on my knees. I looked up at the low gray sky; the rain had stopped and the only sound was the surrounding trees dripping fragrantly. Suddenly I thrust my hands wrist-deep into the snuffy-black earth. The air was pure. All around me the clean smell of earth and water. Keeping my hands buried I stirred the earth with my fingers and I knew I loved Iowa as much as a man could love a piece of earth. (14)

What we see in the film is Kevin Costner, as Ray Kinsella, pull a stalk of corn from the earth and plunge his hands into it just as the disembodied voice interrupts his moment. In this scene, he angrily cast the stalk aside as he challenges the voice to identify itself. We are not told, by action or sound, why he is examining the stalk's roots.

One might imagine Phil Alden Robinson, who wrote the screenplay and directed the film, mulling over whether to include this scene. How would it be filmed? Would it add to or diminish his version? Or would it, perhaps appear too melodramatic for a contemporary audience? Whatever may have been his motives, he chose not to include it in the film. W. P. Kinsella, the novel's author, obviously thought it important in establishing his alter ego protagonist's character. Because Ray Kinsella is an archetype, a man who measures life in terms of family and the primal forces of nature, does the omission of such a descriptive scene lessen the emotional bonding between reader and protagonist? Or does Robinson at some other point in the film provide a scene where this aspect of Ray's character can be felt and understood? Only a careful study of the film structure allows judgment.

One method is to look at each scene semiologically; focusing on each scene as both a revelation and a structural component. It is a given that the order in which scenes are placed is fundamental in conveying the story. However, within that organization of scenes, a director and his or her staff must consider the composition of each frame. This brings into focus the spatial arrangement of character, objects, and background. Film, as a visual medium, must be concerned with a specific and limited space. A novelist has no need to concern himself or herself with space. An author may take us into the mind of the character, who at any given moment may take us on a memory trip, recalling a time and place located in the past, present, or even the future. Directors and cinematographers are therefore somewhat more limited than a novelist regarding space and time. Michael Ondaatje, in his novel *The English Patient*, observes no rules in manipulating space and time in the minds of his characters. In fact, when reading the novel, there are times we have to pause and reconstruct what we have previously read to place the events being described into an understandable order. As the plots and subplots become more complex, the pauses may become more frequent. Anthony Minghella, the film's award-winning director, does not have that privilege. His film version is a continuous movement from one scene into another and does not allow a viewer the opportunity to pause and reconstruct the events mentally. Minghella, in remaining somewhat true to the novel, uses flashbacks to convey the story. He does this by bringing the camera in for a **close-up** of the English Patient's face, using a dissolve to convey we are entering the memories of the character. When we return from the flashback, we are brought back into the scene we left. The novel, narrated by an anonymous voice, is free to move to another character, switch to another memory, or return to real time. Minghella, using the camera as his narrator, must conform to cinematic limits. The director must move smoothly from one scene to another, keeping the audience informed as the story develops.

Being visual does have some advantages. In constructing his story, the director has the opportunity to locate the film in a setting that will not only provide a sense of realism but can also enhance the story. The background of a scene can act as a metaphor amplifying a theme or specific idea the story wants to convey. George Stevens, producer and director of *Shane*, a popular western of the 1950s, selected a location near Jackson Hole, Wyoming, a flat valley at the base of the Grand Teton Mountains, to film what became a modern western classic. The mountains become a frame for many of the outdoor shots. The use of a lens filter causes the mountains to be bathed in a lavender tint providing a subtle "purple mountain majesty" to underscore the romantic idealism of the film. In addition, the camera is placed near ground level, and the camera lens thus becomes an "active observer," presenting to the audience a view of the characters as large as their Rocky Mountain background. We subconsciously see them as larger than life. This is film semiology. The filmmaker is manipulating our minds to see a perspective that influences judgment.

For literature, the language for its presentation is grammar and syntax. For film, we move to the shot, a series of single frames making up a sentence or paragraph. For the episode or incident, film may substitute the scene. Keep in mind that film is a sequence conveying action, dialogue (words), and background, with each functioning independently *and* together as a single unit. Sequences are then spliced together, creating a plot. A sequence will merge many camera perspectives. As an active observer, the camera lens, within a single sequence, may show us faces, hands, wide angles, deep perspectives, actions, reactions, background sights and sounds, symbols, or any other visual or audio possibility the director or cinematographer feels will enhance the concept he or she is trying to provide.

Although this concept tends to oversimplify the comparison dramatically, it does provide a perspective suitable for comparative discussion. Paradoxically, motion pictures are much more and at the same instant much less. An author using words, is limited to the number of words that will apply to the presentation. For the film director, the possibilities for the use of multiple cameras and angles, real and created settings, artificial lighting, and film technology are unlimited. Consider the **denouement** (literally the "untying of the knot"; the solution, explanation, or outcome) in a recent film, *A Few Good Men*. The trial has been concluded, and two young marines have been exonerated of murder, yet because of their actions, they will receive a dishonorable discharge from the Marine Corps. The protagonist, a naval officer played by Tom Cruise, stops the young and very dedicated marine corporal before he exits. Prior to this moment, the negative tension between these two characters has been very strong. That was before Cruise, as the marine's defense attorney, had placed his own future in jeopardy by accusing a marine general on the witness stand of dereliction of duty, thereby doing what the marine corporal had failed to do. Cruise faces the young man who has been told his marine career is finished and states: "You do not have to wear a patch on your arm to have honor." The camera goes to a medium shot of the marine, and you see him realize the truth of the moment. He seems to swell to attention and in a very steady and commanding voice calls, "A-ten-hut! Officer on deck." He follows this with a very precise and smart salute, holding it until Cruise returns it just as militarily and, for his role, totally out of character. The line was meant for both of them, and at that moment the characters *and* the audience know it. In a few seconds of film, the camera captured a moment it might have taken an author a page or more to describe. The statement is made, language is unnecessary. This brief scene speaks volumes though its images. It is its own language. It is the archetype of spring: the birth of a hero and the defeat of the powers of evil and darkness. It makes the audience feel good even though it ends the corporal's career.

This brings into focus what may well be the most complex and important aspect of filmmaking: film editing. This is truly where film, literature, and art come together. There are two editing techniques applicable for evaluation. The first, **mise-en-scène**, is that part of the filming that takes place on the set. We have all seen pictures of a film director getting ready to shoot a scene, where he makes a square frame with his hands and peers through the square at the setting and actors before adjusting the camera or the actors. Or he or she may have a monocular hanging from his or her neck that will identify precisely what each camera lens will photograph. All of this allows the director to fashion the scene with the perceiver in mind. At this point, the director is concerned with what the audience will see and hear. This includes placement of the actors in relation to the camera, the location of the camera regarding angle and distance, the actor's directions, or any other immediate choice the director makes at the moment the scene is being filmed. Modern cameras have amazing capabilities regarding distance and focus. Camera lenses can telescope for close-ups or open to a wide angle incorporating large vistas. They can invert to give the appearance of a distance. A cinematographer may photograph as much or as little as is selected. In addition, with modern techniques of graphic enhancement, a computer may place an object or character into a scene at a later time. Forrest Gump can be seen shaking hands with a dead president; a more elaborate example of this technique is Steven Spielberg's *Jurassic Park*. In all but two scenes involving dinosaurs, the actors performed without the presence of any animals. All of the chase scenes involving *Tyrannosaurus rex* and the velociraptors were added by computer graphics during the editing process. The actors are running from an empty space, to be filled at a later date.

The second form comes when the many pieces of film are spliced together into a single unit. This splicing is called the **montage**. During this process, the director, the film editor, the cinematographer, and selected staff will review all of the film and piece it together using various types of transition. One of the most famous and successful montages came in Alfred Hitchcock's *Psycho*. The shower scene, in which a young women (Janet Leigh) is murdered, is filmed using six cameras from different angles, and produces several minutes of film. The final splicing the audience sees lasts seventeen seconds. This was the final montage. The transition Hitchcock uses is the **quick** or **flash cut**, switching quickly from one viewpoint to another.

This scene is considered a masterpiece. A more common form, and one to which we have become accustomed, is the manner in which we see and hear a conversation between two or more characters. The camera may show us the speaker, or we may hear the speaker and see the reaction of the listener. There is no limit to the possible variations in just one conversation. This technique is available in all scenes where multiple cameras are used.

Transitions occur within scenes and between scenes. Other techniques to facilitate scene changes include the **fade**, where one scene appears to go to black slowly. A good example of a unique fade occurs in Steven Spielberg's *The Color Purple*. Rather than simply fading to black, the camera focuses on an open mailbox, moving slowly into the darkness of the inner box until the screen is in total darkness, opening on a new scene in Africa. Metaphorically the audience has just been mailed to Africa. Another method is the **dissolve**, where one scene fades as another enters and for a brief second we, as viewers, are mentally moving through time and space into a memory, a simultaneous occurrence or perhaps just a new image. A dissolve can be accomplished very slowly or extremely fast. In *Field of Dreams*, a young Archie Graham is very quickly converted into seventy-two-year-old Doc Graham by the camera's focusing on a pair of baseball spikes stepping over a rock path and becoming a pair of well-worn wing-tips. As the camera opens its lens, we see first his medical bag and then a full body shot of the doctor moving quickly to aid the choking child.

A third method of transition is **multiple imaging**, by which we see on the screen more than one image. This technique is frequently used to place us into the mind of a character. In older films, inserts are used to move the audience in space or time: the clock with the hands turning, newspaper headlines, dates falling from a calendar, subtitles, and fireworks exploding or waves crashing on the rocks following a love scene.

The motion picture is not limited to strictly visual images; action is accompanied by sound. In filmmaking, there are three types of sound present in practically every scene. First, and probably most important, is the **dialogue**. It is important the audience hear and understand every line. A good sound mixer can separate each track and augment where necessary to heighten and control communication. A second use of sound is **musical accompaniment**, for which there are two types. Orchestral background music is generally written to enhance the mood and action of the film. A second type of musical background has recently become very popular. The film *American Graffiti* (1973), instead of using orchestral music, used contemporary music as it would be played on a radio. This started a trend that is both popular and in many ways more economical for the production. Stop into any record store, and you will find a category of recorded **sound tracks**—music in both forms that accompanied the film. The third type of sound is **natural sound** in whatever setting the scene is being performed—

automobile horns, or trains, or traffic, or voices, or whatever else would be present in reality. Sound is always within the control of the director and audio engineer. **Special effect sounds** are categorized under the umbrella of total special effects. One real advantage that film has over other media is the ability to add, subtract, augment, or rerecord sound at any time prior to presentation. Everyone has seen the opening of *The Sound of Music* with Julie Andrews singing with full orchestral accompaniment while romping alone on a mountaintop. The actual sound recording was made in a studio and later dubbed into the film's action. The dubbing process is a major part of filmmaking, particularly for outdoor and action scenes and in every case, singing.

In evaluating the quality of film, one must consider the **actors** beyond the descriptions that appear in the literature. **Characters**, whether developed by literary authors or screenwriters, are creations. Authors may pattern a character after a living person or persons, but they are just as likely to develop a character to fit a particular set of functions, both physically and psychologically. In casting a film, the casting director does not have that prerogative. He or she must select a living person to portray the literary creation. Sometimes the actor chosen fits and other times does not. Actors may be chosen to play a role because of their celebrity value as well as their talent. In some cases an actor may select a particular story he or she wants to play, secure the story, and develop the project. One fact must be accepted: incidents and characters in a novel are *not* the characters and incidents we view on a screen. Jack Nicholson, regardless of the fact he won an Academy Award for his portrayal of Randle P. McMurphy in *One Flew over the Cuckoo's Nest*, is not "red headed with long red sideburns . . . as broad as papa was tall, broad across the jaw and shoulders and chest." Nor is Tim Robbins as Andy Dufresne in *The Shawshank Redemption* a "short, neat little man with sandy hair and small, clever hands." Unlike literature, where the reader develops his or her own mental image of the character based on whatever physical description an author may provide, the director selects the person he or she believes fits the role or, in some cases, the film's commercial requirements. Who plays the lead roles may or may not determine the success of the film at the box office.

Fundamentally, there are two types of actor. A **personality actor**, such as John Wayne, Jack Nicholson, Goldie Hawn, and Roseanne, has a personal quality that dominates his or her presence on the screen. John Wayne could not believably play a hairdresser or Goldie Hawn a nuclear physicist. The public would not accept them even if their skills would allow them to play the role. Technically this type is known as presentational: they present themselves as the character an author creates in fiction, be it a play or a novel. Robert Duvall, on the other hand, can play a reformed alcoholic country singer in *Tender Mercies*, for which he won Best Actor, or Major Frank Burns, an oversexed religious zealot in the film *M*A*S*H*, and be quite believable in both. He is a **character actor**, attempting to internalize the role in order to "become" the created character. This division of acting style is present in both male and female actors and does not in any way determine the quality of a performance. Two females noted for their ability to create character are Meryl Streep, who won an Oscar for her portrayal of a holocaust survivor in *Sophie's Choice*, and Jessica Lange, winner of the 1994 Best Actress Oscar for her portrayal of a woman losing herself in *Blue Sky*. These actors are representational. They attempt, as physically and psychologically as possible, to represent the character an author has created.

According to Konstantin Stanislavski (1863–1938), a Russian stage director who literally wrote the book on acting,

While the art of living an image strives to feel the spirit of the role every time and at each creation, the art of presenting an image strives only once to live the role, privately, to show it once and then to substitute an externalized form expressing its spiritual essence; the hack actor disregards the living of the role and endeavours to work out once and for all a ready-made form of expression of feeling, a stage interpretation for every possible role and possible tendency in art. In other words, for the art of living representation, living the role is indispensable. The hack manages without it and indulges in it only occasionally. (qtd. in Pudovkin 246)

In film and on the stage, it is the job of an actor to so completely "live" the role that a viewer does not see the person playing the part but sees the character an author created. For a John Wayne, it would happen rarely; for Dustin Hoffman, it happens most of the time.

What is important to remember is that when we are looking at films constructed from a novel, we must consider the choice of actors as well as the quality of performance in portraying the roles created by the author. Does the actor's physical presence overshadow the story, or by giving a poor performance harm the story? Or was the actor simply miscast, rendering the original story ineffectual?

Or perhaps the story or the characterization is altered to conform to the actor rather than the cultural archetype. One very well-known story involves John Wayne in his final film, *The Shootist*. The novel, written by Glendon Swarthout, was successful as a western novel. When production rights to the book were purchased by Wayne's company, there was a discussion regarding changes. Swarthout wanted final script approval and apparently felt he received it. However, when the film was shot, the ending of the novel was considerably altered to fit the image of John Wayne the actor rather than the novel's character. This was also true of the **ingenue** role played by Ron Howard. The novel portrays Howard's role as a loss of innocence into a future of gun fighting, but one could not expect to find our little Opie or Richie Cunningham descending to such an evil end. In

The Shootist, he is "forced" to use a gun, but then dramatically casts the gun aside, implying a gunless future. John Wayne, true to his image, goes down in a blaze of glory, heroic to the end as he disposes of the two evil men who might otherwise threaten civil society. A court suit attempted to prevent the opening of the film, but failed. The movie opened on schedule and met with reasonable success. An interesting sidelight to the making of the film was that Miles Hood Swarthout, son of the author, adapted the screenplay, emphasizing how little control the screenwriter has in the final editing.

In many films, it is not the stars who ultimately determine the overall quality of the presentation. In many cases, it is the smaller parts that when done extremely well make the overall picture memorable. For example, while Whoopi Goldberg was deservedly nominated for an Oscar for her performance as Celie in *The Color Purple*, Desreta Jackson, who plays the teenaged version of Celie is rarely mentioned, yet she did a superb job in establishing the character in the minds of the viewers and certainly provided the audience a base for Goldberg's characterization. Whatever accolades may go to the star, a film's ultimate success, as in any other group endeavor, will require the supporting cast to perform equally well. Anyone who has seen Coppola's masterpiece *Apocalypse Now* will remember a very small scene in which a young black actor (Herb Rice), moving slowly and deliberately, turns off a blaring radio, calmly listens to a distant voice, and quietly loads and fires his grenade launcher, silencing the taunting. What haunts the screen is that his expression never changes. All we know about him is his expressionless face, his native-like adornments, and his title, *ghost*. When we leave the theater, we take with us his image. Perhaps he as much as any other character in the film is Coppola's symbol of the Vietnam War. A stage director's mantra as he prepares the cast for performance is an old cliché and is as true for film as for the stage: "There are no small parts, only small actors."

Film technology includes a **point of view**, which in most cases is the camera lens. However, it is possible to film in such a way as to present the scenes from a character perspective. For example, in both the novel and film, *The Shawshank Redemption*, Red, a long-time prison inmate, functions as its narrator and as a major character in the story. This allows the director to use Red as **voice-over**, providing transitions connecting scenes that are years apart. This technique is also used in Spielberg's *The Color Purple*, a novel conveyed in letters. Films that are presented from the viewpoint of a particular character provide opportunity for both transition and perspective. In both cases, the "objective" observer is the camera, while the subjectivity results from our knowing, that the story is being told from a single character's memory. A voice-over occurs when a disembodied voice makes observations about the scene, filling in gaps in time or as a motivation for the action. The voice-over is a kind of vestigial **soliloquy**, a theatrical device occurring when a character speaks directly to the audience, providing information the audience needs to know in order to follow the plot. The voice heard is generally that of the protagonist, although it can be another character, as when a letter is being read by its author. Subjectivity primarily enters in the editing of the film rather than the filming.

Originally a camera position was stationary and could only pan vertically and horizontally. As technology expanded, the position became extremely mobile through the use of tracks, dollies, hydraulic arms, aircraft, automobiles, balloons, and even a bicycle. A more prominent upgrade came with the advance in the quality and type of camera lens. A camera with a telephoto lens and fast film can focus on a single feature of the actor, such as an eye or a tooth, or it can pull back and photograph a very wide angle. However, because film, like literature, is dependent on character, there are stock shots conveying a total characterization: **head shot** or **close-up; medium shot**, which includes the torso; a full body shot called a **long shot**; and a **two-shot** covering two people in the same frame. These shots make up the majority of most films, but there are as many variations as the imagination of the cinematographer or director will allow.

One important perspective is to view the camera as an eliminator. The camera becomes a directional viewfinder as a director focuses on a specific aspect, eliminating from sight all extraneous objects or action that might distract an audience from seeing precisely what he or she wants them to see. This is a major difference from stage performance. During a play, the entire space in which a scene is being performed is always visible to the audience. Every character within the scene is also visible. Film has the ability to eliminate everything except whatever specific object or action is desired—a tear, slowly descending a cheek (accomplished by using a drop of mineral oil, since tears, being water, descend rapidly), or perhaps an object. In *The Color Purple*, Steven Spielberg, during a romantic scene in which Shug and Celie kiss, the audience is treated to a view of a pink wind chime. Its delicacy of color and sound adds a rather sentimental innocence to the encounter. Chances are that if the camera had not eliminated all other aspects of the scene, the audience would not have noticed the wind chime.

Lighting, like sound, has advanced dramatically as equipment, particularly the quality of film and cameras, has been technologically improved. From the beginning of motion pictures at the turn of the century until the late 1930s, almost all films were black and white. It was believed even into the 1970s that black and white film had an advantage over color because it seems more real. However, by the mid 1960s and the proliferation of color television, if a film was to make it to television, it had to be in color. American filmmakers (with few exceptions, one being Peter Bogdanovich's *The Last Picture Show*, 1971), producers, and directors would not take the chance on losing that commercial reward. (To be accurate, it is most notably the investors who demand the insurance of video options.) Peter Bogdanovich had great difficulty in convincing the studio that black and white was appropriate for his film. In the end, he was proved correct, but his success has not led others to attempt to film in black and white.

Quality of film is the determining factor with regard to lighting. The two technologies are interwoven. The faster the film, the less lighting is required to illuminate the shot. Technicolor, the first real color process, was invented in 1935. The difficulties it created had to do with its high light requirement, which created problems of where scenes could be shot. With today's high-speed color film, the director can use less light and use filters, altering the tint in order to create a mood. Audiences who have viewed any of the *Dick Tracy* or *Batman* films will recognize this process. For our purposes, we will concentrate on the color values presented in two general categories. For black and white films, we need to be aware of the amount of shadow and gray the film uses—how much contrast exists between **white to gray to black**. This will also relate to the amount of **backlighting** (lighting behind the action) the director uses in filming the story. An interesting technique recently developed for commercial television has found its way into motion pictures: inserting color into black and white frames for communicative purposes. *Pleasantville* (1998) interweaves color as reality with black and white, which is fantasy. As characters discover reality, they are seen in natural color. It does make sense; the real world is in color, and we certainly think of emotion as color. When we are angry we see red, or we become green with envy. Computer graphics now allow the cinematographer to color a face or hand or whatever else and leave the rest of the frame black and white. We will certainly see more of this rather than less. Color becomes a trope enhancing meaning within the structure of the story.

For color, we will become aware of **contrasts, hues,** and **tints** within a scene and as an overall picture. *The English Patient* was partially filmed in North Africa, much of it conveying the vastness of the desert. Color and shadow are used to enhance the open space, forming a background that is integrated into the action demonstrating the smallness of humans in relation to their environment. This is further enhanced by the actor's costumes and makeup. Everyone in the desert seems to blend into the surroundings conveying one of Michael Ondaajte's themes: man is not the center of the universe but simply one of its many features.

Color film, even high-speed film, requires more light than does black and white to bring out the contrasts.

APPLYING THE ARCHETYPE TO NOVELS AND FILM

Art, in whatever form it may be presented has been defined as "the embodiment of the spiritual matured to the point of revelation" (Jaffe qtd. in Jung *MS* 250). It is an act whereby the artist creates a work that will reveal to the public an aspect of human spiritual nature. An artist sends a message; a reader, viewer, or listener must be present to perceive or art cannot exist.

One way to perceive and comprehend is to analyze the work within the context of a previously defined set of standards and approaches to it. For literature and film, there are available some general categories into which a work may be placed that will provide a form for analysis and evaluation.

Realism is a fidelity to actuality in its representation in literature or film, or its level of **verisimilitude**. A third term, coined by Edgar Allen Poe, added the ingredient of **probability**. No matter a story's setting, characters, or plot, the reader must be able to believe in a level of probability. What matters for each of the terms is to create within the mind of the reader or viewer a sense of **believability**. In drama, whether stage or film, this requires suspending disbelief on entering the theater. In a theater the audience sits in the dark and, for the time there, suspends awareness to the obvious and accepts that what is happening on the stage or screen is real. In literature, it means being willing to accept the story on the terms supplied by the author. This implies the reader or viewer will place his or her imagination under the control of an author. Rod Serling, writer and narrator of a 1950s television, show labeled this the "twilight zone." In this application, realism (with a small r) applies to the level of believability the author or director communicates to the audience.

A more literary application of the term is for an entire genre of literature—the school of realism. This can be defined only in comparison with its adjunctive terms, romanticism and naturalism. These terms have very broad and overlapping meanings when applied to either literature or film. A very simplistic but workable explanation is that when the character seemingly controls the environment, or the environment is shaped in such a way to conform to the needs of the characters, it becomes **romantic**. When the environment appears to control the character, it is **naturalistic**. Realism appears in between, allowing some control over and some influence by the environment. Historically, romanticism is generally associated with idealism, as in creating an environment as you would like it to be rather than as it is. In an ideal world, a world of spring and summer, good always triumphs over evil, and for the moment, it appears that everyone will live happily ever after. Nineteenth-century England is most noted for its romantic literature, particularly the novels of Jane Austen (*Pride and Prejudice* and *Emma*) and the Brontë sisters Charlotte (*Jane Eyre*) and Emily (*Wuthering Heights*). The great adventure stories, past and present, also are a major romantic genre. America contributed Edgar Allen Poe and his many stories of the grotesque along with Nathaniel Hawthorne (*The Scarlet Letter*), Herman Melville (*Moby Dick*), and the bridge between romanticism and early realism, Mark Twain (*Huckleberry Finn, Tom Sawyer*). Each of these has been made into film, some of them several times.

A major difference between the novels listed above and modern romance novels and films is that contemporary stories generally incorporate elements of realism in even the most romantic of stories. There are several devices each medium possesses in order to connect romance and realism. One example for film is the use of actual locations, particularly with familiar settings. Alfred Hitchcock did this frequently; his famous *North by Northwest* finale was filmed on the faces of the presidents at Mount Rushmore. A novel or a film may incorporate real people or actual historical events or places to enhance believability. Robin Hood, one of the most famous mythological heroes, occupied an actual forest, Sherwood Forest in western England. Romanticism by tradition also includes all imaginative literature— when imagination overshadows reason, focusing instead on horror, fantasy, or adventure, and including those films relying on special effects rather than plot or character to attract an audience. Romantic novels make no attempt to present the world realistically but instead create a world to fit the needs of the story. In American literature, romance is most often associated with the movement west with the novels of Zane Grey and Willa Cather, and present-day authors Larry McMurtry and Louis L'Amour. As can be readily seen by the diversity of romance writers, the genre is alive and well represented throughout both centuries. Its popularity remains high as contempory novels and films continue to rely on romantic characters and settings, and while they may be in one sense mythical, they are not bound to maintain a *mana identity*. The general focus of modern romance literature is primarily directed toward entertainment and caters more to satisfy our popular culture.

It is in the area of realism where literature and film are at one point closest to each other and perhaps semantically the furthest apart. It is paradoxical to discuss fiction, be it novel or film, as being real. Paradox or not, it is in realism, connecting to actual experience, that the idea of film as mythopoiea becomes most closely united. "People only respond to the mythic nature of a story when they recognize the inherent truth of it" (Monaco *AFN* 253). In realism, just as in myth, there exists the aura of truth. The closer the novel or film represents a primeval reality, the closer the story relates to myth. The closer the story connects to myth, the more direct the connection between the story being told and the reader or viewer of that story. "Real myths, those artistic evidences of our collective consciousness . . . spring directly from roots in reality" and are of our genetic inheritance. We cannot resist connecting with these stories as they tend to "heighten reality and condense it" (251). For the moment in time in which we are participating in the story the unknown becomes the known.

In addition, there is a form of realism where fiction and fact come in direct contact. One example is a film made from a "true novel," Truman Capote's *In Cold Blood*. Capote moved to Kansas, the setting of the brutal murder of the Clutter family, and spent a great deal of time researching the events surrounding the crime, the subsequent capture of the young perpetrators, and their execution. Capote was first and foremost a novelist, not a historian. The book that resulted from his research contains much factual material. At the same time, because of Capote's personal beliefs, the novel presents a strong argument opposing the death penalty. The 1967 black and white film version, directed by Richard Brooks, followed the novel's form by appearing as a semidocumentary in relating the details of the crime, the capture, and subsequent execution. Through excellent performances by the cast, particularly Robert Blake and Scott Wilson as the young killers, the audience was made to feel great sympathy for the youthful criminals during their last moments of life. This follows the book in highlighting and enhancing Capote's theme, that capital punishment is unnecessarily cruel, to a much wider audience than the novel did. The result of this type of narrative is a presentation of the story realistically but not precisely objectively, that is, events were shaded to present a subjective reality. The plot of a story can present a theme of why seemingly good boys become violent killers and simultaneously attempt to sway the audience to a particular ideology. In Capote's mind, there was little difference in how the youthful murderers killed the Clutter family and how the State of Kansas subsequently treated them. As fiction, the story possesses a high level of verisimilitude; as fact, it becomes subjective reality. It also contains all of the elements necessary for myth. Two young men, crazed by alcohol and greed, lose their innocence and commit a multiple murder for which they ultimately try to "redeem" themselves, but society exacts full payment for their transgressions by requiring them to forfeit their lives.

A very contemporary entry into this mode is John Berendt's *Midnight in the Garden of Good and Evil*, a "true novel" about a murder and the subsequent trials in Savannah, Georgia. The novel was published in 1994 and almost immediately rose to the best-seller list, where it remained for over a year. The film version, directed by Clint Eastwood, arrived in theaters in 1997. The film received mixed reviews.

Some other excellent combinations of film and novel based on historical circumstances are *Compulsion* by Meyer Levin, a story of Chicago's famous Loeb and Leopold crime and trial, and *All the President's Men*, concerning the Watergate burglary and the ultimate resignation of President Richard Nixon, written by reporters Bob Woodward and Carl Bernstein. Oliver Stone's 1991 retelling of Kennedy's presidency and assassination, *JFK*, according to many critics attempted to rewrite history by rejecting the Warren Commission's conclusions and reviving the conspiracy theory. Another novel that sought to rewrite history is Robert Penn Warren's *All the King's Men*. Although many critics consider the novel biographical in nature, Warren, admitting to similarities between the novel and the life of the late Huey P. Long, colorful senator from Louisiana, assured readers that the connections were present only to provide a realistic base for a fictional story. What he really wanted to show a public emerging from World War II was the dangers of demagoguery. By incorporating actual events or settings in a fictional novel or film the author used a literary device that imposes a sense of verisimilitude to their presentation. By attaching fictional rather than real names, the novel has a universal and timeless appeal. By connecting the plots and the characters with a mythical archetype, the novels and films provide that spiritual revelation Aniela Jaffe spoke about.

Whether a novel or film is romantic or realistic, the author or director must include an element of real truth, which then becomes the means by which the story connects to the audience. When the reality of the story represents a metaphysical truth, the story connects to a recurrent archetypal theme and reaches toward myth. It does not matter if the story is based on actual events or is totally the creation of the author. The critical measurement is in how effectively and to what extent the author or director is able to incorporate truth in his or her work of art.

Our focus is not on the historical content but on the author or director's ability to portray the complete story with a sense of the actual. In a practical sense, realism requires the novelist or filmmaker to stay within the laws of natural science in portraying the character, the action, and the setting. As simple as this sounds, any avid reader or film aficionado knows that nature is often bent to conform to the needs of the story. In reality, seldom does a clap of thunder occur at just precisely the right moment to punctuate the character's statement or action. A stack of cardboard boxes does not always appear in an alley when police are in hot pursuit, and a parked car never becomes a ramp for one car to catapult into the air before exploding. (My personal favorite is the uncanny ability to find a parking place directly in front of the character's destination.) When action, setting, or character become recognizably contrived, verisimilitude becomes lost, which in turn loses truth, which compromises the story's mythopoeia.

By the presentation's incorporating a concrete sense of reality, the story has a base from which the reader or viewer may connect to a truth that provides a base for myth. If it is myth that brings the known (reality) closer to the unknown (abstraction), it would follow that the more realism or truth a fictional story develops, the closer it would bring us to a fundamental metaphysical truth. The more *real* a spiritual experience (*mana*) is, the closer we get to whatever exists as ultimate reality. For archetype and myth to connect, "realism [must reach] an artistic critical mass, at which point the record becomes transformed into myth" (Monaco *AFN* 252).

The final broad category into which we can place literature and film are those stories employing an aura of naturalism. This term is applied to realistic literature or film that tends to subjugate people to the extrinsic forces of culture and nature. It "attempts to describe life exactly as it is, and ends, by the very logic of that attempt, in pure irony" (Frye *AC* 49). John Steinbeck, one of America's foremost naturalistic authors, demonstrated this form in his great American novel, *The Grapes of Wrath*. Whether you read the novel or view the 1940 film, the dark and violent world of the migrant fieldworker is deeply real. From a literary perspective, it is so real that it becomes somewhat surreal, attaining a nightmarish quality. The elements of character and setting, through their symbolic reference, create a reality beyond the visible. When what you see in your imagination or on a screen is presented to conform to an exodus from depression- and drought-ridden Oklahoma to a "promised land," California, and manifests itself fully in the humiliation and degradation of a family that was "perfect and upright, and one that feared God and eschewed evil" (Job 1:1), a metaphysical reality is simultaneously created. As such, the story moves into the realm of naturalism. The environment dominates the characters. It is an environment over which the Joad family has no control. Drought, ignorance, poverty, violence, and societal indifference become forces that control the Joads' very existence even though they have seemingly done nothing for which punishment would be deserved. They allegorically represent the exodus of the Jews from Egypt and the story of Job.

Naturalism dominated American literature during the 1930s and 1940s. It was also a strong aspect of *All the King's Men*, as the protagonist, Willie Stark, succumbs to the power of corrupt politics. The theme of the novel and film follows the admonition of British Lord Acton when he warned, "Power tends to corrupt; absolute power corrupts absolutely." Willie Stark begins his quest an honest man and loses. When he fights corruption with corruption, he wins. Like the Joads, Stark is consumed by the environment. The characters in these two novels seem physically and intellectually unable to combat the evil influences of the environment and suffer grave consequences. This does not diminish the reality of either story. In fact, *The Grapes of Wrath* was so real that, when it was published, it had an impact on the social order in the United States. People became outraged that good families were being treated in the manner of the Joads, and in many states, especially California, laws were enacted to protect migrant workers.

When discussing a modern novel or film, it is not necessary to classify the story formally as romantic, realistic, or naturalistic. However, it is necessary to understand the level of influence that extrinsic forces, such as the environment or contrivance, impose on the characters. Be careful not to confuse literary realism with believability. Literary realism is more synonymous with being true to life, as in verisimilitude. A story, such as *Interview with a Vampire*, can be completely believable to those seated in the theater or reading the novel and not in a literal sense be realistic. A purely imaginative story will always be romantic, for it exists in a world created solely to fit the needs of the characters. For analytic depth, it is necessary to identify the amount of compliance the author of the original story gave to realism. This is an area on which much critical analysis and judgment will be made—how many laws of nature are contrived or subverted to fit the story. We will critically assess the level of believability, realism, and verisimilitude in character, setting, and plot.

A third area involving the term realism occurs when it is contrasted with abstraction. An abstract quality in novel or film occurs when an idea or event goes beyond sensory perception for its comprehension. A **realistic** quality, on the other hand, is comprehensible in concrete terms. George Bluestone, in *Novels into Film*, seems to feel this is an area of great difficulty for film to compare favorably with a novel. However, it is not an area film directors tend to omit. The good ones attempt to develop cinematic methods that will, even in the brief space of time given to such devices, convey a feeling that will amplify or enhance the narrative meaning.

This would compare to the use of imagery and figurative language in poetry. **Images** are sensorially perceived, while **tropes** or **figurative language**, as in metaphors, similes, allusions, and allegories, require a more abstract ability to connect two different objects or ideas. For example, a novel or film utilizing symbol to enhance or amplify a particular theme is relying on the ability of the reader or viewer to connect the symbol with the action. In the theater, you perceive the action visually and audibly; this is real. The symbol, which may or may not be directly associated with the action, connects in a superconscious or subconscious or abstract sense to amplify the meaning or theme. In film, as in the transition following a passionate love scene, the camera will move to waves crashing on the rocks. This acts as both a transition and a symbol. One of the classic love scenes from film, duplicated many times, originated in *From Here to Eternity*. This scene is able to interweave the symbol into the action. Burt Lancaster and Deborah Kerr emerge from the sea, symbolically cleansed from all past transgressions and, as if they were Adam and Eve, fall upon a blanket on the beach and immediately engage in a passionate embrace. The camera pulls back to focus on the sea breaking on the rocks. What takes place on that blanket occurs completely in the imagination (this is a 1954 film). However, the sea crashing against the rocks should provide some concrete images based on each individual's past experiences.

This type of realism as symbol also occurs in literature. In Walter Van Tilburg Clark's classic western novel, *The Ox-Bow Incident*, concrete language describing the harshness of the environment is used in tandem with the behavior of the characters, implying they are connected. The story involves a lynching of three innocent men by an angry mob. At the point of the lynching, Clark describes the seconds prior to whipping the horses from under the three victims:

We all moved out of the circle to give the horses room. In the last second even the Mex was quiet. There was no sound save the shifting of the horses, restless at having been held so long. A feathery, wide-apart snow was beginning to sift down again; the end of a storm, not the beginning of another, though. (186)

The mob, the victims, the horses, and the weather were bound together, acting in unison. It was not simply an act of good or evil, but a reflection of the time and place. Combining reality (action and setting) with the abstract (the implication that the men were only what their environment made them) amplifies and enhances a mythopoeic theme that a person is not a superior entity created by a benevolent God to dominate the land, but instead is merely an intelligent animal incapable of exercising the will to go against the pack (nature), even when he or she knows the pack is wrong. The novel, being narrated by an active participant, made this connection much better than the film version did. Critical analysis shows the novel's presentation to be naturalistic, while the film version was termed "starkly realistic."

One other form of metaphor we need to know is **allusion,** a specific type of comparison when the symbolic idea or object is derived from a previous literary or historical source. A flood, or a snake, when incorporated into a literary work or film as a symbol, will signify God's wrath or the presence of evil. Both of these originated in a literary sense in the Bible. An "Achilles heel" signifies a weakness or fatal flaw (**hamartia**) and comes from Greek mythology. The great Greek tragedies and for the most part all of Shakespeare's tragedies occurred as the result of a protagonist's flaw. A recent movie built around an allusion was *Don Juan DeMarco,* in which the actor, Johnny Depp, believes himself to be the reincarnation of the great lover Don Juan, a renowned romantic hero of seventeenth-century Spain, immortalized in an opera by Mozart and a poem by Lord Byron. The novel *Jaws* was, according to author Peter Benchley, a modern and considerably less literate version of Herman Melville's *Moby Dick.* An allusion can be a **symbol** or an entire story.

Film not only uses literary allusion effectively but also creates allusions all its own. Two of the best known are the shower scene from *Psycho* and the beach love scene in *From Here to Eternity.* In addition to scenes, memorable lines from film have become a part of our culture. Rhett Butler's famous line, "Frankly my dear, I don't give a damn," and the maid's line, "I don't know how to birth no babies," from *Gone with the Wind* have found their way to other movies and certainly to television. "What we have here is a failure to communicate" from *Cool Hand Luke* is another well-used line. Such well-known television shows as *The Carol Burnett Show* and *Saturday Night Live* rely on film classics for many of their skits. Television's situation comedies frequently use both classic and current movie scenes and lines, mainly due to their quick recognition by the audience; a thirty-minute show must rely on shortcuts.

One other important device present in good literature and film is the effective use of **irony,** which occurs in three forms: **verbal, situational,** and **dramatic.** Irony exists when the language or action conveys a meaning beyond what you read, see, or hear. It is through the use of irony that the abstract quality is conveyed. Verbal irony is obvious when the language, description, dialogue, and tone of voice convey meaning beyond the denotative intent of the words. Also, a metaphor, symbol, or allusion can be used to create verbal irony through **hyperbole** (exaggeration) or **understatement**. The English language has many words that may denotatively convey the same object or action but when written or spoken, they convey a different quality assessment. For example, a dining establishment can be referred to as a restaurant, diner, café, ptomaine tavern, or greasy spoon. Each means a place where you can purchase food, but each term conveys a different picture in the imagination of the reader. An action may be performed savagely or sadistically, or at another time sensuously or graciously, each supplying a tone to the expression. Everyone can relate to a time when a mother or father admonishes, "Don't use that tone of voice with me." The voice inflection conveys to the parent the child's discontent, which in turn, creates their discontent. Where a writer uses word choice and syntax, a speaker uses inflection to create the same outcome, a meaning beyond what the senses actually perceive.

Situational irony occurs when the action implies a meaning greater or less than what is being presented. Just as hyperbole and understatement apply to verbal irony, **parody** or overacting and underacting or subtlety, conveys in many cases meaning far beyond the literal action. Compare the performances of Dustin Hoffman in *Tootsie* and in *Rain Man*. In *Tootsie*, the role called on Hoffman to exaggerate his character to become a "raging feminist." In *Rain Man*, the demand was for subtlety. The character is required to be withdrawn and confined within himself. This type of irony includes body language, facial expressions, and hand gestures, as well as interaction with other characters or objects within the environment. In acting, this is known as **subtext**. The actor, through body language or expression, communicates something more than the dialogue conveys. In literature this is developed through the conflict and a narrator's subjective diction used to describe the action.

Dramatic irony is somewhat different. In literature, theater, and film, dramatic irony exists when the reader or viewer knows information the character or characters do not—a subtle but very important device. For example, in *The Last Picture Show*, readers or viewers know the truth about rich and pretty Jacy, Duane, and Sonny's love interest, long before the boys realize they are being used by her. Knowing this prepares the reader for Jacy's eventual rejection of both young men, and as a result, we accept without question her behavior, knowing, even if the characters do not, they are better off. This is one way an author uses dramatic irony to create verisimilitude. In many cases, the difference between contrivance and verisimilitude is in how well the author uses dramatic irony to foreshadow the action.

All of the technologies for both media are merely devices available to the author or director in conveying the reality and abstraction of the stories. In order to assess the presentation critically, we will evaluate how effectively the author or director made use of these devices. We certainly will not always agree, nor should we. We may not even agree on the archetype, but what we will have is a base from which to discuss and evaluate the quality of each medium.

For literature, we will focus on the author, for film, the director. They are the creative intelligence responsible for the final entity. In each of the novels and films we analyze, we need to keep in mind that the director has some advantage. First, the film will have followed after the novel was published. In some, such as *The Shawshank Redemption*, the time lapse is substantial, while in others, like *The Color Purple*, the film follows closely enough that the reader will also be a prime viewer of the film. In addition to the technological advantages, the director has the advantage of any literary criticism, as well as public acceptance and popularity of the novel. This, of course, is a two-edged sword. The public, particularly professional critics, and, where the film is contemporary to the novel, the reader, will have a preconceived notion of what the film should accomplish. The director knows what has been considered good and what was not so well received about the novel. In the final analysis, however, the director must make choices. He or she will choose those characters and actions that may be developed and spliced together to convey the story. A professional screenwriter, or in some cases the novel's author, will create a screenplay that will be used by the director as a base upon which to build the final product. Ultimately the director creates the film, for it is he or she that who brings together the technologies. This is the major point at which semiology becomes a prime factor. A film director may continue to film and edit until that particular scene meets the precise criteria he or she wants the audience to see and hear. In essence, a film director represents each member of the audience. Also, a director can be more objective than an author because the story being filmed is the actual creation of the author. The director may not have a personal interest in the story, only in how the story can be conveyed visually.

The choices a director makes may be obvious, such as in *The Color Purple*, where the story is told in the form of letters written by the protagonist, first addressed to God and later to her sister, Nettie. It would not make much of a movie to have a woman sitting at a table and reading aloud for 152 minutes what she is writing. Literary critics for the most part agree that for this story, the point of view is effective, although at least one scholarly critic felt that a poor, abused black woman writing letters to God was a little contrived. Steven Spielberg, the director of the film version, chose the scenes the letters described that he felt reflected the essence of the controversial Alice Walker novel. You will read the novel in its letter form and then view the film. You will be a judge of whether Spielberg selected the correct scenes to convey the story's essence. You will evaluate whether the correct actors were chosen to play the parts. You will determine to which seasonal phase this story of one woman's passage from adolescence to womanhood belongs. The novel created controversy in both the black community and among many whites. Much of the controversy occurred because people either do not agree on what Walker wants to say or they agree about her purpose but disagree with the way Walker *and* Spielberg tell the story.

In other films, the choices are less obvious. Some novels adapt easily to film. Practically everything Ernest Hemingway wrote has been converted to film. Because of his terse style of writing and the fact that he constructed straightforward dialogue, his stories seem to be easily adapted. Stephen King is a contemporary author whose work has been made into film. Some critics state that he structures his novels with the film version in mind. One short story of King, "Rita Hayworth and the Shawshank Redemption," was published in a four-story volume entitled *Different Seasons* in 1983. Critics are split when reviewing the stories, some stating that King should stick to horror stories while others say it demonstrates King proves he can write more than horror tales. The film version of this story came twelve years later and is considered one of the best pictures of 1995, with Morgan Freeman nominated for an Academy Award for his portrayal of the institutionalized long termer, Red. It is an excellent film, but there is much more to the novella than what the audience sees. It is the overall story that translates, although style certainly plays a part. It is the story through its primeval reality, its mythological truth, that connects to the reader or viewer.

One final aspect to consider is the context of the time in which the novel was written and the film produced. In older films, such as Henry King's *The Sun Also Rises*, made in 1957 and based on Ernest Hemingway's 1926 novel of the same name, restrictions on what could be filmed and what could be published are much different from today. The language contained in the novel is by today's standards very mild, and it is even milder in the film. This is one reason we do not want to compare a 1926 novel too closely to a 1983 novel. This is why beginning with the archetype provides a basis on which we, as familiar as we may be with novels and films of the 1990s, can find a common ground. Does the archetypal essence and mode of the story emerge from the form, be it film or literature, 1926 or 1998? What does it tell us about the culture that produced it? Is the inclusion of graphic sex and profane and obscene language an enhancement? Will any of the novels or films be available to audiences fifty or more years from now? What do these stories tell us about us?

In each case, a novel and film must be judged on its own context. Although we will analyze stories according to their archetype, the study will focus on a novel and its companion film as a single entity. The bond between them comes not only from their using the same archetype to tell the story, but the creative idea of one became the source for the other. Discussions relating to comparisons of different novels and films will reflect cultural changes incorporated in the presentation.

The stories we read, view, analyze, and criticize are modern versions of archetypal myths. Each represents in its treatment of the archetype a seasonal genre. The story is not only a romantic, realistic, or naturalistic comedy or tragedy, but it is a product that enters our minds by connecting to our natural instincts regarding the rituals and celebrations related to seasonal changes.

Following a midterm project, you will be required to complete an outside project where you will select a novel/film combination to work on individually. There will be a list (Appendix C) from which you may select a novel/film combination to evaluate. You may want to review some of the examples mentioned in the prior text material. Any combinations mentioned will be acceptable excluding the class selections. In this book, we explore selections beginning with a look at contemporary heroism, segue to modern rites of passage from youth to adulthood, and conclude with an evaluation of morality and magic. For each, we will archetype them in order to categorize their significance, discuss their form and content, and attempt to determine what they tell us about out culture and their relationship to our world. As Malinowski stated, "We can say that the narratives being constructed during the late 19th and early 20th century are the stories from which future generations will construct our mythology. These then are the stories reflecting 'a narrative of [our] primeval reality '"(104).

PART II

KNIGHTS AND HEROES

A major recurrent archetype in every culture is the concept of the hero. Within our American culture, a version most familiar is the western novel or film as a form of the messianic-hero myth. This is the stranger who arrives at a time when the local inhabitants are being persecuted by an evil enemy and by using his or her strength and skill overcomes whatever obstacles may be present, righting the wrong. The hero may sacrifice his or her life, move on by riding or walking into the sunset, or, in some narratives, finding his or her own paradise. A biblical source for these stories is the story of Jesus Christ. The Gospel of John (15:13) quotes Jesus saying, "Greater Love hath no man than this, that a man lay down his life for his friends." Upon that tradition, King Arthur establishes a chivalric code. A knight of the round table will be "a faithful Christian," possessing "courage, loyalty, generosity, and honour," including, "protecting women, children, the weak and defenseless" (Cavendish 40–41). Messianic quests are not confined to the Judeo-Christian tradition. An even more ancient story of sacrifice is found in Hesiod's *Theogeny*, probably taken from oral myths originating in the Balkan Mountains of Northern Greece (Puhvel 217). It is the story of the god Prometheus, who willingly accepts eternal punishment for giving mortals the secret of fire and therefore saving humanity. From Asia comes a Japanese story of the legendary Seven Samurai, some of whom sacrificed their lives in saving a small rural village. This story, which was made into a classic Japanese film (*The Seven Samurai*, 1954), came into our own movie lore as *The Magnificent Seven* (1960), a western film about seven gunfighters, who, because the American West had become civilized and had no use for their services, travel to a small community in Mexico to save its innocent villagers from a roving gang of cruel bandits.

It would seem that this story in which a person places his or her life in jeopardy for the benefit of less fortunate others is deeply embedded in a universal human psyche as how a human *ought* to live. Year after year, novelists and filmmakers the world over present versions of this story as a model. Part II looks at three contemporary examples of how we view heroism in this last half of the twentieth century. Heroism, in its most romantic and respected form, is expressed as a conscious choice of one individual to sacrifice him or herself for the benefit of others.

"Rita Hayworth and the Shawshank Redemption," written by Stephen King (1982) (the film was directed by Frank Darabont, 1994), is a short story contained in an anthology of four novellas entitled, appropriately, *Different Seasons*. Each of the novellas represents a season. For King, "Shawshank" connotes spring. The anthology received mixed reviews, mainly because it was a departure from the usual literary style and subject matter of previous King novels. The film, entitled *The Shawshank Redemption*, received high acclaim, being nominated for Best Picture. Morgan Freeman (Red) was nominated for Best Supporting Actor, Darabont for Best Screenplay from a Previous Source, and Roger Deakins for Cinematography.

One Flew over the Cuckoo's Nest by Ken Kesey was published in 1962, and the film version, directed by Milos Forman, opened in 1975. The novel from the beginning was both a critical and commercial success, having sold several million copies to date. The film version won Academy Awards for Best Picture, Best Actor (Jack Nicholson), Best Actress (Louise Fletcher), Best Director, and Best Screenplay Adapted from another Source (Lawrence Hauben and Bo Goldman). It also received nominations for Cinematography, Editing, and Original Score.

And finally we look at a most romantic of stories, *Shane*, originally serialized in *Argosy* magazine in 1949; its film version, directed by George Stevens, opened in 1953. The film version received nominations for Best Picture, Best Supporting Actor, Direction, Cinematography, and Screenplay, winning only for its cinematography. (Most of the Academy Awards for 1953 went to Fred Zinnemann's blockbuster, *From Here to Eternity*, based on a novel by James Jones.) The serialized version of *Shane* was published in novel form in 1954 and remains in print.

Each book and its companion film in this part begins with the stereotypical entrance of a stranger into a situation that has need of a savior—not because the group faces annihilation but something more important in the American culture: its individuality and personal freedom are threatened from both extrinsic and intrinsic dangers. *Shane* is a rather typical western story: the small farmer being forced to vacate his land because of the arrogance and power of a big rancher, a "sodbuster versus cattleman" conflict. In a more modern setting, the mostly voluntary inmates of the

"Cuckoo's Nest" and the involuntary inmates at Shawshank Prison can survive, but at a price to themselves. The inmates of the "Cuckoo's Nest," an unnamed mental institution, are being manipulated and controlled by an arrogant nurse and her authoritarian, machine-like program. For the inmates of Shawshank Prison, the changes imposed on the inmates are more subtle and gradual. In addition to a cruel and dehumanizing environment, they face the problem of becoming institutionalized. In the case of the institutional patients and inmates, before anything can change in the environment, a change must occur within each individual. Each man will require an infusion of courage and hope as much as they require protection from the antagonists. *Shane*, being more romantic, follows the simplicity of a more traditional myth, whereas *Shawshank* and *Cuckoo's Nest* bring into the mythic archetype a more complex vision of modern American culture and individualism.

What is common to all three narratives and connects the stories to a primeval base is an outsider—a stranger possessing unique skills who enters into a threatening situation and provides what each group requires. From this commonality of plot, each story goes its own way in portraying how a modern conflict fits into the mythological hero mold, what attributes are important and what is not important personally in a modern hero, and how a modern version of a mythical hero will perform. In *Cuckoo's Nest*, the story is complicated. R. P. McMurphy, before a solution to the overall problem is reached, must first teach a small group of men who have accepted living their life as mental defectives a sense of individual self-confidence. McMurphy's personality is split between a worldly approach to life and a serious problem in a basic naiveté with regard to his own safety. In contrast, Andy Dufresne, the stranger in *Shawshank*, is under the greatest pressure, for, like Dante, he is required to descend into hell and live to tell about it. (Dante Alighieri, a twelfth-century Italian poet, wrote *The Divine Comedy* describing a visit by the poet into hell, the *Inferno*, into heaven, *Paradiso*, and purgatory, *Purgatorium*. It is Dante's description of hell, not the Bible, that provides a traditional Christian picture of this place of punishment for the damned.) A structural difference exists as McMurphy's quest involves a group, while Dufresne's quest is focused on a single character. This may be simply explained by one being a fully developed novel and the other a **novella** (long short story or short novel). In a form reminiscent of King Arthur's knights, Shane a gunfighter with "courage, loyalty, generosity, and honour," protects a family and its home by singlehandedly "slaying the dragon."

Each of these narratives presents three perspectives. First, the author or director must keep the basic structure of the messianic myth sufficiently intact in order to tap into the collective unconscious of the audience while simultaneously incorporating structural techniques providing something unique enough to make this retelling of an old story special. A third and equally important perspective, particularly for the student, is involved as each of the narratives, intentionally or not, reflects how the author defines current hopes, fears, values, and/or aspirations of American culture at a specific point in time. This is not to imply the author's intent is didactic, but rather provides one individual's insight into how the myth may be replayed within the culture of his time.

These narratives, along with selections in Part III, cover a quarter-century between the 1950s and the 1980s. Some major events that affected the life of every American during that period include the return to civilian life of millions of service personnel and the baby boom (1948–65), and the politics and legislative programs of Presidents Eisenhower (1952–60), Kennedy, Johnson and Nixon/Ford (1960–76), Carter (1976–80), and the beginning of Reagan's term. It includes the years of the Vietnam War (1958–75), the development of intercontinental ballistic missiles capable of world destruction (1955–85), the cold war (1948–1989), the assassinations of John Kennedy (1963), Bobby Kennedy (1968), and Martin Luther King, Jr. (1968), school desegregation (1954), Vietnam War protests (1968–73); the Manson trial (1971), space exploration and walking on the moon (1958–71); the Cuban missile crisis (1962), and the fall of Saigon (1975). These were the events that dominated national newspapers, magazines, radio, and television. Discounting the political administrations, you might note that of the events listed, thirteen would be considered negative and only two, space exploration and desegregation of schools, are positive. In other words, the major events affecting our lives are not very uplifting.

One additional major occurrence that slowly and inexorably influenced change in our culture during this period was the growth of television. It began in major cities in the early 1950s. By the 1980s television sets were in over 90 percent of American homes, affecting America's culture more than any single event since World War II. For example, television is credited as the prime cause of Vietnam War protests. Through television, war was brought into the homes of ordinary Americans, who for the first time saw war's realities and began to oppose it openly.

The events listed above received the greatest publicity, but we also know that each year, the majority of people, then as well as now, went about the daily business of living. On the local news you might have heard about your or a neighboring city's having a disturbance due to racial problems. The price of groceries continued to rise, as did the cost of living generally. (Parents then and now like to remind their children what a dollar could buy when they were teenagers.) Citizens began to move to the suburbs, leaving the inner cities to deteriorate. Rock and roll became the music of choice for adolescents. Drugs, particularly marijuana and LSD, became as acceptable as alcohol in escaping from reality. Dr. Benjamin Spock, a noted pediatrician, published a book on child rearing that henceforth changed the manner in which parents disciplined their children. Women demanded equal rights in all things. At one point, some draft-age males publicly burned their draft cards, while some women of every age burned their bras. School became laboratories for new and unproven educational technologies, lowering the overall quality of learning. There seemed to be less tolerance and more corruption everywhere. Personal responsibility, adolescent discipline, business ethics, and family values were subjugated to an individual's desires. These, along with other cultural changes, all occurred before the proliferation of talk shows, cable television, the home computer, and the Internet.

The modern versions of myth explored here did not occur in a vacuum. They are continuations of old myths, yet, as an integral part of their context, they are representations of who we are and how we viewed life in the years from 1960 to 1982. Ken Kesey and Stephen King created a strange microcosm of life: an insane asylum and a maximum security prison. By placing us with men confined to their surroundings, we experience with them an existential world, one seemingly without exit. Yet each author developed his form of optimism, of how, even in hell, we can find a meaning or purpose for life. With the right leader, we can be led, but each person, regardless of surroundings, must find a meaning for himself or herself. What do they tell us about ourselves? Our responses will come from insights gained by comparing and contrasting the stories with each other and with our own existence.

Chapter 3

Hope Springs Eternal

"Rita Hayworth and the Shawshank Redemption" by Stephen King

Possibly, this story, from beginning to end, is one most directly associated with mythopoeia. It has to do with survival. Humans are not the strongest or the swiftest in nature, yet they have been able not only to survive but, acting collectively, to dominate all other forms of life. In fact, humanity has "progressed" to the point that we now possess the means of our own destruction. From a literary perspective, this concept treats humanity as a single entity, and when writers attempt to deal with it, the stories tend toward broad symbolism and allegory. Writers such as H. G. Wells (*The Island of Dr. Moreau*), Isaac Asimov (*Nightfall*), Mary Shelley (*Franken-stein*), and, to a certain extent, Michael Crichton (*Jurassic Park*) draw a broad picture of human arrogance, far beyond what would be considered reality. The unique characters are not intended to deal with ordinary problems or ordinary people.

Most contemporary writers prefer to focus more on the ordinary individual. This variation in perspective can be seen in how we view the Bible's first narrative story. Consider for a moment that first man, Adam, who was exiled from the Garden and forced to make his way in what was probably a very hostile world. How he dealt with his daily problems of food and shelter were never explained. We simply see Adam as a very broad symbol representing the fall of man, an obvious allegory conveyed to us in myth or parable form. We can neither sympathize nor empathize with Adam. Except for artists' renderings, we have no idea about his appearance, and the content of the story does not reveal any details regarding his skills, feelings, or any other aspects of his life. We can only interpret and hope to understand the meaning of such a story in extremely broad terms.

Most modern writers prefer to focus on the common struggles one individual has with one or more other individuals and various conflicts pertaining to the environment. It is important to a writer that the reader have something in common with his or her characters and to some extent the environment. This common bond can be found in the two overlapping obstacles involved in the human struggle to survive and grow. One obstacle exists abstractly and therefore beyond the scope of science: how we ought to live (the search for a meaning to life). This quest occurs primarily within the individual. The second obstacle is somewhat broader: how ordinary individuals cope with the natural, cultural, and societal forces of the environment in fulfilling a meaningful life. In good literature, the protagonist confronts elements of both conflicts.

With this thought in mind, we begin our study with this story's connection to the familiar biblical story of Eve in the Garden of Eden. Eve literally means "first woman." The generally accepted interpretation of this story teaches us that the female of the species was responsible for the presence of evil in the world when Eve, tempted by the serpent, ate of the fruit of the tree of knowledge and in so doing, has her mind and mankind opened to both the knowledge of good and evil and their presence as forces conflicting for man's eternal soul. For this transgression she was forever condemned to subjugate herself to her male companion, in addition to suffering pain during childbirth. For his part in following the lead of Eve, Adam is to survive only by the sweat of his labor. In other words, Adam and Eve become free agents in a hostile world, forced to become a part of nature rather than its overseer. What is important mythologically is the belief that this story confirms that there exists within our world a force for good and a force for evil, both available to people and between which each individual must choose. As long as people choose good (how they ought to live) over evil, human life will be protected by its creator. Adherence to God's law then becomes the means by which humanity survives. This story, in essence, establishes a basis for moral law.

A Greek version of this myth, and one that obviously influences Stephen King in "Shawshank," is the story of Pandora. In primordial time, the Olympian gods and the Titans battled for supremacy. The gods, led by Zeus, won and established dominion over the universe. Two Titans, Prometheus and his intellectually challenged brother, Epimetheus, fought on the side of Zeus and are rewarded by becoming the creators and overseers of mankind. Prometheus, in addition to his creative abilities, is a trickster. He plays a practical joke on the great god Zeus regarding the disposition of the choice parts of a sacrificial bull. When the parts are divided, Prometheus takes the choice parts and covers them with fat and bone. The rest of the fat and bone is placed in a container and covered with a layer of prime meat. Zeus, having first choice, takes the camouflaged fat and bone. He becomes angry and punishes Prometheus by having his creation, man, prevented from having fire. Promethus, in order to protect his creation from starvation and annihilation, steals fire and gives it to humanity, thereby ensuring human existence.

Zeus, being furious with Promethus, commands Hephaestus, the smith of the gods, to create a female from clay. Hephaestus creates a woman, to which Aphrodite adds beauty and Athena domestic skills. She is named Pandora, "all gifted." Pandora is given to the brothers along with a clay jar containing all of the evils of humanity. Zeus and the early Greeks felt it was punishment to impose the presence of a female in a previously all-male world. Prometheus, being wary, advises his brother not to accept the gift, but Epimetheus, being intellectually challenged, is captivated by Pandora's beauty and welcomes her. Because he warns Epimetheus, thereby violating a command, Prometheus is condemned to be chained on a mountain where a huge vulture will descend and on a daily basis, rip out his liver. He will be restored during the night, only to have the entire cycle repeated the next day and forever.

Pandora becomes the wife of Epimetheus, and although both have been warned by Zeus and Prometheus not to open the jar, Pandora, just like Eve in the Garden of Eden, allows her curiosity to overcome judgment and opens the jar. From the jar emerge the evils of the world to haunt humans: greed, lust, sickness, old age, famine, and death, among others. There was one aspect that catches on the lid and is returned to the jar—*hope*. With hope, individuals will be able to cope with all of the evils that escaped. This alteration in the ending of each story conveys a basic cultural difference. For the Judeo-Christians, survival depends on man's remaining in the grace of God, whereas the Greeks tend toward a more humanistic view, leaving the ultimate choice to human reason.

These myths provide an appropriate entry into Stephen King's "Rita Hayworth and the Shawshank Redemption," a short story contained in an anthology of four novellas appropriately titled *Different Seasons* (1982). Each of the novellas represents a season and a specific attribute of humans. For King, "Shawshank" represents spring, the season of rebirth and hope. The anthology received mixed reviews. For example, *Kirkus Reviews* stated that although "Shawshank" was "the best of the lot . . . the climax is feeble (especially after such a long build up), the redemption then is murky—but the close observation of prison life offers some engaging details." Kenneth Atchity, in his *L.A. Times Book Review*, was more complimentary: "To find the secret of his success, you have to compare King to Twain, Poe,— with a generous dash of Philip Roth and Will Rogers thrown in for added popular measure. King's stories tap the roots of myth buried in all our minds." The film version, entitled *The Shawshank Redemption* (1994) and directed by Frank Darabont, was nominated for Best Picture, and Morgan Freeman for Best Supporting Actor.

Both the novel and the film are noted for their realistic approach. King tells the story in a terse and straightforward style reminiscent of Hemingway. However, in the novella, King, perhaps because his principal claim to literary success is in the horror and mystery field, seems more concerned with suspense than with probing the full depth of his characters. Even in his narrator, Red, we never see the depth to which prison life has changed him from a young man convicted of murder and, one would expect, dominated by anger and resentment, to the novella's character, a fully institutionalized prisoner who is slowly changed into a hopeful parolee. The result is that this is a realistic story that suggests allegory more than it creates one. In fact, King suggests this when Red describes Andy: "You may also have gotten the idea that I'm describing someone who's more legend than man, and I would have to agree that there's some truth to that. To us longtimers who knew Andy over a space of years, there was an element of fantasy to him, a sense, almost, of myth-magic, if you get what I mean" (38–39). The "if you get what I mean" would seem to acknowledge the presence of the reader and suggest the story has an abstract component.

This allegorical aspect, however meager, does enhance its mythological roots. The story has many connections to the Pandora myth, the obvious one being hope. As for evil, one could not find a more malevolent and corrupt place than a maximum security prison. The guards, the administration, and the various sadistic groups exemplify as Atchity described, "[to] show us a natural shape of the human soul—a shape even more horrifying, for it protean masks, than the ghouls he [King] has conjured up in the novels." Every contemporary evil seems to be described: greed (the wardens), murder (Andy and Red, the guards), sadism (the guards and the sisters), jealousy (Andy's hamartia that sent him to prison and the warden's reason for not aiding Andy), hypocrisy (Norton's religious facade), old age (Brooks), and, perhaps the greatest of all evils for the institutionalized Brooks and Red, the loss of hope. Red states in both media, "They give you life, and that is exactly what they take, at least the best part of it" (26, film). What is there left to hope for?

A second connection is the symbolic replication of goddesses: Rita Hayworth, Marilyn Monroe, Raquel Welsh, and Linda Ronstadt. Although the film omits Linda Ronstadt, who perhaps refused permission to use her poster, the mythical symbolism is equally present. These women represent American icons of beauty during different time periods, which in turn connects them to a centuries-old archetype: the seductiveness of female beauty. From a practical standpoint, the literary function of the changing posters is obviously to show the passage of time. Symbolically, however, the images suggest a connection to Pandora, whose beauty was fashioned by the goddess Aphrodite and whose clay jar contains both evils and the means of coping with them, hope. Those pictures keep for the men a connection to what is beautiful on the outside and also to remind them that there are females in the world. King superbly creates an ironic twist: it is the beauty that provides the shield for man to escape the clay jar (Shawshank) containing its nest of evil. In Shawshank, a sustaining hope is the only means of remaining human.

Dufresne's obsession with rocks is another connection to myth. The earth has a mythological female connotation. Andy Dufresne is given direct connection to Mother Earth in his love of geology. Andy, when he finished polishing a rock, "would put it carefully on his window ledge, which faced east. He told me [Red] he liked to look at them in the sun, the pieces of the planet he had taken up from the dirt and shaped" (71). Add to this the lodestone, the "piece of volcanic glass," the one that caused Red's nightmare about the "great glassy black stone in the middle of a hayfield; a stone shaped like a giant blacksmith's [Hephaestus] anvil . . . that wouldn't budge" when he tried to move it (78–79). King is connecting his story not only to Pandora and hope, but to the matriarchial origin of all life, Gaea, Mother Earth.

King has made his reputation through images of evil and supernatural forces in novels such as *Carrie, Pet Sematary, The Shining,* and *Salem's Lot,* to name but a few. "Rita Hayworth and the Shawshank Redemption," and the three others in the anthology focus on subjects that rely on natural causes. A critic, Paul Gray, writes, "*Different Seasons* is, in fact, his bid to be recognized as something other than a writer in a fright wig" (*Time* 30 Aug 82). This story does demonstrates that King can connect with a general audience when the material is right. The mythological archetype of this story is a journey into the underworld; the story's theme centers on an understanding that one must have hope to withstand the evil in this world.

In this novella, King modifies his style in order to connect with our natural instincts toward the seasons causing each story to affect us deeply. In general, King's novels do not make this connection. For example, academic critics generally relegate Stephen King's literary efforts as not worthy of critical analysis. The public seems to like them, to the point they are a commercial success in both media. Are the novels successful because of the films, or vice versa? Literary critics cite two reasons his stories would not achieve classic status. First, his subject matter generally represents the horror genre. Horror may be very entertaining but it is written to cause fright rather than direct itself toward a mythological truth. The primary intent would seem to be to shock or scare. Very rarely does a horror novel go beyond its original popularity. Second, King has a tendency to focus more on action than on character. This leaves his characters underdeveloped and subjects his style to negative criticism. King may be "the author of some of the best horror stories since those of Ambrose Bierce and H. P. Love-craft" yet, his desire for understanding and acceptance as an author "led him to publish [*Different Seasons*], an uneven, though surprising volume" (Cheuse 17).

"Rita Hayworth and the Shawshank Redemption" is a story about two men and how each adapts to the life that circumstance has dealt them. It is written in a manner to appeal to the masses. The characters are made believable through descriptive detail. Andy Dufresne is vividly portrayed by the descriptions of his actions and for most film critics is psychologically replicated by Tim Robbins in the film. Clearly Robbins is not a "short, neat little man with sandy hair and small clever hands" (16). Nor would a reader picture Morgan Freeman as Red, "a kid [who] had come in back in 1938, a kid with a big mop of carroty red hair, half-crazy with remorse, thinking about suicide" (54). In his role as Red, it is Freeman's acting ability to perform the subtleties of the role that complements Robbins's performance and makes the film work, at least up to the ending, as believ-ably as the novella. Note that the character name given to Morgan Free-man, "Ellis Redding," provides a degree of verisimilitude for his being called Red.

The story concerns these two very likable men who have nothing in common other than the setting (time and place), yet find in each other something missing from themselves. For Andy Dufresne, the missing ingre-dient is adaptability. Andy, as a bank accountant, always controlled his world in the same manner he controlled the bank's accounts. Everything in his world had a place and could be evaluated and categorized efficiently. For Red, Andy's only real friend at Shawshank, the missing ingredient is hope. Red has become "institutionalized." He has adapted so completely to the confines of the prison that being free no longer is an enticement; in fact, it is something to be feared. The story takes place in a maximum security prison in Maine between 1947 and 1975. In 1947, Dufresne is sentenced to two consecutive life terms for allegedly murdering his wife and her lover, a professional golfer. His story, and how it changes the life of the narrator, forms the plot.

The narrator, Red, is also a convicted murderer, who at the time of Dufresne's arrival has been in Shawshank ten years. He is known to the other inmates as a supplier—a convict who over the years has made per-sonal contact with the guards and service personnel to bring items into the prison for which other inmates are willing to pay. For this service, he re-ceives a 10 percent commission. We learn from the beginning that Red is an honest man, which establishes a sense of irony early in the story. Red's business allows him to have access to almost everyone and, because of his ability to provide for their necessities, receives little or no interference from the other inmates or guards. Most important for the reader, he under-stands the effects of prison life and the individuals sent there. Red, like the Chief in *Cuckoo's Nest*, observes and provides insight into the prison's daily operations and informs us how the prisoners adjust, or not, to prison life. The author has provided a means for access, just as Kesey does for the Chief in *Cuckoo's Nest*. While the Chief pretends to be a deaf mute, Red is respected by both the guards and the other prisoners as a self-made "trustee." As Red moves freely among the inmates and as a trusted member of the prison black market, he is able to know what is happening throughout the prison, which makes the narration very believable.

The story may be approached from several perspectives. It is a story of male bonding, of isolation, of what it means to be human, and a how-to story on surviving in a cruel and violent environment. It is a search for a meaning of life. It is a retelling of Dante's *Inferno*. The motivation for his journey into the underworld becomes one man's search for paradise. The man in this case is an inmate in a maximum security prison. If he can accept the pain and degradation of being buried behind prison bars as a test, if he passes (survives), he will be rewarded by entering paradise, freedom. What makes the story appeal mythologically is that it clearly defines the importance of hope for all of us. The flyleaf, we assume written by the author, states "HOPE SPRINGS ETERNAL" above the title. Each of the three words has a mythical meaning independent of the others. Hope is not only fundamental to religious belief, but, as we know from Pandora, is the key to survival in an evil world. Spring has two meanings. First, it is a season that invokes a sense of being reborn, which is what happens to Andy and Red. And as a verb, it is an action involving elasticity or resilience—the ability to bounce back from defeat. The use of the word *eternal* connects the story directly to paradise, to Eden. The essence of the story is that humans can stand almost anything if they maintain hope. Scarlett O'Hara, Margaret Mitchell's heroine in *Gone with the Wind*, expresses the feeling when, after having lost everything, including her wealth and her husband and child, she looks toward the sunset and says: "Tomorrow is another day." As Red says, "It comes down to two choices. Get busy living or get busy dying" (105). When you reach bottom, the only way is up. If you have hope, you will not only survive, but will have the motivation to overcome.

The film version follows for the most part the story as presented in the novella. What becomes readily apparent is how the film extends the novel to include incidents and characters far beyond the literature. Leonard Maltin, in his 1996 *Movie and Video Guide*, explained that this "widely praised film is well crafted but terribly overlong" (1170). Roger Ebert, noting the same circumstance, added, "If the film is perhaps a little slow in its middle passages, maybe that is part of the idea, too, to give us a sense of the leaden passage of time, before the glory of final redemption" (693). It is an aspect of the film's structural semiology that causes the audience to feel the slow passage of time that imprisonment brings. This may result from the novel's first-person point of view. Adaptation of a novel told through the eyes and mind of an individual character other than the protagonist provides a unique set of problems for the screenwriter and director. The perspective becomes dramatic rather than subjective. For this narrative, the brevity of the story, the limited setting, and the inability to contrast the fullness of Red's explanations with the graphic experiences provide material for criticism.

In this story, it is difficult to find a truly good person. We do learn that Dufresne has been wrongly sentenced and that Red has been fully rehabilitated, which certainly qualifies them to be redeemable. However, this is not a story portraying human weakness, rather, it is a story of hope. One interesting difference between the novel and film occurs when, in the novella, there is no reference to an active payback to society, the brutal guards, or the sadistic and perverted inmates. Only in the film is an overt revenge motive established. The film, in contrast to the novel, chooses to focus the antagonism on one or two characters. Warden Norton and a composite guard captain named Hadley. In the film, Hadley is arrested for multiple crimes, and Norton commits suicide, clearly showing the triumph of good over evil, whereas in the novel, King tends to personalize guilt by having Norton live out his life consumed by regret and Hadley, having provided the initial incident involving Dufresne's rise above the ordinary, simply disappears. The film complicates King's theme by allowing Dufresne to use extorted money to finance his paradise rather than money he had saved prior to his incarceration. Both forms, however, have happy endings, which would normally label the story as romantic. Stories told with great realism seldom end happily. In this case, because the theme is hope, a happy ending may very well be the story's saving grace. All of the elements of tragedy—violence, betrayal, indifference, isolation—that are so prevalent in realism are present, yet Dufresne finds his paradise. It takes place because of a graphic yet metaphoric rebirth. It is not an act of God, a deus ex machina, or the efforts of a romantic hero that bring about this rebirth, it is the eternal hope and the patient work of one man. In the final analysis, everyone receives what he ought to get, implying that right will eventually triumph when or if one does not lose hope; at the very least, it has a chance. What may go beyond believability is the effect of hope on Red. King's narrative provides one scene involving Red that strengthens the eventual outcome. Red, listening to the turmoil following the discovery of Andy's escape route and hearing the guard's exclamation, "It's shit oh my Gawwwwwd," begins to laugh uncontrollably, stating, "And oh dear God didn't it feel good" (88). At that moment, Red epiphanically knows what it means to feel free. The scene was omitted in the film, instead having Red brought into Andy's vacant cell for questioning. More importantly, the film relies on a promise Red gives to Andy rather than the character's depending on hope for the trip to Buxton and subsequent action and actually diminishes the full effect of hope as a motivator. Red's final epiphany occurs as he remarks to himself: "No, what he [Andy] needed was just to be free, and if *I* kicked away what *I* had, it would be like spitting in the face of everything *he* had worked so hard to win back" (102–3 my italics). The two men are irrevocably bonded, and Red, recognizing the moment, begins his weekend trips to Buxton in search of an anvil-shaped rock, not knowing what, if anything, he will find there. It is simply a matter of hope.

Andy Dufresne fits into Frye's second phase of comedy. A "complex irony is formed when a society is constructed by or around a hero, but proves not sufficiently real or strong to impose itself" (180). Dufresne is confined to a society, Shawshank Prison, in which he refuses to conform. The prison society (the wardens, guards, sisters and the system) expends every possible effort to make him one of their own, as they did to the institutionalized Red. Dufresne is placed in the dungheap of society and through ingenuity and will is reborn into paradise.

QUESTIONS

Cite page numbers for quotations and/or references in your responses.

1. Identify three similarities between Andy's method of escape and a sense of rebirth.

2. One of the major aspects relating to long-time prisoners was the idea of becoming institutionalized. What does this term literally mean when applied to long-termers? How do they change physically? Psychologically?

3. King, through the commentary of Red, seems to be making a point about the intrinsic nature of men in his descriptions of the guards' actions as they interact with the inmates. Select two comments Red makes about the guards and explain what King may have wanted the reader to infer.

4. Both of the two principal characters, Andy and Red, are convicted of murdering their wives and others. From the story, we are given to believe that Andy is innocent while Red is admittedly guilty. In the end Andy escapes, and Red is paroled. What makes this ironic? What thematic insight may be gained from this action?

5. Literary critics have written negatively about the novella's ending. The film made considerable changes in the ending, but film critics, like the literary critics, felt the ending was the weakest portion of the story. What do you think? Explain how you came to your conclusion.

Chapter 4

A Search for Laughter

One Flew over the Cuckoo's Nest by Ken Kesey

One of the best-known mythopoeia in Western culture is the legend of King Arthur, particularly in the search for the holy grail, the cup that Jesus Christ used during the Last Supper. According to legend, Joseph of Arimathea came to England as a missionary, bringing the cup with him. Legend holds that he secretly buried the cup for its protection, providing the basis for a search. Eight hundred years later, during a celebration of Pentecost, the cup appears in a vision to King Arthur and the knights of the round table. Four knights take upon themselves the task of finding the cup. The quests of the four knights—Galahad, Gawain, Lancelot, and the ultimate locator of the cup, Percivale—are the stories making up the myth. The grail, which becomes a Christian icon in the Arthurian sagas, is magical in the sense that it will provide food and drink for the believer.

This is not the first encounter with a magical grail. According to mythologist Jessie Weston, the holy grail is an extension of the horn of plenty, better known by its Latin name, a cornucopia—a magical goat's horn capable of supplying human needs. In Celtic mythology, the cornucopia became a *graal*, a serving platter or cauldron capable of producing food for some while denying it to others. Before the presence of the Romans and the introduction of Christianity, the Celts were druids. Druidism as a religion tends to be pantheistic rather than deistic. God is within all of nature rather than a singular being to be found on a mountain or in the sky. By the twelveth and thirteenth centuries, due to the domination of Christians, the object known to the Celts as a magical serving tray became the holy grail. Joseph Campbell confirms to some extent Weston's opinion by

agreeing that the grail as a metaphor existed in Celtic mythology long before the advent of Christianity in the British Isles. (*MC* 406–7). What we
have is the confluence of two entities—druidism, establishing a mystical
symbol, and Christianity, adopting the form—but placing the symbol into
its own historical perspective. In Christian Britain, the grail quest represented "the restoration to life, health, and fecundity of a land, its people,
and its king" (Segal 136). The common bond for all of these representations
is the cornucopia, graal, or grail, a physical object that represents the source
of a good man's sustenance. God will provide for those who obey his laws.
Metaphorically, our cultural mores are directly descended from the Anglo-
Christian culture of the twelfth and thirteenth centuries, with the grail coming to symbolize salvation, the means by which humans may be saved, for
only those who truly believe can "know and see" its presence.

This leads us to a study of the life and times of a modern knight/messiah,
Randle Patrick McMurphy, a red-haired, freckle-faced Irishman and by
ancestry a Celt, as portrayed by Ken Kesey in his classic novel, *One Flew
over the Cuckoo's Nest*. For McMurphy, the grail and the means of re-
storing to "life, health, and fecundity (fertility)" is laughter; his quest is to
guide this small group of mental defectives in finding the means to save
themselves from a wicked ward nurse and an indifferent medical system by
getting them to laugh at the absurdity of their lives and environment.

This novel appeared in February 1962 and received immediate critical
and commercial success. A *Time* magazine review stated that the novel is
"a roar of protest against middlebrow society's Rules and the invisible
Rulers who enforce them." A critic writing in the *New York Times Book
Review* stated, "What Mr. Kesey has done is to transform the plight of a
ward of inmates in a mental institution into a glittering parable of good
and evil." Over the next decade, a million copies of the novel were sold.
Apparently something very important within it touched a large part of the
American public. Its broad appeal as both a popular novel and a literary
work of art is enhanced by the continuing study in college classrooms. (It
has been supplemented by both Cliffs and Monarch notes.) Not everyone
enjoys the story; Kesey's chauvinistic attitude toward the females in the
novel has produced some of the strongest negative criticism. Marcia L.
Falk, in a letter to the editor of the *New York Times*, stated after viewing
the play version, "The novel/play never once challenges the completely in-
human sexist structure of society . . . the only right-on women in the play
are mindless whores."

The complexity of this novel may create some difficulty in identifying
the genre but not the archetype. The first problem occurs when the "hero"
fails to conform to those romantic ideals we have come to expect from our
knightly representatives. McMurphy introduces us to the antihero—a character who performs good works, although he is not necessarily a good

person, nor are his motives and actions particularly good. Kesey has given us an intriguing character. McMurphy is capable of being admirable and repugnant, occasionally at the same moment. Is this summer romance or autumn tragedy? Is this romantic heroism, realistic tragedy, or a contemporary satiric version of an ancient Greek tragedy? Is this a myth of eternal return, a dramatic confrontation between the forces of evil and good, or simply a retelling of the hero and the dragon—or perhaps a synthesis of all three?

A literary analysis of this novel identifies several unique effects. The point of view is first-person retrospective, with narration by a patient, Chief Bromden, suffering from paranoid schizophrenia. He is a Native American, who ranges in mental perspective from calm understanding to nightmarish hallucinations. The Chief inserts into the narration his hallucinatory dreams. At the time of insertion, particularly in the first two parts, these "trips" do not appear to have relevant meaning. Literarily, the dreams serve several functions. First, as exposition, they contain flashbacks relating background information. In addition, they provide a device for us to witness Chief's progress in his illness as his dreams gradually diminish in their distance from reality while adding an element of suspense. The point of view and the nonchronologic plot sequencing require the novel to be read through completely before everything falls into place. Also, *Cuckoo's Nest* provides an excellent example of why point of view frequently creates a major problem in transferring a novel to the screen. The screen version chooses to downplay the Chief's character to somewhere between a major and a minor role, resulting in a loss of much of the metaphoric quality of the novel.

One very important aspect creating additional difficulty for the film director is the novel's inclusion of symbolism. Two types of symbol are used in the novel. First, there are the traditional symbols in the form of literary allusions: McMurphy as Jesus Christ, a connection to *Moby Dick*, water as life and freedom, and fog as a deterrent to knowledge. In addition, Kesey creates symbolic metaphors to amplify specific attributes for individual characters. In the case of Nurse Ratched, in addition to the suggestive name, it is large breasts (not present in the film), perhaps suggesting a relationship to Gaea and a thematic rejection of matriarchy. McMurphy's initials, R.P.M., would seem to counteract the tightening effect of the "ratchet." Over all, of course, is the aura of the children's nursery rhyme of migrating geese, evoking a question in the real world, How do we identify just who is "cuckoo"?

In a novel that on its extremely realistic surface is trying to portray a mental hospital as it really is, the presence of so many symbols would appear out of place. When one combines these with Kesey's straightforward use of diction and detail, ranging from the graphically accurate to the metaphorically surreal, it would suggest a film director's nightmare. For the novel, it is an archetypal harmony with ancient myth that gives us a sense of verisimilitude. The inclusion of closely related dream and reality causes the reader to connect with both through the use of symbol, or that "part of the psyche that retains and transmits the common psychological inheritance of mankind" that forms our "collective unconscious." (Jung *MS* 107). It should be noted that Kesey attributed several breakthroughs in the writing of the novel to his use of peyote, a mental stimulant derived from the mescal cactus, while working in a Veterans' Hospital mental ward. A symbol acts as a literary mental stimulant, "intermediate between event and idea, example and precept, ritual and dream" (Frye *AC* 243). It is the unconscious making contact with conscious mind. The film, in not making effective use of symbol, must rely more heavily on character and the actor's subtext to convey the theme and in so doing may diminish the novel's depth of conscious-subconscious connection.

The beautiful manner in which Kesey creates character is worthy of mention. He presents the inmates and the antagonistic ward chief, Nurse Ratched, with precise detail, engaging the imagination of the reader in a believable manner. The situation seems bizarre, but the patients in that situation are people with whom we feel empathy. It would seem we know them personally. This, particularly with regard to the inmates, may also be one of the film's great strengths. The actors, being visually portrayed, are able to evoke sympathy in ways the novel may not. In this area, an interesting comparison is to *M*A*S*H*. Both novels and films approach their subject using a medical facility as their setting. In each, chaos would seem to be the order. However, the focus of *M*A*S*H* emerges from the medical staff's perspective and *Cuckoo's Nest* from the patients'. It is this change in perspective that establishes *M*A*S*H* as a satire and *Cuckoo's Nest* as somewhere between a romantic comedy and a story of a tragic hero. *M*A*S*H*, the novel and film, is satirizing war, the military, and human absurdity. *Cuckoo's Nest*, even though the setting presents a sense of irony, chooses to focus on the individual, McMurphy, and his quest to find and deliver the holy grail that will bring salvation to his flock.

The novel is divided into four parts rather than chapters; in fact, the chapter divisions are not numbered because they represent random thoughts, not in any numerical or chronological order. The parts indicate the changes that occur in both McMurphy and the narrator. Part I introduces the characters and covers the first five days of McMurphy's conflict with Nurse Ratched. Chief Bromden, the narrator, introduces the fog and the machine, which become metaphors for the Chief's illness. Part II focuses on the conflict with Nurse Ratched, who for the moment is apparently winning. Like most other tyrants, she goes too far, and McMurphy chooses not to capitulate but to fight to the end. Part III lifts McMurphy to the role of savior as the men begin to laugh at themselves and the hospital environment. Laughter, McMurphy's holy grail, is both a motif and a theme, but like Ratched in Part II, McMurphy goes too far and places himself in a vulnerable position. In Part IV, McMurphy assaults an attendant and undergoes electroshock treatments, causing him to act out a final and tragic end. His hamartia, his personal code of honor requiring him to "hold up his end of the deal" (226), is his undoing, although his legacy appears to be very successful. This particular aspect of McMurphy's acting on honor is unfortunately omitted from the film. Underscoring each part of the novel is the steady improvement in the narrator's mental illness; the fog is literally lifted, and by the novel's end, the Chief feels ready to face the outside world.

Another interesting use of symbols comes from the conflict between nature (geese, dogs, the sea, the moon, fish) and Ratched's machinery (grinding and moving walls, subbasements, tubes, wires, and rust and ashes for human organs). This conflict also has its roots in mythology as the age-old battle between man and machine. Most myths teach that man is most pure when he is closest to his natural origins—the admonition of "earth to earth, dust to dust," returning man to the bosom of his origin, Mother Earth.

One major difference in the novel and the film concerns the element of religious allusion. The novel makes frequent and in some cases extremely obvious references to the Messiah concept found in the Bible: In the fishing trip with McMurphy and his twelve followers; the references to him as a saint, martyr, and savior; and the shock treatment, when the attendant places "conductant" on his head. McMurphy comments, "Anointest my head with conductant. Do I get a crown of thorns?" (237). The placement of the patient on the table during shock therapy has already been alluded to as a cross. The connection to Jesus Christ is not in any way hidden. However, the film's director, Milos Forman, decided to minimize the direct religious connection and chose to focus primarily on characterization as his communicative device. In the novel, Kesey uses the Christ allusion effectively, but to a great extent sarcastically. McMurphy will never be confused with a benevolent savior. However, it is through this religious symbolism that the book connects most closely to the messianic myth.

The mythological portions of the novel are complex. On one hand, "the hero of a romance is analogous to the mythical Messiah or deliverer who comes from an upper world, and his enemy is analogous to the demonic powers of a lower world" (Frye *AC* 187). This obviously describes McMurphy and his hospital nemesis, Nurse Ratched. We can look to Celtic legends and specifically to Percivale, one of the three knights to complete the quest for the holy grail, for a similar challenge. Percivale, a subject of both English and German mythology, is a likely source for McMurphy. Percivale, also known as Parsifal and Parzival, is the most human of all the knights of the grail epic. He possesses great strength and profound weakness. His name means "straight to the center," which explains to a degree why he is realistic. His is "a life responsible to itself, to its own supreme experiences and expectations of value, realized through trials in truth, loyalty, and love, and by example redounding, then, to the inspiration of others to like achievement" (Campbell *MC* 480). We have a perfect definition of Randle P. McMurphy.

For a specific plot reference we can look to Thomas Malory's *Le Morte D'Arthur* as he describes one of Percivale's adventures leading up to completing his quest. Percivale, while resting on a river bank, encounters a beautiful seductress:

And then Sir Percivale proffered her love and prayed her that she would be his. Then she refused him, in a manner, when he required her, for the cause he should be the more ardent on her, and ever he ceased not to pray her of love. And when she saw him well enchafed [hot], then she said, Sir Percivale, wit you well I shall not fulfil your will but if ye swear from henceforth ye shall be my true servant, and to do nothing but that I shall command you. Will ye ensure me this as ye be a true knight? Yea, said he, fair lady, by the faith of my body. Well, said she, now shall ye do with me what so it please you; and now wit ye well ye are the knight in the world that I have most desire to. And then two squires were commanded to make a bed in the middes of the pavilion. And anon she was unclothed and laid therein. And then Sir Percivale laid him down by her naked; and by adventure and grace he saw his sword lie on the ground naked, in whose pommel was a red cross and the sign of the crucifix therein, and bethought him on his knighthood and his promise made toforehand unto the good man; then he made a sign of the cross in his forehead, and therewith the pavilion turned up so down, and then it changed unto a smoke and a black cloud, and then he was adread and cried aloud. (398)

Like Sir Percivale, McMurphy faces a choice. Nurse Ratched begins her seduction by describing how the men must receive "some manner of punishment . . . for their unspeakable behavior concerning the house duties . . . [and] the rebellious way you acted." Dramatic irony tells us that while the punishment was verbally for all, in fact, the entire action is aimed directly at McMurphy. He can choose to accept her punishment, "taking away the privilege of the tub room," and thereby succumb to her judgment, or "uphold his end of the deal" and become the savior. McMurphy, relying on personal honor rather than a "red cross" as Percivale did, chooses a heroic path, for "he was the logger again, the swaggering gambler, the big red-headed brawling Irishman, the cowboy out of the TV set walking down the middle of the street to meet a dare" (171–173). In that moment, McMurphy is tied directly to the western hero, America's romantic knight, and by continuum to Percivale, Galahad, Gawain, and Lancelot and before that to Hercules and Ulysses and back into primal history.

On the other hand, "the typical tragic hero is somewhere between the divine and the 'all too human'" (Frye *AC* 207). There is no doubt

McMurphy exhibits both extremes. He is constantly reminding us of his human side with his ever-present gambling and whore chasing. Just when he seems to be an amoral manipulator, the Chief will describe an action or expression that reveals a deep sense of commitment, as if an inner voice was making contact with his conscious self and of which even the character seems unaware. One such moment occurs on the trip back from the fishing excursion. The car passes the locale where McMurphy grew up and he was recounting his loss of innocence, when Chief noted, "Then—as he was talking—a set of tail-lights going past lit up McMurphy's face, and the windshield reflected an expression that was allowed only because he figured it'd be too dark for anybody in the car to see, dreadfully tired and strained and frantic, like there wasn't enough time left for something he had to do" (218). The moment reveals "not how men think in myths, but how myths think in men, unbeknown to them" (Hawkes 41). Interestingly, the film does not use the automobile setting but captures a similar moment near the end when McMurphy has the opportunity to escape. While waiting for Billy and Candy to complete their tryst, Nicholson, utilizing an actor's subtext, visually conveys the feelings described above and in the film quietly goes to sleep awaiting the moment when he will be discovered. To maintain realism, according to Frye, elaborating on a line from Milton's *Paradise Lost*, "If the hero was not sufficient to have stood, the mode is purely ironic; if he was not free to fall, the mode is purely romantic" (*AC* 212). McMurphy on several occasions had demonstrated he was "sufficient to have stood" and, as the scene above shows, was obviously "free to fall." Something from deep within causes him to place the need for Billy to develop a self-identity above his own need to escape. What emerges from his character is the choice to do what he ought, even if it means his fall. This is a point where the film and novel may separate in meaning. By the film's altering not just the placement of McMurphy's self-reflection but ignoring the Chief's many insights into his inner consciousness, we lose much of the character's motivation—*why* he chooses to act as he did. To what degree, and at what point, in each medium is McMurphy aware of the final outcome? Or, from a practical perspective, is the point for each action merely how the author and director chose to foreshadow the ultimate end for the reader or viewer?

This action connects McMurphy, not only to the mythical, but to one of the foundations of American culture, the principle of reciprocation—a society built on a principle where the recipient of a good deed has an obligation to return it in kind, to the one who gave it or to pass it on to another. When someone does something for us, we acquire a debt, not because it is demanded, but in a sense of voluntarily returning loyalty for loyalty. McMurphy, in responding to the Chief's complaint, "You're always winning things," stated, "Winning things! You damned moose, what are you accusin' me of? All I do is hold up my end of the deal" (226). This statement occurs shortly before McMurphy physically comes to the defense of George. George, who is obsessively paranoid about foreign objects' touching his body, uses his experience as a sea captain to bring the fishing boat in safely during an unexpected storm. McMurphy simply, and in an ironic way, was holding up his "end" of the deal by saving George from the enema (228–31). In this episode, tastefully omitted from the film, we are witness to Kesey's skill as a writer. He incorporates a cultural theme and simultaneously creates a very entertaining and ironic pun: If someone saves your——, you have an obligation to save his or her——, if the opportunity arises.

The novel also brings in a mythical forbidden road motif, "where the young hero deliberately violates the taboo, which has been given to protect him and so enters the field of one or more malignant powers, whom he overcomes, to release mankind from their oppression" (Campbell *MO* 110). McMurphy violates this taboo when he decides to defeat Nurse Ratched; he is fully aware that all he has to do is remain quiet and acquiescent, and he will be released. Exemplifying a very American cultural value, he chooses to take the conflict personally and seek individual triumph. In so doing, he becomes a model for the patients in addition to their advocate. Americans traditionally prefer the leader who leads by what he does rather than by what he says. On this point, the film may actually surpass the novel by creating a stronger empathetic feeling. Two scenes in particular emphasize this attribute. The first is McMurphy's futile attempt to move the water therapy machine. Forman uses close-up shots to portray the effort McMurphy/Nicholson is making. The actor is truly attempting to move the machine. Members of the audience become personally involved in the action as they visibly strain against their armrests in an attempt to help. We want McMurphy to succeed. A second, and more important, focus comes in the final scene, as Forman shows us the anger and hatred manifest in the character of McMurphy prior to attacking Nurse Ratched. At that moment, we know the conflict is reduced to personal hatred, and for a split second, we hope McMurphy will do precisely what he does. The camera's lens is able to create empathy, making us a part of the action.

The setting, the many characters, and the novel's reliance on allusion create a complex forum. In the novel, the basic quest for the holy grail remains the same for the inmates of Kesey's asylum as the knights of medieval England. What this conveys is how our present-day heroes are no longer larger than life. They are ordinary men of honor placed in a situation requiring them to live up to that code even though their own lives may be placed in jeopardy. The cliché "a man has to do what a man has to do" may be hackneyed, but when you consider that each use of the term *man* means something different, the progression becomes meaningful. A male must do what the culture requires of him to earn the title, a man. As the knights of King Arthur's round table are bound by their code of honor in order to earn knighthood, McMurphy must adhere to both his and the culture's code of honor, simply stated by Kesey as holding up one's end of the bargain. As McMurphy moves toward Nurse Ratched for the final time, the Chief tells us, "I suddenly realized with a crystal certainty that neither I nor any of the half-score of us could stop him. . . . We couldn't stop him because we were the ones making him do it . . . it was our need that was making him . . . perform a hard duty that finally just had to be done, like it or not" (267). Once McMurphy accepted the challenge, it was his responsibility to hold up "his end of the deal" and do what "had to be done." This adds a little realism from American culture to King Arthur's romantic and idealistic code for knights.

As the title implies: "One flew east and one flew west, one flew over the cuckoo's nest, O-U-T spells out." The "out" refers to the world outside the security of their asylum. When the inmates learn to laugh at themselves and the world around them, it is the beginning of coping with reality. On the fishing excursion they become aware that being insane is not without power. Harding comments, "Think of it: perhaps the more insane a man is, the more powerful he can become. Hitler for example" (202). Even at the climactic moment when McMurphy breaks the glass between the dayroom and the nurse's office, it is done with a smile: "I'm sure *sorry*, ma'am," he said. "Gawd but I am. That window glass was so spic and span I com-*pletely* forgot it was there" (172). For McMurphy, like "Wolfram's *Parzival* the boon is to be the inauguration of a new age of the human spirit: the *secular* spirituality, sustained by self-responsible individuals acting not in terms of general laws supposed to represent the will or way of some personal god or impersonal eternity, but each in terms of his own developing realization of worth. Such an idea is distinctly—and uniquely—European" (Campbell *MC* 480).

It is a part of a collective consciousness rooted in those European forebears that established American culture and remains one of our prime virtues.

QUESTIONS

In your responses, identify a specific reference by quotation or page number:

1. Select one of the Chief's dreams or hallucinations and explain in detail how it metaphorically represents a theme.

2. Identify three actions or events and explain how the diction and/or detail connects McMurphy and the Christ allusion.

3. The novel makes a clear distinction between what is natural (and good) and what is mechanical (and evil). One use of this distinction functions as a motif,

laughter. Identify one incident in which laughter proves therapeutically beneficial to the inmates. How do we know it is beneficial?

4. In your opinion, is McMurphy or Chief Bromden the novel's protagonist? In explaining your answer, you will determine if you view the novel as a comedy (protagonist succeeds) or a tragedy (protagonist fails).

5. In the tradition of the Greek theater, McMurphy dies because of his tragic flaw. Describe the flaw by citing one example from the novel that clearly demonstrates this weakness.

QUESTIONS FOR GROUP ANALYSIS

1. Evaluate the extent to which myth identity is lost by omitting the Christ allusion.

2. At what point, and to what degree, in each medium is McMurphy aware of the final outcome—that he is forever giving up any hope of freedom?

3. Read Joseph Campbell's statement on the previous page and discuss its accuracy and relevance to or applicability in modern American culture. To what degree does this concept emerge as an archetypal theme in each medium?

Chapter 5

Romantic Heroes Never Die

Shane by Jack Schaefer

That a nation's image of itself emerges out of its myths is a kind of chicken-and-egg dilemma. Whichever comes first is of little consequence because the two inevitably become interwoven as a nation develops. As an example, consider the English. Much of their image is derived from the myths surrounding King Arthur and the knights of the round table. A short summary would include a high idealism supported by a regimented set of rules governing the motivations and behavior of its citizens. In each adventure, the knights' actions are bound by an oath to King Arthur and to God. This, in essence, became the guidepost for all citizens of Great Britain; a strict adherence to the rules and full submission to the Crown. The models advocating just how to apply this behavior can be found in its more famous knights: Sirs Tristram, Lancelot, Gawain, Percivale, and Galahad. The exploits of these five, plus the Arthurian rules of chivalry and the wizardry of Merlin, establish a persona that serves as a base for what it means to be British.

America too has its knights and a heroic code. Film director George Stevens, according to Harry Schein in an article for *American Scholar* magazine, "expressed his desire to 'enlarge' the Western legend and to have said that the pioneers presented in the Western fill the same role for the Americans as King Arthur and his knights hold in English mythology" (Summer 1955). The knights of Great Britain and the knights of America have much in common. They travel alone on horseback and routinely find themselves in situations where they must defend the weak against the strong. Although they are separated by geography and time, what really separates the American knight is a factor inconceivable in any place other than that vast territory west of the Mississippi River. Paradoxically, the American model is first an individual and then an American. What makes him an American is an ability to act individually *and* honorably. Where the British knight is always bound to the round table and King Arthur, these American knights are most likely a "mysterious stranger," apparently without any overriding authority except personal honor. The origin of this idea emerges out of the transcendental Puritanism of Henry David Thoreau and Ralph Waldo Emerson. In "Civil Disobedience" Thoreau wrote, "I think we should be men first and subjects afterward." His compatriot Emerson stated, "Whoso would be a man must be a nonconformist" for "no law can be sacred to me but that of my own nature" in an essay, "Self Reliance." Transcendentally, we know what is right and are obligated by nature to act accordingly.

There is no question that people living in other countries tend to associate American principles with the western heroes they see in American films. What *Shane* accomplishes in novel and film is to define those attributes that are good about America. Shane then becomes a model of American knighthood, and wherever the film version may play, in Europe, Africa, or Asia, the viewers see Shane as a representation of what it means to be an American. They react to the idealism personified by one man, willing to stand alone if necessary, against the evil personified by an arrogant rancher (landowner), corrupt government, or dictatorial oppressor. It had taken the Europeans centuries to overcome the oppression of feudalism. American individualism, which more than any single attribute opened the West, did not allow it to happen here. What makes the American hero stand out are his courage, skill, and inner morality that disallows using his skills to subjugate the weaker or less skillful. What gives it a mythical quality is that the highest skill is possessed only by the most moral, suggesting that good will triumph in the end.

Shane takes on the character of the knights of the round table, except that he is being presented in an arena of reality. Were there really men like Shane—men who do not possess trickery, or magical weaponry, or direct connections to a deity yet are able to "slay the dragon" regardless of its power and skill? Shane is portrayed a quiet man whose possessions include a horse, his manner of dress, and, most important, his Colt .45. He must rely on speed and accuracy to overcome whatever enemy he must face to make things right. Shane, like the reader or viewer, simply knows he will win.

There are two perspectives from which a successful modern western saga may be evaluated. First, the story may be a myth in which those idealistic values of what it means to be an American are defined. On a broader scale, it can be viewed as a story about those forces that come into play in forming a nation out of a wilderness. *Shane*, a novel written by Jack Schaefer, who ironically, was born in the East in 1907, on its surface would not appear to be worthy of either assessment. The first publication of *Shane* was as a serial in *Argosy*, a glossy man's magazine popular in the 1930s, 1940s, and 1950s. The response to the publication of the novel and film was so positive that Schaefer was able to move to a ranch near Santa Fe, New Mexico, and devote full time to writing stories of the Old West. Admittedly, this story is just one of many that through the years have catered to America's fascination with the romantic stories of the westward movement. Of the thousands of stories published or filmed, a few, such as *High Noon, Red River, The Searchers*, and *Shane*, seem to possess that hard-to-define ingredient that causes it to connect in a way others do not.

The novel was not reviewed until after the film was shown. Since that time, several criticisms have been included in texts concerning western novels. James K. Folsom in his book, *The American Western Novel*, seems to have discovered the key to this novel's success. He asserts that the novel is "heavily flawed" in that it contains too much "platitudinous wisdom" and "Schaefer himself seems uncertain at times of what Shane is meant to symbolize" (126). On the other hand, in the novel, by not relying on suspense, "it becomes clear that the world of the Western town in which the story of Shane is unfolding is a symbolic one in which Schaefer can present a basically allegorical concern. For Shane is a walking figure of God's providence in the confusing world of flux" (127). Jenni Calder in her book *There Must Be a Lone Ranger* comments "Shane, in Jack Schaefer's story and George Steven's movie is the best of all possible examples of the mysterious stranger" (18)— that allegorical figure who is able to represent the best of the individual and simultaneously contribute to the success of the community.

The film, titled *Shane*, opened in 1953 to immediate success both critically and at the box office. The film was nominated for Best Picture, Best Supporting Actor (both Jack Palance and Brandon DeWilde), Director, and Screenplay Adaptation, and won the Oscar for Cinematography. Director George Stevens was able to take this stereotypical western to a new level. Much of the credit must be given to the superb cast; Alan Ladd as Shane; Van Heflin, Jean Arthur, and Brandon DeWilde as the Starrett family; and Jack Palance as the evil gunfighter Stark Wilson. The supporting cast—the settlers, the cowboys, and the townspeople—using an ensemble style of performance ably gave these larger-than-life characters a sense of verisimilitude. In fact, the film's popularity led to the story's being reissued in novel form and remains in our culture in an educational format. When the myth connects, it remains a part of the culture, perhaps forever.

At first glance, this is a reasonably typical story of a western hero built around the essence of the hero myth. Shane, the mysterious stranger of Schaefer's novel, fits nicely into the typical hero mold. We are never given the details of Shane's birth, except that he comes from Tennessee. We are given proof of his strength in his attack on the stump, his fight in Grafton's saloon, and in his fearless attitude (Campbell *H* 31). A shadow of fate begins to enter the story when Shane, for the most part, is accepted by the farmers even though he is obviously not one of them. When Marian comments that Shane appears "mysterious . . . dangerous," Joe replies, "He's dangerous all right . . . but not to us, my dear. . . . In fact, I don't think you ever had a safer man in your house" (8). Schaefer at this point is incorporating a sense of fate or destiny, some greater force *(mana)* that brought this stranger to these people just when they have greatest need. The settlers, even in their most fearful moment, seem to sense intuitively that his presence is ordained.

A major subplot enhancing the story beyond the conflict between farmers and ranchers is the personal relationship that develops between Shane, first with Joe, then Bob (Joey), and finally, Marian. The reader is made aware of the bonding, perhaps in a little different manner from the usual western story. Shane becomes more human, more personal, and more real as a man who, even against his will, becomes a hero rather than just a hero who happens by. An attempt at suspense is manifest in the early neutrality of Shane in the conflict. He seems to withdraw from any direct participation, other than the personal insult, before the intrusion by Wilson. This is enhanced by the author's not giving us any direct background on Shane. Schaefer wants the reader to feel Shane is uncertain whether to intervene. In the beginning, it is his desire to protect the Starrett family. When he realizes they are intertwined with the entire community following the death of Torrey, he fulfills what the audience has known from the moment Stark Wilson arrives in town.

In this unique subplot, the family relationship develops and matures around Shane. They become a unity of individuals, each with his or her own relationship to Shane, and each other. They share each other's friendship without jealousy or resentment in the most honorable way possible: mutual respect. Whatever Shane's feelings are toward Marian, or her feelings toward him, there is a clear recognition of what is morally correct and neither party would do anything otherwise. It is in this subplot that the point of view works best. By telling the story through the innocent eyes of Bob, the details are presented in a simple yet believable form.

The references to the garden, the farm, and its relationship to the family convey an Edenic quality to their world. Their world is being threatened by a powerful and greedy rancher (the devil?) who sees the land, not the people, as having value. The lines of the conflict are clearly drawn. On one side is the "evil" rancher, the man who opened the territory and now feels it belongs to him because he was the first white man to occupy it. He has chosen to forget the land was previously "owned" by Native Americans, whom he has driven off by force. When a wandering knight, Shane, enters into the conflict on the side of the farmers, the rancher counters by calling in his "serpent," Stark Wilson, to convince them to leave.

Schaefer enhances the biblical allusion with the diction and detail in describing the gunfight between Wilson and Torrey (88–89). Note the dominant *s* sound in, "I'm handling his business affairs" and "His business with stubborn jackasses," conveying a subtle hissing sound and again in the first confrontation between Shane and Wilson (98–99) when he is described as "sure of himself, serene and deadly." Each detail is alluding to the fact Wilson is evil personified as connection is made with the evil serpent from the Garden of Eden.

A major difference in the novel and film occurs when Shane and Joe argue about who will face Wilson and Fletcher in the big showdown. The novel provides a much quicker and cleaner assault on Joe. Schaefer obviously feels the character of Joe does not require being elevated to Shane's level of physical performance. The novel's climax occurs when Shane and Wilson face each other; a long fight sequence would add nothing to the plot. For Shane, the confrontation with Joe is a minor impediment in what has already been set into motion—the final showdown. George Stevens thought differently. He stages a battle royal between Shane and Joe, possibly to build suspense, or perhaps to strengthen the character of Joe in the eyes of the audience. Whatever his reason, it was a semiological choice. It could be because Stevens alters the ending, omitting the denouement. By having the fight, Shane is free to ride on, setting up the most memorable line from the film: "Shane! come back Shane!"

In one episode the film totally surpasses the descriptions in the novel: the death and burial of "Stonewall" Torrey. Wilson's execution of Torrey has become a classic. The silence is punctuated by the single shot from which Torrey flies backward into the mud with arms flung wide and legs crossed at the ankles in the form of crucifixion. The scenes that follow amplify Steven's directorial talent. At the burial, as the camera begins with a long shot showing the community cemetery located on a small hill above the town, we slowly are presented with several individual shots showing the community together. It is not the ranchers that will bring community to the West; it is the settlers with their small children. As a harmonica plays a mournful rendition of "Dixie," the men slowly lower the rough-hewn coffin. Everything seems to stop when, during the playing of "Dixie," the harmonicist segues into "Taps" and the camera slowly pans around the groups showing the families not as individuals but as the future. When Little Joe attempts to pet a new foal trying to nurse, the camera cuts to the smiling face of a little girl who says, "He's gonna bite'cha." The future is in the faces of the children, and a feeling of optimism overcomes the aura of death. As an audience, we know the turning point has arrived. Shane, who has been standing somewhat isolated, will now take control and make this small part of the West safe. This scene is also an excellent example of Stevens's cinematography. He uses a low camera angle, causing the characters to appear larger than life when photographed against the background of the Grand Tetons. His filters also bathe the mountains in a light "purple mountain majesty."

One other interesting difference is the costume Shane wears in the novel and in the film. In the novel he wears dark trousers "tucked into tall boots and held at the waist by a wide belt, both of a soft black leather tooled in intricated design. A coat of the same dark material. . . . His shirt of finespun linen . . . and a handkerchief . . . of black silk" (1)—a costume more likely to suggest a gambler or professional gunfighter than a savior. In the film, Alan Ladd, who physically is a much smaller man than the novel's character, is wearing buckskins. One reason might be Stevens's desire to represent Shane as different from everyone else. Another possible reason is to try, by using buckskins, to connect Shane more directly to the West and simultaneously suggest a suit of armor.

We know, through dramatic irony, that Shane is going against an ambush as Fletcher's men are placed in such a way that whoever arrives will be killed, and the battle between the settlers and the rancher will end. The quick disposal of Joe emphasizes what the reader has known since the moment Wilson is introduced. We know he and Shane will engage in a final gunfight. Yet in both media, the author is able to create an aura of suspense, or at least anticipation. Structurally, was the right amount of suspense created? Obviously, this was the climactic moment, but was there ever a doubt as to who would win? Could anyone possibly believe after all of the buildup of the quality of Shane's character that the author would allow Fletcher and Wilson to win? What, if not a subconscious desire to witness the hero triumph over evil, causes us to become emotionally involved in the story? Collectively, we see the American ideal triumph and for one brief moment feel all is right with the world.

QUESTIONS

In your responses, identify a specific reference by quotation or page number.

1. The point of view of the novel is first person, participant, retrospective. What advantages are relevant for this point of view?

2. The novel seems to be told in three parts: Part I, chapters 1–5: Part II, chapters 6–14; Part III, Chapters 15 and 16. Which part most clearly conveys the theme? Explain why.

3. A real lesson is being taught to Bob by Shane when he tries to explain his fight with Chris (see page 66). What point is the author making for the reader that Bob found "beyond his comprehension"?

4. At the end of Chapter 8, Shane makes a promise to Marian. How does his promise relate to his reason for getting an axe and starting to remove the stump in Chapters 2 and 3? What does the stump symbolize?

5. The final two lines of Chapter 12 describe Shane's actions and motivations. What does this detail of what Shane is seeing and how he views it contribute to his characterization?

6. How are the ancient mythological qualifications of a hero altered for this story? What alterations can you relate to the story being set in the American West of the 1880s?

PART III
RITES OF PASSAGE

At the end of World War I, as the Western world began to assess the terrible price paid by both sides, a new appreciation emerged in the West for the philosophy of existentialism. The rise of existentialism, particularly among intellectuals, advocated a somewhat depressing concept regarding teleology or a meaning of life: nihilism. What nihilism denotes is that life is without any knowable meaning. Life is merely existence in a world of reality we cannot really know; that is, we can know only what our experience and intellect allow us to know based on the limits of individual perception. Before World War I, Friedrich Nietzsche (1844–1900), a German philosopher, had written an essay, "Thus Spake Zarathustra" (1883), proclaiming "God is dead." The essay, considered an early foundation for existentialism, was not intended as a direct attack on religion but was based on the "facts" that science had produced regarding physics, cosmology, and biology which by the very nature of the information, contradicts many previously held religious beliefs. Later, Jean-Paul Sartre (1905–1980), French philosopher and playwright, expressed the reality of the new philosophy in his best-known short story, "The Wall" (1948), and his major philosophical work, *Being and Nothingness* (1956). These stories, as the titles suggest, refer to a world in which individuals are in essence, condemned to live. Sartre, in a lecture entitled "Existentialism is a Humanism," stated, "Man simply is. Not that he is simply what he conceives himself to be, but he is what he wills. . . . Man is *nothing* else but that which he makes of himself" (my italics). In other words, you and I are whatever we are as a result of our choices. Each of us possesses an individual will, a means by which we make our choices. What we cannot do is refuse to choose, for that is a choice.

Just how free are we to make choices? We are born into an environment with all manner of traditions, mores, institutions, and expectations. Geographically, we are simultaneously residents of a nation, state, county or city, and neighborhood. Physically and psychologically we are functioning members of a family (past, present, and future), a social group, a church, a political party, a workplace, and so on. As participants in each of these diverse groups, we are expected to adhere to certain traditional, historical, geographical, environmental, governmental, and social obligations. All of these entities have the possibility to enhance or limit our options.

However, there is one universal stage in life where a combination of nature and social forces provides an opportunity for each individual to reshape his or her own destiny, *if* he or she chooses to do so. It is that moment in time when a young man or woman is recognized as an adult. Adulthood may be defined in a variety of ways, but the reality remains unchanged. Adulthood truly occurs at that moment when we are free to make our own choices. If we choose to follow the path our environment provides, we may, but it is important to know that we, particularly as citizens of a free society, have the right to select a different path if we choose to do so.

This idea is a subtle but important cultural influence into literary plot formation. Old World tradition, whether East or West, expects a child to follow closely the way of the family. Americans, from the very beginning being a restless culture, alter the Old World tradition into one that fully expects the next generation to be better educated and financially superior to their parents. This, by any standard, is unique to American culture. In order to accomplish this, the adolescent must first choose his or her own path, with, of course, varying degrees of help and influence from family and friends. Following the confirmation of passage into a new stage of adulthood, each individual must continue to choose between being the controller or the controllee.

Placing this ritual into a literary context, when the protagonist becomes a controller, a circumstance where he or she instigates the action and controls to some extent the environment, the story then tends toward romanticism and conforms to the seasons of spring and summer. When the conflict engages the forces of fall and winter and the protagonists are forced to supplicate themselves to external pressures, the story tends to be naturalistic. Realism, the mode most nearly conforming to life as we know it, shows the young adult as working within the environment to control what can be controlled and adapting to that which cannot. This mode, by infusing elements of summer romance with some of the tragedy of fall, is true to life and therefore more realistic. When dealing with fictional narrative, it is the author who, in relation to how he or she perceives the current culture, presents the story as romance, realism, or naturalism. If the author presents the story as an example to follow, the hero may triumph, fall, or die, but will have control of his or her own destiny. If the author is highly critical of the culture, the hero will be forced to submit to forces beyond his or her control, resulting in a tragic mode. When the protagonist is in conflict with both the forces of comedy and tragedy, the higher the level of verisimilitude will be.

The ritual aspect to be explored in novel and film for Part III is one in which we all participate: the passage into adulthood. In many primitive societies, it was, and still is, a seasonal rite, generally attaching itself to spring, celebrating rebirth. A common form among many primitive and some modern groups is celebrated as a spiritual rebirth in which children, having physically attained puberty, will be initiated into spiritual maturity at the same time. For example, Judaism, in addition to its ancient rite, bar mitzvah, celebrating a young boy's passage has more recently added a bat mitzvah ceremony for young girls. Both ceremonies convey upon an adolescent that he or she is now a "son or daughter of the commandment" and must assume personal responsibility for his or her spiritual life.

Coming-of-age rituals are not always limited to a spiritual act. In many primitive tribes, and perhaps in some not so primitive, noting the popularity of modern tattoo and body piercing parlors, the passage is marked by a physical ritual recognizing the individual as both an adult and a member of the tribe. An African ritual that we will encounter in *The Color Purple* involves male and female circumcision and facial scarring. It is explained as one way in which they attain a cultural identity as opposed to seeking individuality. In contemporary society, street gangs are known to require a tattoo or specific color costume as acknowledgment of membership. This, as initiation rituals have since the beginning of recorded history, tends to make one a part of a larger group, suppressing, to some extent, a growth in individual identity.

In contrast to customs advocating tribal identification, the U.S. Constitution, particularly the Bill of Rights, stresses the importance of individuality. What exists in North America, and to varying degrees in every other free society, is a conflicting group of activities representing a passage into adulthood. One individual may participate in graduation, club or gang initiations, religious rituals, teenage rebellion, the first driver's license, a serious love affair, military service, or employment, with each event implying in its own way a stage of maturity. Whereas at one time required rituals (initiations) were the way a culture or subgroup would differentiate itself from all other groups, young men and women in the New World may choose to participate or not. This does not diminish in any way the importance of the rite of passage. The difference comes from the individual's being aware he or she chooses; whether by submission or commission, it is a choice. Our contemporary society may not promote this transformation as ritualistically as other cultures, yet, for a young American, it remains a series of major steps.

Because America is a free society stressing individuality, Congress has arbitrarily set the age of eighteen as the first legal step. At that point, a young man or woman is required by law to accept some responsibility for his or her life. Complicating this in today's world are the very intricate economic and social forces that make it extremely difficult for the eighteen-year-old to do so. In another contradiction, several states have recently approved laws lowering the age at which an adolescent may be tried as an adult in a criminal prosecution. Complexity breeds confusion.

It is on these complexities that a broad view of literature can help to sort out reality. Literature, by connecting to its mythical base, has a means of reducing the problems to individuals in whom we, as readers, can more easily understand and with whom we can empathize. Although contemporary literature and film may in fact tend more and more to embrace a nihilistic perspective, it cannot escape a connection to a ritual past. Just as the young Greek or Native American had to pass a test to become a member of his or her culture, the youth of today must acquire what our culture demands before attaining adult status.

What has become increasingly clear is that in our society, a young man or woman must first develop a self-identify, which will expand to include a meaning for his or her own existence. Literature defines how we may, within our culture, choose a way of life with those values that conform to a cultural norm and simultaneously evolve a strong self-identity. This is an important distinction. Whatever the background or setting, young men or women today must first recognize themselves as possessing self-worth before they can evolve as fully developed members of society. Literature, by focusing on a single protagonist, demonstrates how an individual may overcome the obstacles society imposes in a natural effort to subvert individualism. For a contemporary man or woman, it is a combination of self *and* society that gives an individual life meaning.

The narratives for this part will help us better understand what we, as citizens of a new world, create as obstacles and what aid and encouragement we impose on young adults. What is expected, within each microcosm of culture, the maturing adolescent must know and accomplish in order to establish a *self* and a *citizen*. The range of cultural microcosm includes one semiclosed society, mired deeply in Old World tradition (*The Color Purple*), a society fractured by war and alienation (*The English Patient*), and the trials and travails of a society on the decline (*The Last Picture Show*). In each, a young person or persons will face a rite of passage, not in the ritualistic sense, but in a modern version of that primeval reality. The rite of passage is defined by three completely different groups of young adults from three very different New World subcultures, yet each individual is still expected, in the words of Shakespeare, "to thine ownself be true" (*Hamlet* I:3:83).

Chapter 6

A Return to Matriarchy

The Color Purple by Alice Walker

An old story, and one that perhaps was a forerunner of Greek myths, comes from ancient Babylon, successor to the ancient Akkadian Empire. Around 3000 B.C.E. in what is now Iran and Iraq, an empire arose known as Sumeria. In the first known written story of creation, composed around 2500 B.C.E. by the Babylonians, Marduk, a sun god, fought an epic battle against Tiamat, goddess of the oceans and creator of Marduk. When Tiamat was slain, her body was severed into two parts, the top half becoming the heavens and the lower half the earth, both land and sea. In this act, as in later Greek myths and the Bible's Genesis, Marduk, being masculine and the more powerful, establishes a male dominance that probably spread throughout the Middle East and into Europe by Greek and Roman conquests. (It should be noted that Asian myths do not separate the powers of male and female gods; however, the female deities are more involved in creation.)

Early creation stories are similar in that they begin with chaos, which is in some way organized into the earth and the sky (firmament) by a creator. In communicating this story, most primitive cultures anthropomorphize (give human form to nonhuman entities) the forms by assigning the sky a male identity and the earth female. As all known life emanates from the earth, this would account for the almost universal concept of Mother Earth, or, as she was known by the Greeks, Gaea (English prefix *geo*). For the Greeks, Gaea and Uranos (the heavens) created the Titans, who created the gods. In the battle for domination between the Titans, led by Gaea and Uranos, and the gods under the command of Zeus, the gods won. Zeus, like the Babylonian Marduk, being the dominant figure, established male domination over the universe. A contemporary archetypal connection for this conflict is derived from the natural act of an adolescent offspring reaching adulthood and challenging parents for domination. Again we see how the origin of a myth is possibly deduced from a natural human order. A male and a female come together to create new life, and the natural order continues in that at some point in time, the new life will assume domination. The question then arises, is this also a base for the male figure's being dominant over the female?

During the past fifty years, along with many changes in our culture regarding race and ethnicity, has been a movement within women's groups to deemphasize male domination with regard to many aspects of the culture, including religion. Why is God, creator of humanity, male? Does referring to God as *he* establish rules for dominance? For all we know, there may well have been a time in the ancient past when the creator god was neither male nor female. Let us hypothesize that the creator is either both male and female or gender neutral. If God is not a he, would any observation of nature logically determine which gender of the creator's creation will dominate?

There is no stronger basis for a patriarchal culture than one based on Judeo-Christian principles. The creation story found in Genesis establishes in no uncertain terms the relationship between the sexes. While this may be the traditional Western approach, there is at least one respected historian who looks beyond these stories to a time when the world possibly was matriarchal. A Swiss classicist, Johann Jacob Bachofen (1815–87), studied the earliest myths of Europe. His conclusions, later confirmed by British writer Robert Graves (author of *I, Claudis*), "found within many Greek myths a record—at times thickly veiled, at other times obvious—of a prehistorical battle between a matriarchy (society ruled by women) and the emerging patriarchy (society ruled by men) that supplanted it" (Bierlein 271). Bachofen's theory, accepted by Graves and Joseph Campbell, held that culture in Europe began with no gender truly dominating. The first groups organized into families and communities were established under matriarchal domination, females at a later point losing domination to their physically stronger male counterparts. One example from Greek mythology that supports this hypothesis is a tribe of warrior women, the Amazons. Because a reason for this group is never fully explained, it is possible this is a myth explaining how humans moved from barbarism to a civilized community. Female values, according to Bachofen, are characterized by "changelessness, passivity, peace, selflessness, and equality." Male values, on the other hand, are characterized by "change, activity, ambition, fighting, self-centeredness, and hierarchy" (Segal 101). When one looks at the structure of cultures today, this would seem to be a logical hypothesis.

Women warriors are common in Celtic myths; one in particular is the Irish Queen Mebd (Maev). The legends concerning her skills as a warrior and lover are magniloquent. Following a battle, one defeated warrior, Cethern, describes his assailant:

A tall, fair, long-faced woman with soft features came at me. She had a head of yellow hair and two gold birds on her shoulders. She wore a purple cloak folded about her, with five hands' breadth of gold on her back. She carried a light, stinging, sharp-edged lance in her hand, and she held an iron sword with a woman's grip over her head—a massive figure. (Cahill 87)

On another occasion Mebd bragged: " 'I never had one man without another waiting in his shadow.' She is said to need thirty men a day, and only those who were her equal in stamina could remain her lover" (Rutherford 110)—hardly a female who subjected herself to the demands of her husband or to any other man for that matter.

Another connection to a once-feminine domination is a contrast in the character of Apollo (Greek god of the sun) and Artemis (goddess of the moon). Apollo is responsible for arts and culture, while Artemis is goddess of the hunt, normally a male activity. It is also known that most primitive cultures measured time by the moon because its changes were easily measured. It is also true the moon cycles are much more attuned to a woman's menstrual cycle than is the sun. In our contemporary world, *Xena, Warrior Princess* has become a very popular television show, as has *Buffy the Vampire Slayer*. What all of these metaphoric myths tell us is that the conflict between males and females for domination is not a new one, nor are we likely to settle it soon.

This may be one reason the next selection has had such a controversial impact on both the literary world and the world of motion pictures. An interesting archetypal theme one can take from Alice Walker's *The Color Purple* is how male domination, when left unchecked, can be sorely abused—how males in their seemingly natural tendency toward violence are nearer to barbarism than to socialization. For Alice Walker, it is an opportunity to explore how American culture and a subculture of black Americans evolved from a pattern of dominance that has both a moral and a religious base and how it affected particularly the black cultures, and what might be done about it. The novel was published in 1982 at a time when America was recovering from the terrible experiences of the 1960s and 1970s. For black Americans, the country had gone through desegregation (1954) and the Civil Rights Act (1964), and the nation had come to a tenuous acceptance at best. While most Americans think of civil rights in relation to race or ethnicity, there is another strong component: feminism. The feminist portion of the civil rights movement was, and to a certain extent still seems to be, plagued by contradiction. In one sense, women demand equal treatment in the career world. On the other hand, many want to maintain a more traditional role, allowing (encouraging) men to act as providers while women maintain the role of homemaker. For black women, according to Alice Walker, their culture presents two additional burdens. They must function while living in a world dominated by white society and also face a slightly different perspective with traditional expectations of black men. When some critics complained she was excessively negative toward black men in her novel, she responded:

Their [black men] apparent inability to empathize with black women's suffering under sexism; their refusal even to acknowledge our struggles; indeed, there are many black men who appear unaware that sexism exists (or even of what it is), or that women are oppressed in virtually all cultures, and if they do recognize there is abuse, their tendency is to minimize it or to deflect attention from it to themselves. (Walker "In the Closet of the Soul" *Ms.* Nov. 1986)

Walker, although her major characters are black, goes beyond the black culture and recognizes in a female's rite of passage, regardless of race or locale, a specific obstacle that does not exist for males. "For Walker, the black American woman is a universal symbol representing hope and resurrection; through her female characters, she advocates the importance of bonds between women who contend with negative social mechanisms" ("Walker" 422). Walker's main point is that for a female to reach full and equal status as an adult, she has to, like the male, learn the skills she will need as an adult, separate from family, and accept responsibility, but because she is a woman, she must overcome male sexism, which in the black subculture is particularly restrictive. Although Walker's setting is two generations removed from today and in a southern community, the idea, in the opinion of the author, is omnipresent and will apply to all races and times.

One other factor determining ritual passage into adulthood that must be considered is the influence and control imposed by the beliefs, mores, and customs intrinsic to the family or community, which due to the immigrant and migrant nature of America's inhabitants, occasionally involves an Old World influence. In *The Color Purple*, the influence is twofold. First, the Old World influence comes from the African ancestry of the characters and is illuminated in Nettie's letters from Africa. The second influence is more subtle, yet it plays a major part in communicating the novel's archetypal theme. Walker places the novel's setting in the American South prior to World War II and long before any organized civil rights activity. This emphasizes its focus. While the novel deals with race much more than the film does, particularly with the situation in which Sofia finds herself, it is obvious that Walker wants the reader to focus on how one female adolescent, who happens to be black, becomes her own person. The novel does not ignore the problems of racial bias; it is merely one of the many hurdles Celie must overcome. This makes Celie a more universal character and is certainly more representative of a female's coming of age.

The Color Purple was published in 1982, and the film, directed by Steven Spielberg, was produced in 1985. The novel was awarded a Pulitzer Prize. The film was nominated for, but did not win, Best Picture, Best Actress (Whoopi Goldberg), Best Supporting Actress (Margaret Avery and Oprah Winfrey), and for its Art Direction, Cinematography, Costume Design, Make-up, Best Original Score, Best Song, and Best Screenplay. Whoopi Goldberg and Steven Spielberg did win Golden Globe awards for, respectively, Best Actress and Best Director.

One of the most striking aspects of this novel is the epistolary point of view. The story is epistolary, being told in a series of letters by the protagonist (Celie), who addresses her letters first to God and later to a sister (Nettie) whom she believes is dead, but is discovered to be a missionary in Africa. In the latter half of the book, we will read, with Celie, letters to her from Nettie. These letters are written over a period of thirty years, from the early part of the twentieth century to the years leading up to World War II. This rather unique point of view is important because Walker tells us how essential it is for an individual to have someone in whom to confide. By being able to write these very personal confidences, Celie gives them a much deeper meaning. The second important aspect is the unique character of the protagonist. Celie paradoxically is a nondescript and quite ordinary African American girl who falsely believes herself to be ugly, ignorant, and without self-value. Her stepfather raped her when she was in her early teens. He continues to abuse her, getting her pregnant twice and selling the babies to a black couple for adoption. Celie is rendered sterile by the birth of her second child. Later he trades Celie to a cruel and brutal neighbor as a common-law wife. She is totally subservient and finds it difficult to challenge the status quo. She explains to Nettie, "But I don't know how to fight. All I know how to do is stay alive" (26). Her expectations are explicitly expressed when she tells her stepson Harpo that if he wants to be successful in his relationship with his new wife, Sofia, he must "beat her" (43). Ironically, Walker uses the character of Sofia as both comedy relief and to show there are some women who, like the mythical Mebd, are too physically and mentally strong to be beaten by their husbands.

A second major stylistic aspect of the novel is Walker's use of dialect. "When these people talk, there are no self-conscious apostrophes and contractions to assure us that the writer, of course, really knows what the proper spelling and grammar should be. Celie just writes her heart out, putting words down the way they feel and sound" (Steinem 89). Celie's language confirms the reality of her world and causes the reader to know that what emanates from her is the truth, in its most simple form.

The story involves a multitude of trials and tribulations as Celie passes from the adolescent described in the previous paragraph, into a confident and secure woman. Structurally, the novel uses character contrasts, presenting five women, each at a different level with regard to personal freedom, to portray the cultural variation present in rural Georgia and to some extent as it exists in Africa. Celie not only survives the personal abuse, but grows through what she learns from her relationship with each of the women. She suffers humiliation, beatings, the loss of her children, and the indifference of the world around her and yet in the end is able to reach, if not true happiness, at least personal fulfillment. Thus, the novel is more than a story of survival. It dramatically extols the value of women as individuals and provides a road map showing the route one individual can travel with the fortitude and patience to make it happen.

Interwoven within the novel is the story of Nettie's experiences as a missionary to Africa. Nettie's life in a strange way parallels the life of Celie—not as a reflection but rather in a symbiotic way, providing a cultural background that seemingly explains why the relationship between the sexes exists as it does. It is not a matter of morality or the result of slavery that produces the chasm between black men and women; it is a deeply embedded ritual in the culture as far back as their African traditions, which probably have their origins in Egyptian and Sumerian cultures. The addition of the African segment adds a great deal of depth to the novel and separates it from what might be considered a novel of feminist triumph. By showing the sexism as a hangover from Old World traditions and not necessarily an inherent part of the American or any other New World subculture, a woman (in this case, Celie) has every right to be free and succeed on her own. It is in the African segments that the novel transcends race and moves into the larger social arena of gender. Most traditional Old World cultures, be they African, Asian, or European, deny women equal rights. Throughout the African segments Walker communicates through Nettie's New World comparisons how an American woman feels toward the tribal rituals requiring physical scarring and total subservience to a male counterpart; an Olinka woman becomes complete only after she attains a husband (144). In contrasting this custom with the rite of passage that transforms Celie, Walker rejects the idea that old traditions automatically carry over into a new society. She implies that changes are matters of choice, for they occur within the individual. For Celie, becoming a successful businesswoman is as much internal as it is external. It contrasts a contemporary American cultural idea—a woman does not require a husband to be complete or free—with the mythological base for the story. When Thomas Jefferson wrote, "All men are created equal," an egalitarian principle entered into American culture. Twentieth-century women such as Alice Walker have, by their actions and writings, revised Jefferson's gender reference to a more inclusive term.

It is this portion of the story the viewer of the film will need to consider most carefully. Film treatments of the African portions are brief and some-what disjointed. Spielberg decided to focus the film on the American fe-males; however, even there, the character development is diminished in both Sofia (Oprah Winfrey) and Shug (Margaret Avery). It is not that they have minor roles; it is more that their actions are confined to their rela-tionship to Celie (Whoopi Goldberg). A controversial aspect of the novel, and to a certain extent in the film, is the lesbian relationship that exists between Shug and Celie. It is interesting to consider how the author treats this in the novel; because the novel is first person, the reader receives an intimate and at times graphic description of the circumstances and feelings that are involved. The film chooses to soften its impact as the novel's sub-plots are submerged into the major plot of Celie's passage into adulthood. The novel includes her more deliberate development as an individual played against the trials of Sofia and the county and Shug's family problems. As we read Celie's assessment, we become aware of how her analysis of these events contributes to her overall growth as an individual. This mode of transference is not unusual, as noted in *Cuckoo's Nest* and other examples. In reading a novel, "we observe that word-symbols must be translated into images of things, feelings and concepts through the process of thought. Where the moving picture comes to us directly through perception, lan-guage must be filtered through the screen of conceptual apprehension" (Bluestone 20). Development of a subplot will only diminish the focus of the story by tending to distract from our direct perception during the brief time we sit in a movie theater. "Its substance does not lie in its style, its original music, or its syntax, but in the story it tells" (Levi-Strauss *SA* 210). The meaning of any fictional story is always communicated through the whole story. To omit or alter any part will to some degree change the totality of meaning. A reader controls the pace and depth of his or her attention to the story by pausing, rereading, and thinking about a passage before moving on. Film viewing does not offer these luxuries. A film's com-munication is dependent on the semiological choices of the director and the concentration of the viewer.

Another obvious difference between the book and the film is a general alteration in the major theme. The novel, being more comprehensive, fo-cuses first on the struggle of women in reversing the domination by men and then on the part that real love plays in the total experience. The film seems to alter the focus to one more concerned with the effects of love in a romantic vein. Special attention should be given to the final chapters of the novel, when Walker specifically draws the reader's attention to the interrelationships of the characters as they develop a mature understanding of love in its broadest sense—not love as a soap opera romance but love as one part of human experience that encompasses not only emotion but also an interdependence in which each partner complements the other in strength and weakness. This caring includes, but also extends beyond, gender relationships to inter- and intra-family feelings. Shug, in explaining to her son the estrangement from her parents, states, "They had a lot of love to give. But I needed love plus understanding. They run a little short of that" (235–36). Albert, in explaining his maturation, says, "But when you talk bout love I don't have to guess. I have love and I have been love. And I thank God he let me gain understanding enough to know love can't be halted just cause some peoples moan and groan" (237). Perhaps the strongest point made is that before one human being can truly love another, they must first love themselves. "They [women] receive and accept the *right* to love themselves and each other. Love of self energizes them to the point that they break the chains of enslavement, change their own worlds, time and Black men" (Parker-Smith 483).

Interwoven with Celie's story, Nettie describes how she came to love and marry the widowed Samuel, and Adam, Celie's natural son, looks beyond the physical in his love for the scarred Tashi. In the lives of the characters, there comes that moment when physical love and appearance become a part of the equation and not the substance. When Walker adds Sofia's relationship to both Harpo and Miss Eleanor Jane into the mix along with Shug and Germaine, Mary Agnes and Grady, the contrasts are interwoven much more than in the film. As in *Cuckoo's Nest*, the choice of the director to omit the denouement proves diminishing to the novel's comprehensive theme.

For the naive and innocent Celie, we see another common tragic mode framing the story: revenge. Like Hamlet, Celie suffers the "slings and arrows of outrageous fortune" placidly. And, like Hamlet, in the end she is able to reverse the situation and take revenge on all of those who persecuted her. There is little question that Walker's antagonists violated moral law, if not social and legal law as well. Albert (Mr. ____) and his father, as well as Celie's stepfather, all violated Celie personally in addition to violating common moral values. For Celie, Shug's love and caring lifted her from self-deprecation to self-esteem. If Shug, whom she respected as an individual, could care for her beyond any personal gratification, then obviously she has personal value. In *The Color Purple* as in *The Last Picture Show*, love, not lust, provides the means by which characters acquire an identity.

As in the other selections, *The Color Purple* takes a rather negative attitude toward organized religion. First, Celie, who from the beginning has communicated with God, begins to question the relationship. She questions Shug why, if she believes in God, she does not attend church. Shug responds: "Any God I ever felt in church I brought in with me. . . . They [other folks] come to church to share God, not find God" (176). Celie replies, "Us talk and talk bout God, but I'm still adrift. Trying to chase that old white man out of my head" (179). Celie seems to associate God closely with male domination, and this causes her problems. Celie and Shug come to the conclusion that there is more of God in the purple flowers growing in the fields than in men or the church. The idea of seeing God in nature confirms that God is within each of them, further adding to self-worth. If God is within you, you obviously have value.

Walker extends this idea to the Christian church in Africa, which not only fails to protect its missionaries but also abandons the Olinkas in the face of colonial power. In contrast, the film relegates the Olinka problem to an innocuous voice-over narration. This idea is softened for the film as a conflict resolution is created between Shug and her estranged father, the local church minister. This provides an opportunity for a musical production number and a placation of any church group, thereby defusing any religious criticism, which, had Spielberg followed the novel closely, certainly would have occurred. At the least, it would have increased the rating from PG-13 to R.

Applying this novel to our analysis process, it would seem to fit somewhere between romance and tragedy. While the experiences of Celie—sacrifice, isolation, and rejection—would seem to suggest tragedy, the outcome tends to the romantic. The film version amplifies the romantic aspect of the narrative. The film, more than the novel, fits into a transitional phase in which the circumstance is identified not as tragedy, but as a "fourth phase of summer: romance" (Frye *AC* 201). In that phase, the heroine, Celie, although forced to enter an evil environment, retains her innocence. When Shug discovers Celie has never enjoyed sex, she comments, "Why Miss Celie . . . you still a virgin" (79). It may be the same base myth that fosters a *Beauty and the Beast* or *The Phantom of the Opera*: the inability of evil to overcome the deeply embedded goodness of the heroine that eventually causes the evil one to change. "The fourth phase image of the monster tamed and controlled by the virgin" (Frye *AC* 201). It becomes Daniel being delivered from the lion's den, convincing King Darius of Persia that his God is supreme (Daniel 6:16–24), or in this case, Celie, as the novel ends, sitting on the porch watching "Mr. ___ patterning a shirt for folks to wear with my pants" (247). The "my pants" at this point may be a thematic pun. It just might be, based on the novel's ending, that Alice Walker is not satisfied with equality of the sexes; she believes a better world requires a return to matriarchy.

QUESTIONS

In your responses, identify a specific reference by quotation or page number.

1. Celie's growth into womanhood comes from her awareness of the best attributes of each role model. What attribute did she take from Shug? From Nettie? From Sofia? From Mary Agnes?

2. A major theme of the novel, and an area of strong controversy, emerges from the portrayal of black men as oppressors of their wives specifically and women generally. The theme emerges through the dynamic actions of character. In order to develop this theme fully, the novelist must identify those characteristics that categorize them in relation to the term *manhood*. What attributes of Albert, Harpo, and Grady does the author advocate? Which attributes are condemned? What conclusions do your results suggest?

3. The novel suggests a comparison between the African Americans of Georgia during the early part of the twentieth century and the Olinkas of Africa as they are described in the letters from Nettie. What traditions and customs do the two groups have in common? What traditions and customs are unique to each? Identify by quotation and page number a minimum of two each.

4. This novel has a strong moral, even didactic, purpose. As such, it follows Cassier's theory of a story's reflecting "primeval reality . . . a dramatic world—a world of actions, of forces, of conflicting powers." What is primeval (based on cultural tradition) in this story? What is the reality found in the present culture? What lesson is being taught?

5. In your opinion, what in the story is directed specifically toward African Americans? Toward men? Toward women? What is universal?

QUESTIONS FOR GROUP DISCUSSION

1. Read again the quotation from *Ms.* magazine on page 100. In what way does Walker interject 1980s moral concepts about women's rights into the story's setting of 1930s America—concepts that are understood now but were not particularly meaningful at the novel's setting?

2. Assume you did not know Alice Walker was an African American woman. What clues exist within the text of the novel and film that show an African American or a feminine bias?

3. *The Color Purple* includes a historical segment, the African Olinkas. What does this story contribute to the overall novel? What might we have missed if the story had not been included?

Chapter 7

Finding Yourself in a
Lost World

The English Patient
by Michael Ondaatje

The novel, published in 1993, received the prestigious Booker Prize for Fiction and The Governor General's Award for Fiction in English. The 1996 film version, directed by Anthony Minghella, won seven Academy Awards: Best Picture, Best Director, Best Supporting Actress (Juliette Binoche as Hana), Cinematography, Sound, Costume, and Film Editing. These awards indicate that both versions are recognized as outstanding. However, anyone who has both read the novel and viewed the film will recognize that although there are many similarities, the versions are more different than alike. The novel presents a strong theme about a young couple's search for individual identity, while the film seems more concerned with entertainment.

This novel is similar in form to Ernest Hemingway's *The Sun Also Rises*. Hemingway's novel, about five members of the "lost generation," expresses the existential nihilism prevalent among survivors of World War I. A much more optimistic view emerges from *The English Patient*. Ondaatje also brings together five seemingly lost souls; all but one has survived the war, and by a series of strange circumstances are placed in a unique setting. On this point, the novel and film agree. The time is 1945 and the place is a bombed out-convent, which, after having been abandoned during a land battle, is being used as a field hospital. As the Allied invasion of Italy is moving on northward and a field hospital must follow closely behind the battle lines, the convent is again practically abandoned. Remaining at the convent as refuse from the war is a Canadian nurse, Hana, who chooses to remain with a critically burned patient, known at the beginning only as the English Patient. As they patiently await the death of the English Patient, two very different participants in the war's action enter their domain. The older one, David Caravaggio, is a middle-aged Allied spy, who, as chance would have it, knew both Hana and her family in Toronto before the war. The other entrant is a Sikh Indian, Kirpal "Kip" Singh, who has been drafted into the English army and trained as a bomb disposal expert, known idiomatically as a "sapper"—one who "drains" unexploded bombs and mines. As much of the novel is told in flashback, a fifth character, Katherine, plays a major role, although she is deceased by the time the others have reached central Italy. Katherine is a married woman with whom the English Patient has had a brief but passionate affair and becomes an integral part of the English Patient's story as the multiple subplots slowly come together, forming the main story.

The novel in a general sense concerns itself with those things that unify us as humans and those things that separate us. Specifically, the novel conveys how the two young participants, Hana and Kip, grow into mature and productive individuals despite, and to some extent because of, the horror each has to experience in performing their roles as nurse and sapper. The focus is on how experience coordinates with conscious understanding to show whom each is as an individual and how, as individuals, each relates to a greater humanity. It is on this point that the film and novel have the greatest separation. The novel conveys to us through its omniscient anonymous narrator how previous experiences interact with what is occurring in the present, which, ironically, by the time we recognize it, is a part of the past and now will affect the future. The film, on the other hand, focuses on the English Patient and how his past experiences have placed him in the unfortunate condition he now finds himself.

This alteration in focus diminishes the overall thematic presentation. Thematically, each character seeks to find a reality and his or her place within it. Ondaatje's method is to show us how the present is, in fact, a continuous motion connecting the past with the future as thoughts are, in essence, an immediate memory. This form makes time, whether one measures by the hour, day, week, or year, inconsequential. Actions and reactions are in continual motion, interweaving events of the near past with events of the early past as they reflect on the present. This gives the novel a kind of thematic stream of consciousness point of view, where seemingly random experience, memory, action, and reaction combine to create one's reality as opposed to a linear sequence or chronology. This point of view maintains a degree of objectivity as, in a very human manner, the action and reaction of characters alters in accordance with whether they are reflecting on an experience or interacting with one or more of the other characters. Underlying this objectivity is a subtle subjectivity imposed by the author in the form of metaphor, simile, and imagery as he enhances his descriptions of both action and reaction. For example, in one tense episode, Hana has just assisted Kip in defusing a booby-trapped bomb by providing a third hand to complete the task. Once the bomb is defused and the tension has cleared, Hana asks Kip to hold her while she sleeps. Kip reflects:

He was still annoyed the girl had stayed with him when he defused the bomb [the present and past], as if by that she had made him owe her something [the future]. Making him feel in retrospect responsible for her, though there was not thought of that at the time. As if *that* could usefully influence what he chose to do with a mine [the present and future]. (104)

The *as if, like,* and *as* are a structural device for the narrator to suggest meaning beyond the action while maintaining a relative sense of objectivity. Stylistically, the lines also demonstrate Ondaatje's ability to incorporate past, present, and future into one series of actions. A third, basically thematic function of the line implies whom Kirpal Singh, the young man from the East, is in relation to Kip, a bomb expert in the British army. He is able to separate in his mind and in his relationship the two roles he is playing in the war. A further function of the diction foreshadows, in his disallowing Hana to "usefully influence" his choices, a reason for his behavior at the novel's end.

The film version omits this entire concept. What we have in the film is a concentration on the relationship between Almasy, the English Patient, and Katherine, particularly their sexual exploits. This, in a way, expresses the degree to which film caters to popular culture; and thankfully, authors of the quality of Ondaatje do not. One scene, which graphically demonstrates this point, comes at a garden party when Almasy and Katherine engage in an almost violent sexual encounter in a pantry, with one wall separating the action from her husband and friends. The scene does little to enhance the theme; however, it no doubt provided audience stimulation, much needed in so long a movie (160 minutes).

One might ask, Who are these people, and why should anyone care about four or five lost souls in a long-ago war? We should care because in many ways, we are one more continuation of the archetype. We, like Ondaatje's dropouts from World War II, are placed into whatever setting we may find ourselves, interrelating with other persons, yet we each have an individual nature that is at that precise moment both similar to and different from every other inhabitant. What emerges is a paradox that will become more divisive by the confrontation involving cultural traditions of East and West. A basic premise of Western philosophy places great value on the individual. In the west, it is necessary to know whom we are as individuals before we can become fully realized. This tends to emphasize differences, while si-

multaneously we try to establish a relationship with other persons by finding a bond on which we can base a connection. This paradox forms a base
for Ondaatje's major theme. It is, like the quest of Sonny in *The Last
Picture Show* and Celie in *The Color Purple*, an archetypal search for identity, but with a twist. By including a Sikh Indian, and by ancestry a product
of the East, the conflict expands to include a clash between cultural ide-
ologies, giving the quest a greater universality. For example, one of the
major ironies evolves in contrasting Kip with the European English Patient
and the North American Caravaggio. Eastern philosophy, from which both
the author and his central character, Kirpal Singh, draw their origins, traditionally holds that all human life is a single entity, devaluing to a degree
the importance of any one individual. Eastern philosophy, as described by
Huston Smith in *The Religions of Man*, draws heavily on Hindu influence,
which tends to gauge reality by its inclusion rather than exclusion:

It would make more sense if we were to gauge a man's being by the size of his
spirit, that is, the range of reality with which he identifies himself. A man, who
identifies himself with his family, finding his joys in theirs, would have that much
reality; one who could identify himself with mankind as a whole would be pro-
portionately greater. By this criterion, if a man could identify himself with being in
general, being as a whole, his own being would be unlimited. (Smith 30–31)

Neither historians nor anthropologists can tell us when primitive people
began to see themselves as separate from the world around them. We know
people arrived at that point because we are able to perform the act. What
can be determined is when this idea was first recorded. It is generally accepted that the oldest known record of when consciousness became reality
was in the Middle East in what is now Iran and Iraq, in the period between
3000 and 2400 B.C.E. Mythologists tell us that that locality is the geographical point of separation between East and West. In the East, emphasis is
placed on the inner being. Humans can accomplish total unity only with
God through meditation and total submission. The more a person medi-
tates, the closer he or she gets to ultimate reality.

Greeks, Romans, and Celts, whose ancient cultures form a base for modern Western beliefs and values, chose a different path, one that eventually
led to monotheism. Monotheism, a belief in one God, tends to place its
emphasis on a form of individual judgment. Reality and being become
measured by how the individual ranks within whatever level of social contact the specific environment demands. What both cultures continue to
share is the simple fact that people are physically and mentally alike and
possess consciousness, which allows us to make choices through the exercise of our will and the ability to evaluate those choices in accordance with
cultural values. It is as if we are performing in first person and simultaneously able to compose mentally a narrative describing the action in third

person. This attribute allows for evaluation and judgment, which spawns the difference in individuals as well as cultures.

What evolves from this diversity gives the novel a uniqueness somewhat missed by the film. The novel includes a confrontation of the two major cultures that is subtle as it occurs in an environment alien to both. The Villa San Girolamo, a convent in its prewar existence, is located on a high point above the village. Having been abandoned by both religion and politics, it becomes an Eden-like setting, isolating the characters from everyone except each other. It brings together a modern Adam (Kip) and Eve (Hana) in a symbolic attempt to rejoin the cultures back to that point in ancient Sumeria from which each came. The union of Kip and Hana is one of childish innocence. Each was raised and educated in a different world while possessing the common bond of an English heritage in language and culture as a part of their environment. Yet in their innocence, there remains a distance; neither seems to know or care if what they feel is love. Perhaps it is just "a game of secrets." Ironically, the more intimate they become, "the space between them during the day grows larger" (127). As much as they care for each other, both seem to know (karma?) it is an interlude, never to be complete. To complete the allusion, Carravagio, sans thumbs, becomes the snake that will ultimately bring the forces of evil into this innocent setting. Minghella's film, possibly in an effort to universalize, or perhaps desiring to play to an American audience, omits any emphasis on how much the diverse origins of the characters provide each with insight into their own being.

An unusual feature of this story that is implied in both media is the fact that none of the four are now or ever have been actual combatants in the war: two, Caravaggio and Almasy, are undercover operatives (one for England, one for Germany), Hana is a nurse, and the sapper follow along behind the battles cleaning up mines and bombs left over by the retreating army. What makes the characters more unusual in a war novel is that each has a primary responsibility toward saving lives. While the work of a nurse and a sapper are obvious, spies are to provide military advantage by preventing surprises and finding weakness in the enemy force, thereby preventing loss. Granted, they were engaged in saving the lives of their side, but it is an important aspect.

Hana, the only female in the group, is the pivotal point on which all of the action revolves. She becomes a conduit through which the men will ultimately see into themselves by recognizing what as individuals each has become as a result of his war experiences. Each man will first establish a relationship with Hana and through her a relationship with each other in coming to terms with his own reality. She is a physically present apparition triggering memories of love and past relationships each will use in comprehending just how his karma (moral law of cause and effect) led him to this point. Kip comes to the realization: "His name is Kirpal Singh and he does not know what he is doing here" (287). At that moment he comes to terms with a reality that has taken him full circle, except now he understands what that means. Each man knows at the story's end what it is that gives meaning to his life as a man.

In addition to the Judeo-Christian Eden allusion, Ondaatje must have made connection with his archetypal knowledge of Indian myths in creating the path for his three male characters. One of the major beliefs, originating in Hindu religion and carried into Sikh beliefs by its founder Nanak, is the concept of a female goddess known as Maya. Joseph Campbell explains her name is

the Indian term for "illusion," maya—from the verbal root ma, "to measure, to measure out, to form, to create, construct, exhibit or display"—refers to both the power that creates an illusion and the false display itself. The art of a magician, for example, is maya; so too the illusion he creates. The arts of the military strategist, the merchant, actor, and thief: these also are maya. Maya is experienced as fascination, charm; specifically, feminine charm. And to this point there is a Buddhist saying: "Of all the forms of maya that of woman is supreme." (*MI* 52)

Carl Jung describes Maya as "the deepest reality in man":

It belongs to him, this perilous image of Woman; she stands for the loyalty which is in the interests of life he must sometimes forgo; she is the much needed compensation for the risks, struggles, sacrifices that all end in disappointment; she is the solace for all the bitterness of life. And, at the same time, she is the great illusionist, the seductress, who draws him into life with her Maya—and not only into life's reasonable and useful aspects, but also into its frightful paradoxes and ambivalences where good and evil, success and ruin, hope and despair, counterbalance one another. Because she is his greatest danger she demands from a man his greatest, and if he has it in him she will receive it. (*EJ* 109–10)

Hana, a personification of Maya in both name and action, brings an illusion of goodness into the madness, and through her, each man is able to find his path to peace.

Theoretically, no person will be the same tomorrow as today, for each day some new experience is added to all past experiences, creating a change ranging from the minute to an epiphany. Experiences are at every moment both physical and psychological. We act and react with and to everything in our surroundings. The degree to which we change is directly related to the intensity with which we incorporate each experience into our knowledge and nature. This factor is obviously why Ondaajte chooses to set his novel in the final days of World War II. Each experience related to the war becomes more intense due to the stress of dealing with extreme horror, which amplifies any small good experiences, causing them to become much more meaningful than they might be during more ordinary circumstances. A small pleasure for Kip is a passion for condensed milk; for Hana, it is seeing vegetables and flowers grow in her garden. The possession of these items enables them to cope by bringing for each a moment of pure pleasure in a world surrounded by pain and death. Structurally, the pleasures reveal aspects of the character rounding out a part of his or her nature. For Kip, a desire for condensed milk expresses his youthfulness, an ignorance of things in the modern West that others would consider ordinary and a contact with a technology that provides benefit rather than death. For Hana, the garden brings a touch of both home and nature into her life, a sense of beauty and security. Abstractly, the milk for Kip and the garden for Hana connect them to Mother Earth, the source of all life.

Another stylistic device Ondaatje uses throughout the novel to convey the changes within his characters is a subtle use of reflection. There are two types of reflection. One occurs externally when one physically sees oneself in such items as small fragments of broken mirrors, pieces of glass, reflective pools of water, shadows on walls, and, perhaps most important, in the eyes of the beholder. A second form of reflection occurs when one is able to bring together the past and present within the mind—to process an experience in relation to a memory and relate it to one's very being. These are the moments of greatest impact for the character and, in a vicarious way, the reader. For the English Patient, this moment is reflected in his description of Katherine's death. Following the plane crash killing her husband and critically wounding Katherine, Almasy carries her into the cave of swimmers where she dies in his arms. He expresses in a much more poetic manner the Biblical admonition of ashes to ashes and dust to dust:

her whole body was covered in bright pigment. . . . The body pressed against sacred colour . . . a naked map where nothing is depicted. . . . Such glory of this country she enters now and becomes a part of it. (261–262)

She has become one with the desert, a part of its topography locatable on a map, which for Almasy means it will remain forever, like the frescoes of the swimmers on the cave walls. It is Almasy's nature to see life's journey as lines on a map.

A very important distinction Ondaatje uses as a motif in the novel is how each character possesses an inner nature or inner being that will ultimately influence his or her decisions. Films are unable or unwilling to spend time in providing character background, even where it is important to the story's theme. For example, one aspect of conscience is shared by each of the characters: all possess a nonpolitical nature. Count Ladislaus de Almasy (the English Patient) is an anthropologist, who because of his knowledge and abilities at mapping the desert is of great value to the Germans. His personal interest is in finding the ancient oasis of Zerzura, known to exist only in folktales and legends about the vast and presumably waterless Libyan Desert. He is asked by the Germans in the late 1930s to aid them in locating travelable routes through the desert and, as a by-product, to show the military outposts of the English. Once he obliges the Germans, he has no choice but to continue if his search for the elusive oasis is to go on uninterrupted. His goal, emerging from his most inner nature, is to find the oasis and locate it on a map. Nothing else matters. David Caravaggio too is somewhat coerced into becoming a spy for the British. In Canada, he is an accomplished thief. But even the best make mistakes, and eventually he is arrested, and because of his unique abilities to burgle, he is "offered" the opportunity to use his skills for the British in North Africa. Caravaggio became a thief because of a natural talent for the job and the appeal of its by-product, great adventure. His nature is to push the envelope of danger, and the government offer was too good to pass up, especially when the alternative was jail.

For Hana, the war has become a terrible weight. She came to the war with all of the right motives: to help injured and dying soldiers. After all, her father is serving in the Canadian army, and the least she can do is offer her services. Tending to the wounded and dying begin to take a much greater toll than she expected. When the news of her father's death came, she quit. Remaining with the English Patient is, in essence, a final payment to her father, who also dies as a result of being burned in an explosion. Her loyalty is not to the causes of the Allied coalition but to her father. Kirpal Singh, on the other hand, became a soldier because his family expected it of him. In his family, it is tradition for the first son to become a soldier and the second to become a doctor. Kip's older brother has broken the tradition by refusing to serve in "any situation where the English have power" and went to prison instead. Kip, being less politically minded and much more non-confrontational in his nature, simply goes in place of his brother (200). Like the others, he has no personal political motives for being there; he is following tradition, which in his ancestral culture is a standard way of life. This knowledge enhances the novel's theme, for it is impossible to know who you are without knowing who you were. It is in not knowing this information that leaves the film without a specific theme.

Four noncombatants—four without any nationalistic fervor—and very diverse individuals with separate natures, agendas and loyalties are placed together in a garden setting with religious overtones. They all recognize from the beginning that this is an interlude in the war. They know the war is ending, and for Hana, David, and Almasy, it is their decision to end their part now. Kip will continue working up to the moment he hears of the bombing of Nagasaki and Hiroshima with atomic weapons and at that point will also become a dropout.

None of the four dropped out of the war from fear. For Hana, it was revulsion, for David, an incapacitation having lost both thumbs in an altercation, for the slowly dying English Patient, a critical wound, and for Kip, the lone Asian, the belief an atom bomb would never have been exploded over a "white nation" (286). In his eyes, it is the West that establishes separation as a part of their reality. For him, he does not reject Hana; it is her culture that rejects him.

Awareness of the motivation for each of the characters is important to an understanding of the story's major theme: coming to terms with one's self. First, the three males are faced with what it means to "be a man," in the present circumstance and within the culture to which each, except Almasy, will return. What Ondaatje presents in his metaphoric style is how Almasy, Caravaggio, and Singh come to realize what, for each, is required to become a fully realized male in a single universe. A universal thematic point is made: ultimately, the process is the same for each person; it does not matter from which of the cultures anyone may evolve. What matters is coming to terms with reality as each perceives it and in the manner his inner being demands. Joseph Conrad, the Polish-born English author of such novels as *The Heart of Darkness* and *Lord Jim*, when asked what he considered the major theme to be in his volume of work responded, "Those who read me know my conviction that the world, the temporal world, rests on few simple ideas: so simple that they must be old as the hills. It rests most notably among others on the idea of fidelity" (136).

Fidelity is the act of being faithful. For Conrad and Ondaatje it means being faithful to one's own beliefs and values. Ondaatje does not proclaim any one of the men to be better or worse than the others. The only morality imposed emerges from within the inner consciousness of the individual. Each of the men comes to recognize this as he interacts with Hana, the seductress, drawing them "into life with her maya—and not only into life's reasonable and useful aspects, but into its frightful paradoxes and ambivalences, where good and evil . . . counterbalance each other" (cf. 112). Political, religious, and cultural differences that exist will remain outside the convent as Hana lights a path between the men and reality. Through her, each man finds a means whereby he may make contact with his own inner sense of reality. In the novel's climax, Kip, after hearing of the atomic bombing, confronts westerners Almasy and Caravaggio with a rifle. In that moment, he condemns the West for all of the evil and since Almasy and Caravaggio represent both sides he has found the perfect foil for his anger. He points the rifle at the English Patient, who speaks, "Do it." The comment seems to throw a new light on the proceedings. Kip, pauses, disarms the rifle by ejecting and snatching its bullet in mid-flight, then tosses the rifle onto the bed where it becomes "a snake, its venom collected" while "Hana [remains] on the periphery" (285). In that tense moment, Kip recognizes it is the West that has imposed violence on the world; by removing the venom from his own snake, he renders the snake harmless. Ondaatje, by including in this most climactic moment the presence of Hana/Maya, identifies the influence of the goddess. Kip catches a glimpse of his very essence and chooses not to become a part of the mayhem. By this action, he affirms his place in the universe. He gets on his motorcycle and starts the long journey home.

In the end, each of the male characters returns to his nature. The war was an interlude, which in a positive sense provides each an insight, bringing them full circle except that now they know who they are. Our last view of Caravaggio has him crossing hand over hand on a rope connecting the convent to a villa next door. At the moment he is attempting to steal a statue of Demetrius (an early Christian martyr, honored primarily by Eastern Orthodox) down the hill. Hana had told him previously that, according to Almasy, "all statues of Demetrius were worthless." Caravaggio, being true to his nature, in a dark and stormy night is trying to steal the worthless statue—not for its value, but probably, just for the challenge of doing it. The last words we read of him are these: "He is halfway across when he smells the rain . . . and suddenly there is the great weight of his clothes" (297). Like Caravaggio, we are left hanging, never to know whether he makes it or not, only to know he is following his passion and now perhaps understanding why he must do it.

Almasy apparently dies quietly in his bedroom: "He sees . . . a figure at the foot of his bed," perhaps the shadow of death. He does not fear its presence, nor does he resent it. He waits, "his hand reaches out slowly and touches his book and returns to his dark chest," seemingly expectant and knowing his life has had meaning as his additions to Herodotus's *Histories* attest (298). Herodotus's book, finding and mapping the fish paintings on the cave wall and the fact that "harpoons are still found in the desert" (19) are symbolic of the meaningless of time. It all connects; now—then—forever are one. He does not, as the film implies, suggest that Hana, in her role as his nurse, administer an overdose, therefore hastening his demise. This alters the characterization of both Hana and Almasy. It would seem to be a film expediency, bringing the story to a quick and dramatic finale.

Kirpal Singh returns to his beloved India and fulfills his original promise, becoming a physician. He has, in accordance with family tradition, become a doctor. He has married and now has two children. His life too has come full circle. He has memories of Hana, which the author assures us will remain a part of his life. He has chosen not to keep in contact, preferring memories to knowing the actual results. When he sees in his mind the episodes of their past, "he is just as fascinated at himself there as he is with her—boyish and earnest" (301). What actually happened then is recurring in his mind now. It appears in his memory, just as it was then. In his mind, the past is now; just as when he looks at his daughter and pictures her future, it too becomes now. The world around him may move in time, but his perceptions are always now. One idea Ondaatje confirms is that now Singh knows who he is and has found contentment in that, for which he must give some credit to Caravaggio and Almasy, with the greatest influence coming from his illusions of Hana.

The novel, at the time of publication, met with both superlative and negative criticism. Cressida Connolly, writing for *The Spectator*, offered high praise: "If there is anyone out there who can write as well as Michael Ondaatje, then I'd like to hear about them" (32). Nicholas Spice writing for the *London Review of Books* was somewhat less enthralled. His evaluation accused Ondaatje of "a style which at best generates things of real beauty, at worst creates effects of tromp-l'oeil [realistic detail] which makes us suspect that there is less to what we read than meets the eye" (5). When an author writes in a highly poetic style, there is no doubt he is treading on very thin ice with regard to public acceptance. For example, Ondaatje seems concerned about the prosody of his diction, and according to some critics he may be going too far by placing sound above meaning. However, what may seem overdone to one critic will appear to be great writing to another. Ondaatje, who has a strong background as a poet, may have been trying to use syllabic sounds to amplify meaning. In one descriptive paragraph comparing his native land to England, Kip recalls how in his homeland, "one cooled an over-heating car engine not with new rubber hoses but by scooping up cow shit and patting it around the condenser" (188). A few pages later, while attempting to locate himself geographically, he pulls down a map and reads, "*Countisbury and Area. Mapped by R. Fones. Drawn by desire of Mr. James Halliday.* 'Drawn by desire . . . '" He was beginning to love the English" (190). Both lines possess degrees of consonance. The first, "scooping up cow shit," in addition to a series of hard consonants, provides tactile, aromatic, and visual images, while the less harsh-sounding, but no less alliterative, "drawn by desire" conveys a sense of humor as well as insight into the more formal English way of life. Both fit perfectly within the context and enhance the meaning of the description. The "cow shit" image is used to relate how his knowledge and the culture from which he comes are based entirely on pragmatism. In his culture, one uses whatever material is readily available and will solve the problem, whereas in England, one tends to look to the more formal and grandiose, seemingly to create a facade. Interestingly, one of the lessons he learns comes in his encounter with Miss Morden, Lord Suffolk's secretary. During a tense moment in defusing a bomb, she calmly causes him to pause and joins him for tea well within the danger area, conveying that the English, at least those whom he has come to know fully, are exactly what they seem to be (202).

There are many delightful moments in the life of Kirpal Singh that are totally omitted from the film version. The film focuses almost entirely on the English Patient and his memories, while the novel is more concerned with Kip. In the film, the affair between Kip and Hana is acknowledged but in a superficial manner. What the film does show effectively is the difference between the tenderness in the Kip-Hana relationship and the near-violent sex of Almasy and Katherine. This diminishes the power of the cave scene when Almasy cares for the critically injured Katherine. By the time this occurs in the novel, we have been privy to the deepest feeling of Almasy, whereas in the film we have been treated to the obsessiveness of their sexual encounters. However, there are some features of the film that all critics agree were extremely well done. Most are complimentary about the cinematography, conveying comments similar to Richard Blake's: "The warm tints and rugged textures that have lured generations of explorers into the desert come to life through John Seale's spectacular cinematography" (25). Anthony Lane appreciated both the cinematography and the interpretation. Writing in *The New Yorker*, he commented: "Minghella has not simply trimmed Ondaatje's book; he has reinvented the story with his eyes," and "together with the producer, Saul Zaentz, the composer, Gabriel Yard, and the director of photography, John Seale, he has made a clear and hard-edged epic." He closes with this compliment: "Man to man, this is awfully close to a masterpiece" (25 Nov. 96). John Simon of the *National Review* is considerably less complimentary: "Anthony Minghella, the scenarist-director, apparently had to do a lot of inventing to tie the many strands into a coherent 160-minute movie, and more or less managed it, although coherence does not preclude oversaturation . . . the film is full of wonderful hokum" (11 Dec. 96).

One scene seemed to impress all the movie critics, and all responded in similar complimentary fashion. Simon wrote, "There is a marvelous scene . . . in a dark church where Kip hands Hana a flare and hoists her up with a pulley, as stunning, starkly illuminated frescoes stare back at her enraptured face" (Simon 53). And, "In a lovely metaphorical scene, he rigs a rope and harness and hoists her to the rafters of a ruined church to show her the surviving murals. As she soars and swings in ecstatic delight . . . she discovers that beauty endures" (Blake 25). Readers of the novel know that this scene, as written, does not show a relationship between Kip and Hana. The novel uses the scene to provide insight into the nature of Kip. In the novel Kip takes a professor, a "mediaevalist who had befriended him" and lifts the very reluctant participant to the ceiling. He locates the suspended professor beneath *The Flight of the Emperor Maxentius*. After lowering the professor, Kip places himself in the sling and elevates to see for himself what the professor saw. What he sees is the "Queen of Sadness," perhaps in his mind, Tara, a Buddhist personification of divine compassion and in that moment, extends his own hand to make contact between the two worlds. He becomes aware of "the liquid sense of it. The hollowness and darkness of a well" (72). It is Kip's nature that is being revealed in the novel—his feelings while making both physical and spiritual contact with Western religion, which in no way feels foreign or alien to him. To Kip, the Easterner, all religion, all spirituality, emerges from the "darkness of the well," and in that moment he feels part of all. A comparison of the two scenes offers unique insight into each media. The inclusion of Hana, rather than a mediaevalist professor, offers an opportunity to speculate that the director sees something the author may have missed. Certainly the picture of Hana, with a long skirt flowing, presents an aesthetic view the novel missed. However, the change emphasizes an oft-repeated idea: films are not as concerned with themes, preferring to emphasize entertainment. Good novels probe the depths of human consciousness in striving to comprehend reality. Ondaajte certainly causes readers to stretch their mind in comprehending the paradoxical nature of reality; Minghella does not.

QUESTIONS

In your responses, identify a specific reference by quotation or page number.

1. Ondaajte, being a poet, would appear to favor strong and meaningful metaphors. On page 91, he writes, "A novel is a mirror walking down the road." Explicate the line and interpret its meaning. Select one other metaphoric line (your choice) and explain its relation to the theme.

2. The climax of the novel occurs when Kip hears over the radio about the atom bombs dropping on Japan in August 1945. Explain, beyond the fact that Kip is from the Orient, why this event had such a devastating effect on him. Did any of the others react similarly? Why or why not?

3. On page 61 of the novel, Hana, following the manner of the English Patient opens a novel and begins a personal entry. If *Herodotus' Histories* amplifies, to some extent, Almasy's character, what does *The Last of the Mohicans* and Hana's entry suggest about her?

4. On page 111, Kip discusses his relationship to Lord Suffolk, described as an autodidact. What is there about being self-taught that appeals to Kip? Connect your answer to both the person and his culture.

5. There are many references to literature, art, and music in the novel: *The Last of the Mohicans* (11), the statue of Demetrius (297), *Peter Pan* (197), *Anna Karenina* (237), the story of Odysseus (241), and others. Select one of the art forms from the novel, and explain what it means in context and what it means metaphorically in relation to a theme. Remember that the author could have chosen any artistic representation; he chose these for a reason. Why one of these?

QUESTIONS FOR GROUP DISCUSSION

1. Compare the descriptions of Amasy's and Katherine's affair on pages 154–158 with the film's love scenes. In what manner did they compare? Contrast? Why did the film go beyond the novel?

2. The film relies a great deal on scenic photography, using deep focus. Define *deep focus* and explain how this technique contributes to the story's theme.

3. The roles for Kip and Hana are considerably diminished by the film. Review the text material concerning the goddess Maya and discuss the level to which the film's *mana* identity is diminished.

Chapter 8

The Steep Hills of Thalia, Texas

The Last Picture Show
by Larry McMurtry

In order to place *The Last Picture Show* into a mythological perspective, we begin by introducing a novelist, playwright, and essayist who was able to overcome the depressive aspects of nihilistic existentialism to find a purpose or meaning in life. In 1940–43, while France was under the occupation of Nazi Germany, a French writer, Albert Camus, a contemporary and one-time personal friend of Jean-Paul Sartre, interpreted a Greek myth as a bridge between existentialism and teleology (meaning or purpose in life). While suffering the oppression of Nazi occupation and serving in the French resistance movement, he penned an essay interpreting into modern terms the myth of Sisyphus. Camus saw Sisyphus as an absurd hero, an oxymoron. He was absurd in the condition of his suffering but heroic in his fulfillment of it. "His [Sisyphus] scorn of the gods, his hatred of death, and his passion for life won him that unspeakable penalty in which the whole being is exerted toward accomplishing nothing." Ironically, it is in the accomplishment of nothing that Camus found the greatest meaning. (For a contemporary application of the principle, Camus may have been the source of Jerry Seinfeld's inspiration for his successful television sitcom, which was, according to its creator, a show about nothing.)

Around 700 B.C.E., the Sisyphus story was included in poetry written by the Greek poet Hesiod (*Theogeny*). This is a story about a wealthy Corinthian (a king in some translations) who was able to defy both the gods and death. Sisyphus, in addition to being wealthy and a community leader was most of all a trickster capable of fooling the great god Zeus and his brother Hades, lord of death; it seems that Zeus had kidnapped Aegina, beautiful daughter of the god of rivers, Asopus. Sisyphus, in exchange for a new spring, for which the city of Corinth had dire need, informed Asopus who had kidnapped his daughter, enraging Zeus. Hades, having been asked by Zeus to destroy Sisyphus, sent Death into the upper world to collect his soul. Sisyphus tricked Death into trying on handcuffs and subsequently took him prisoner. Zeus exploded with anger, sending Ares, god of war, whom he no longer needed since Death was held captive, to free Death and capture the soul of Sisyphus, condemning him to the underworld. Sisyphus, expecting such an occurrence, had told his wife to throw his body into the city square unburied. Because this was a cultural taboo, Sisyphus convinced Hades to allow him to return in order to punish his wife for her callous treatment of the body. Once back in Corinth, Sisyphus refused to return to Hades. When he finally succumbed to Death, for creating all of this difficulty, Sisyphus was condemned to spend eternity pushing a huge boulder up a mountain, only to have it roll down, causing him to push it up the mountain again—a perfect metaphor for eternal futility and a poster boy for nihilism.

As a conclusion to his translation of the myth, Camus writes:

All Sisyphus silent joy is contained therein. His fate belongs to him. His rock is his thing. Likewise, the absurd man, when he contemplates his torment silences all the idols. . . . At that subtle moment when man glances backward over his life, Sisyphus turning toward his rock, in that slight pivoting he contemplates that series of unrelated actions which becomes his fate, created by him, combined under his memory's eye and soon sealed by his death. Thus, convinced of the wholly human origin of all that is human, a blind man eager to see who knows that the night has no end, he is still on the go. The rock is still rolling. I leave Sisyphus at the foot of the mountain! One always finds one's burden again. But Sisyphus teaches the higher fidelity that negates the gods and raises rocks. He too concludes that all is well. This universe henceforth without a master seems to him neither sterile nor futile. Each atom of that stone, each mineral flake of that night-filled mountain, in itself forms a world. The struggle itself toward the heights is enough to fill a man's heart. One must imagine Sisyphus happy. (Camus 375)

Larry McMurtry's third novel, *The Last Picture Show*, presents a familiar archetype involving rite of passage, going from adolescence to adulthood, and in that rite of passage, a quest for each individual to find a meaning in his or her life. *The Last Picture Show* was published in 1966, and the film, directed by Peter Bogdanovich, appeared in 1971. The film version won Academy Awards for Best Supporting Actress (Cloris Leachman) and Best Supporting Actor (Ben Johnson). In addition, nominations were given for Best Picture, Best Supporting Actor (Jeff Bridges), Best Supporting Actress (Ellen Burstyn), Director (Peter Bogdanovich) Cinematography, and Best Screenplay.

To place this novel into a literary perspective, "*The Last Picture Show* is not a novel so much as a satire which occasionally exhibits the essential properties of a novel" (Landess 23). Just as Camus saw Sisyphus as a model for the twentieth century's "absurd man," McMurtry creates his version of absurdity by portraying his characters as "one dimensional and stylized their humanity sacrificed to the ruthless demands of the author's sociological categories" (23). It was not McMurtry's intent to create a real world, but to fashion a world of hopelessness for both the culture and the people who inhabit it. The story maintains a light touch, subtly moving the tragedy into satire. Readers of the novel and most certainly viewers of the film will see the characters more as caricatures of life than as fully developed people, for whom we might feel sympathy.

This novel deals with the transition of the protagonist, Sonny, and three of his friends as they move from teenage high school students to teenage adults. A major element of the plot, obviously influenced a great deal by the setting of the novel in north-central Texas and the time in which it was written, is the emphasis placed on sexual relationships. For McMurtry, sex is a stylistic device, controlling to a great extent how the characters behave personally and in relationship with each other. While the emphasis in the novel is on adolescents, McMurtry expands the influence of sexual behavior to motivate most of the action in the novel, including the adults. In Thalia, Texas, "Sex is the groin level blind eye that directs all the characters and the basis for any philosophic comment and the end result, normal or subhuman, of all their encounters" ("A review" 783).

A second major influence providing a naturalistic mode is the setting. Charles Peavey, biographer and critic of Larry McMurtry, stated "The emotions underlying *The Last Picture Show* are distaste, bitterness, and resentment against the small town." In fact, according to Peavey, McMurtry developed the blindness motif in the novel to reflect "the sightlessness of life in a small town" (325). Janis P. Stout, writing for *Western American Literature* magazine, added, "Thalia has become a place to be escaped, and restlessness dominates. Sonny . . . a central character . . . first appears in the opening chapter struggling to get his old pickup to run. It is a prophetic detail, for Sonny [like Sisyphus] will never be able to escape" (330). For McMurtry, in this novel and his first, *Horseman, Pass By* (film version *Hud*), the movement from adolescence to adulthood is not a pleasant experience. Both novels project a sense of stark realism, moving away from any sense of western romantic idealism and into the tragic or satiric mode, representing the winter phase of the mythic cycle. This would seem to conflict with the traditional concept of adolescence as being a summer cycle, one of happiness and romance, for no matter what else may be present in a tragedy, one aspect permeates: "The tragic hero cannot simply rub a lamp and summon a genie to get him out of trouble" (Frye *AC* 207).

Sonny, protagonist of *The Last Picture Show*, will not have a Lone Ranger suddenly appear on the scene and make things right. Win or lose, the characters in this novel, like most other American adolescents when they reach adulthood, are on their own. For *The Last Picture Show*, there is little, if any, doubt that this is a tragedy because the novel contains all the necessary elements: sacrifice, rejection, and isolation. It also ends tragically, not in the physical death of the protagonist, but certainly in a spiritual death.

While the characters are dying a spiritual death, a physical death is also occurring. The community of Thalia is physically dying due to a cultural change that is still taking place throughout America. Small towns are dying as a result of economic change. From America's beginnings, agriculture relied heavily on the small farmer or rancher, which due to many changing economic factors is slowly dying. Without the family farm or ranch, many small towns lose their economic base.

For Larry McMurtry, this is not particularly disturbing. He, unlike many other Americans who have migrated to a metropolitan area, does not look back nostalgically at the time when life was simple and traditional small town values dominated young lives. The values in Thalia, Texas, at least those of the 1950s, are not those we see in reruns of Andy Griffith's Mayberry, or every Christmas in *It's a Wonderful Life*'s Bradford Falls. McMurtry's town is socially stratified, religiously narrow minded, and hypocritical, especially about sex. His story is as much about the physical death of the community and spiritual demise of the people of Thalia as it is about the difficulty three young men and one girl have in facing the passage into adulthood. The town becomes a metaphor for Sisyphus's rock as its inhabitants struggle to push it forward, only to have it continually fall backward. This extends the realistic tone to a level of naturalism, causing the adolescents to be the innocent victims of a world they did not make.

Structurally, this novel does not contain the totality of problems associated with coming of age in America in the late 1950s and early 1960s, but it does reflect the attitudes and opinions of a large segment of the population. That this story is more narrowly directed emphasizes one major difference between messianic myths and ritual myths. Heroes can make their own rules as they combat their adversary and are generally romantic; that is, they tend to take control of their environment. It is a matter of overt action, and the impending success of the hero is one that requires a character with the strength of an Andy Dufresne or Randle P. McMurphy to control the action. A movement from one stage of life to another is an initiation and traditionally requires a submission of the initiate to the rules and mores of the group and stage to which he or she is passing. Neither Sonny nor any of the other adolescents in *Last Picture Show* can change the ritual or the environment. Their only choice is to survive it and in some way, like Sisyphus, find some degree of happiness in their survival.

In addition, apparent in this novel is an adaptation to geographical and regional demands. Not every place in the United States is like the plains of north-central Texas, a land of cattle and oil wells. Also, most locales do not have the historical background of being settled by men of heroic proportions, such as Sam Houston, Stephen Austin, James Bowie, and the heroes of the Alamo. Perhaps it is knowing the strength and individuality of the Texas pioneers who fought their own war for independence and made Texas an independent country prior to joining the union in 1845 that causes McMurtry to look with such depressing disdain on the post–World War II generation of adolescents. It is through this contrasting absurdity that McMurtry develops his satire and most closely connects to myth. If the reader or viewer see Sonny and Duane as the post–World War II generation of "western cowboys," the story not only connects to the myth of the Old West, but also demonstrates the absurd lack of direction present in today's generation. If his intent is to create a sense of reality, you would think he could have found just one youth who posesses the attributes of their forebears to provide a contrast for the losers. After all, using character contrast as an expositional device certainly amplifies a character's attributes and is common in literature.

This same method of satire is used in McMurtry's creation of setting. One would expect a small town to be conducive to a simple life, providing a safe and secure environment for its youth to mature into stable adults. However, because the problems of maturation are internal and complex, McMurtry implies it does not matter what size or space the town occupies. Whatever world we live in makes the physical rite of passage from adolescence to adulthood a difficult journey for every young male or female. McMurtry's own difficult passage may account to some extent for the depressing theme emerging from the novel. However, what is recurrent and applicable to everyone is the fact that adolescents, irrespective of their culture or locale, must pass through a set of established trials before they can claim adult status. In so doing, they must find an individual identity and a meaning for their lives, wherever or whatever their rock might be. A fascinating aspect of this rite of passage, in deference to the hero ritual, is that the participant cannot fail but will, at least chronologically, become an adult if he or she survives. As Camus explained to us about Sisyphus's rock, even in futility, there can be meaning.

The Last Picture Show is a novel about what happens in small towns when the sons and daughters of pioneers lose the spirit that conquered the West. The place, Thalia, Texas, is a community of fewer than a thousand people suffering a steady deterioration in business and lifestyle. In real time, the novel covers a little more than one year during the early 1950s. *The Last Picture Show* begins as satiric tragedy and completes its story in the same mode. It is "dominated by the archetypal tragedy of the green and golden world, the loss of innocence of Adam and Eve, who, no matter how heavy a doctrinal load they have to carry, will always remain dramatically in the position of children baffled by their first contact with an adult situation" (Frye *AC* 220). The hero of a tragedy may survive but, like Adam and Eve, at a huge price. Innocence will be tragically lost, constituting a fall. The question remains, Will anything change?

When the novel opens, most of the businesses in Thalia have already closed. We are made aware of three that have survived, at least for the time being: the pool hall, a diner, and the movie theater. The three businesses, the high school, along with a reservoir known as the "tanks," and some nearby communities provide the locale for this depressing story of lives lived seemingly without purpose.

All three businesses are owned by Sam the Lion, who along with Jacy's mother, Lois; Genevieve, the diner's waitress; and Abeline, Lois's paramour, represent the older generation of the town. Sonny, the central figure, his best friend, Duane, Jacy, Duane's girlfriend, and a narrow-minded preacher's son, Joe Bob, represent the new generation. They are graduating from high school and by tradition and ritual into adulthood. McMurtry's adolescent characters all seem to be searching desperately for an identity as they journey to other towns and cities, but always end up back in Thalia. The journeys, like their experimentation with sex, end in futility and frustration. They give up their sexual innocence, expecting to become something new and different. What they find is the same emptiness. The past, present, and future appear as bleak as the wind-swept prairies of north-central Texas.

The anonymous narrator (third person omniscient) of the story tells us about the people and their actions in the form and tone of a gossipy neighbor. He seems to be all knowing, particularly about all of the sins of the community, and certainly does not want us to miss any of those. It is typical of small towns that everyone knows everyone else's business. This trait of a small-town gossip works to provide a degree of believability for the narrator. One of the subtle ironies of this story relates to how other people know what you think is your secret. They talk about it to everyone but you. No one, not even your best friend, will mention it to you unless you are the first to speak. For example, Sonny, believing his affair with Ruth to be their secret, never mentions it to anyone. He seems shocked when he becomes aware that everyone in Thalia except the cuckolded coach know and are quite willing to offer opinions about the relationship, especially Lois and Genevieve, but only when asked by Sonny.

The storyline focuses on the problems of growing up in a place where the future is limited and perhaps nonexistent for any who remain there. A dramatic irony exists when we learn how naive Duane and Sonny are, for like many other eighteen-year-old males, they believe they have already attained adulthood; they have voluntarily separated from their families and are working and paying rent on a room in a small rooming house. They support themselves economically, which gives them status among their peers. Both boys, however, come to realize during the course of the novel, they have much to learn about life. They are constantly being forced to look at their behavior as well as the behavior of others in the community, and evaluate it. They discover that some of the acts committed as adolescents no longer produce the excitement they once did, even without fully comprehending why. One example occurs when Sonny and Duane participate in an incident with a blind heifer and in getting a girl for Billy. Sonny demonstrates his being on the cusp between adolescence and adulthood in his reluctance to be active in the action but unable to condemn it. He knows in the incident involving the retarded Billy that he was wrong in not standing up for him. When confronted by Sam the Lion after the incident, Sonny does act responsibly by accepting his punishment without complaint, knowing he did wrong, but not quite understanding why it was wrong (103–13). The vision of a group of high school boys participating in a "gang bang" with a blind heifer would seem to confirm the satiric mode. "Satire demands at least a token fantasy, a content which the reader recognizes as grotesque, and at least an implicit moral standard, the latter being essential in a militant attitude to experience" (Frye *AC* 244). The narrator's matter-of-fact and humorous tone throughout the episode is in sharp contrast to the perversion of the action. McMurtry's choice of detail combined with the narrator's tone, in essence, holding the action up to ridicule, also implies a moral judgment.

A major theme emerging from the novel is isolation. Separation and loneliness permeate the story as the town of Thalia appears isolated from the rest of the world. There is no mention of any event that is occurring outside Thalia except, after Duane has joined the army, he tells Sonny he is going to Korea and will "see you in a year or two, if I don't get shot" (271). We assume this is because of the war, but the lack of discussion emphasizes how the town is unaffected by the outside world and enhances the satiric tone by exposing the extreme naiveté of the characters. The continual references to the picture show demonstrates how the young and, we may surmise, the older generation accepted the movies as a window on the rest of the world. As the town dies, the picture show loses out to television, which has no appeal for the younger adults. This event enhances the feeling of isolation because no common interest exists between generations except the high school, and Sonny conveys what is probably a normal first-year alumnus's feeling while functioning on the chain gang at the football game. "He [Sonny] was an ex-student, he was nothing" (260). He seems to be caught in a no-man's-land, ignorant of both who he is and what his function is to be in the world around him. One world has disappeared and the other is not yet a reality; according to McMurtry, he is ill prepared to choose a direction. In response to Sartre's *Being and Nothingness*, the question becomes just how much of Sonny's dilemma is a matter of choice. An obvious conflict emerges between nature and nurture, realism and naturalism. McMurtry's satiric tone would seem to come down on the side of Sartre: we are what we choose, for even if we do not choose, that becomes a choice. Be it one of omission or commission, it remains our choice.

The final scene in both the novel and film shows Sonny—his only close friends, Duane and Jacy gone, and Billy dead—frantically driving away from Thalia/Anarene, only to put on the brakes and slowly return. In the film, immediately after he passes the city limits of Anarene, he stops, and, to repeat Camus' admonition about Sisyphus: "At that subtle moment when man glances backward over his life, Sisyphus [Sonny] returning toward his rock [the town], in that slight pivoting he contemplates that series of unrelated actions which becomes his fate, created by him, combined under his memory's eye and soon sealed by his death [isolation]." Like the community, Sonny is now all alone except for the pathetic Ruth—a relationship that, the reader knows, has no future, like the town. In fact, at some point, every character in the novel conveys a feeling of isolation.

A summary of the novel might read thus: Sonny, the protagonist, breaks up with his mediocre girlfriend and through an unusual set of circumstances begins an affair with the football coach's forty-year-old wife, Ruth. Duane, Sonny's best friend, after being continually manipulated and finally dumped by his girlfriend, Jacy, "the prettiest girl in town," blames Sonny, causing a fight. Sonny loses an eye, leaving him ineligible for the army. Duane, like many others in his generation, joins the army and is sent to Korea. Sam the Lion, the only person who seems to know who he is, dies and leaves the pool hall to Sonny, who as a part of Sam the Lion's will, is to care for Billy, a retarded adolescent. Jacy sexually teases Duane to the point that when he finally gains access, he suffers a temporary impotence. Duane's eventual success is short lived as Jacy drops him in order to join a group of wealthy and aimless young adults and begins a promiscuous sex life, just like her mother. It sounds like an ordinary small town, where every life touches every other life and reads very much like a soap opera.

What makes this novel more than a soap opera is the emphasis on a series of interconnected vignettes in the lives of the characters. Each satirical vignette represents a ritual in the maturing process of Sonny, Duane, Jacy, and Joe Bob. Into the vignettes, McMurtry interweaves symbols as motifs, connecting each ritual and reflecting the archetypal tragedy of a modern rite of passage from adolescence to adulthood. Symbols such as the deteriorating setting, blindness, the closing movie theater, ridicule of organized religion, and loveless sex function as motifs amplifying the tragic fall of Sonny. Sex, in addition to its symbolic meaning, motivates the action by the characters—talking about it, doing it, or, when neither of those is available, fantasizing about it. This attitude toward and about sex forms the basis for the satirical mode. It is an absurd paradox; the characters' obsession with physical sex blinds them to their real need, a relationship with at least one other human being that could give their life a meaning. The opportunities are subtly suggested throughout; the satiric absurdity is how blind they are to the reality.

The film, directed by Peter Bogdanovich in 1971, was shot in black and white, imposing on its viewer the mood and tone of the novel. A hopeless tone hanging over the characters as they strive to overcome their surroundings seems to be a form that modern authors, such as McMurtry, use to amplify the tragedies in our world. The film version, generally considered Bogdanovich's best, provides several specific images that enhance both the tragic and mythological base for the story. Expressing the images in black · and white also creates an aura of truth, echoing James Monaco's comment that an audience responds to the mythic nature when there exists the "aura of truth." The film presentation enhances the result of several specific obstacles, mostly psychological, that form a test in the rite of passage. One in particular is loss of virginity. We are made aware throughout the novel how each of the characters views the importance of sex, then witness with some varying degree of visual constraint the event; more important, we are made aware of the high level of expectation, followed by the fall when emotional reality sets in. Although the novel presents the same idea, the film seems to make the point more emphatically that the world did not change; in fact, the characters are confused by the outcome. The audience, through dramatic irony and especially the quality of the actors' subtext, understands the reality and truth of the situation. The action in both the novel and the film represents reality in its most painful nature.

Two of the major cinemagraphic aspects of this film are the black and white background and how Bogdanovich is constantly showing emptiness. The viewer's perspective is considered when we see the characters photographed with open space behind them. As we become aware of how space is used both to separate the action within a scene and as a transition between scenes, we realize why this film was nominated for an Academy Award for its cinematography. This is an example of semiology at its directorial best.

The acting in this film by all critical accounts is excellent. The novel, however, was resoundly criticized by literary critics. Peavey criticized by stating, "The protagonist of the book is somewhat inadequately developed. But, *The Last Picture Show* is weaker than McMurtry's first two novels in other ways than characterization" (325). Larry Goodwyn added: "The feeling is therefore induced that we are in the presence of a skilled craftsman who is uncertain what he is trying to portray" (201). The general sense is that McMurtry never was able to say, at least in many critics' minds, what he would like to have said about a small town and its inhabitants. In the analysis by Thomas Landess, these critics missed the point. They did not view the story as satire, but as a traditional realistic novel. It is through the satiric mode that the novel becomes a unique presentation. According to the reception of the film, Bogdanovich was able to manifest this on the screen. Maybe through the exceptional performances of the actors and a good director, the novel's missing subtext was communicated.

Satire, realism, and tragedy may be presented in several forms or modes. For example, we might compare the story of the innocent Sonny with that of Job, a truly innocent individual who ironically must suffer undeserved isolation and loss. For Sonny, there is no obvious tragic flaw, other than youthful ignorance and a lack of will, to compensate the reader in accepting the depth to which Sonny has been condemned. On the other hand, Sonny as a fictional creation is in good company based on some previous innocent victims: Cordelia, the only good daughter of Shakespeare's *King Lear*; Joan of Arc, whose only crime was to adhere to the voice of God; and Jesus Christ. To understand the tragedy of the innocent is one of the oldest myths. If we exist within a moral world, why do the good suffer along with the bad?

The antagonist/dragon of this story is not found in a single character but rather in the environment. Nobel Prize novelist Alexander Solzhenitsyn in a commencement speech at Harvard University, stated, "in the United States the difficulties are not a Minotaur or a dragon—not imprisonment, hard labor, death, government harassment and censorship—but cupidity [lust], boredom, sloppiness, indifference . . . the failure of a listless public to make use of the freedom that is its birthright" (qtd. in Cozic 112). Sonny and his peers face one very important virtue we associate with American culture: individualism. In order to defeat the dragons, Sonny, Duane, Jacy, and Joe Bob must broaden their own awareness by a conscious assessment of who they are and what will become their "boulder." As writers continually tell us, individuality is becoming much more difficult to attain. Modern society seems to be corrupting us both individually and collectively by its focus on personal gratification.

One existential facet that needs to be mentioned is the negativism expressed toward contemporary organized religion. McMurtry's bitterness is manifest during the community revival when he sarcastically describes Joe Bob's father using the perverse actions of his son to elevate his own standing. Whereas organized religion was once the bastion of moral judgments, modern writers, such as McMurtry, if they allude to religion at all, generally show it as being hypocritical and unable to meet the needs of contemporary society. The film version downplayed the author's attitude. Joe Bob's action involving the Clarq girl was included, but except for one line during the English class regarding Keats's "wanting to be a nightingale," the religious fervor was omitted. Joe Bob comes through as a religious nerd.

Can morality and spirituality be separated? The modern writer who is influenced by a century of existential philosophy continually implies that organized religion is unable to answer the moral questions ordinary individuals confront in their daily lives. What seems true is that the more novels and films reach toward reality, the higher the level of verisimilitude, the closer the story adheres to the metaphoric truths found in ancient myth. Protagonists (heroes) continue to struggle with their surroundings (dragons). What does not change is the need for the individual to establish an identity and an individual meaning to life, paradoxically both within and external to the environment in which he or she lives. How one goes about accomplishing this task determines the quality and value of the individual. Religion in modern literary interpretation becomes just one more facet of the dragon.

The solution, implied by Camus and presented in contemporary myth by McMurtry, would seem to be love, for it is in loving relationships that the characters are able to establish their identity. Lois, in explaining how the name Sam the Lion came to her says, "The lion was seventy years old he could just walk in. . . . I don't know, hug me and call me Lois or something an' do more for me than anybody. He really knew what I was worth" (252). At that moment, Lois knew whom she was; no one else in Thalia ever made her feel that way. As Tennessee Williams's gentleman caller explains, "The power of love is pretty tremendous" (Sc. VII, *The Glass Menagerie*). In *The Last Picture Show*, the characters' immature inability to separate sex and love proves to be a fatal flaw, isolating them from life. Maybe if it were a rock and not a member of the opposite sex, the problem would be simpler. However, we can recognize that McMurtry is describing the importance of caring for and about one another. It just might be that when Ruth reaches out to straighten Sonny's collar in the film's final scene, the theme is better communicated by being able to see Ruth not as a forty-year-old predator, but as one of life's castaways reaching out in love to another; a viewer understands more easily than a reader.

QUESTIONS

In your responses, identify a specific reference by quotation or page number.

1. A motif for the novel is blindness. The culmination of the motif occurs when Billy, with both eyes covered, is run down by a semi-truck. Cite a minimum of three other events when blindness or the inability to see clearly appears and explain how blindness amplifies the thematic meaning.

2. The novel is a study in the rite of passage from adolescence to adulthood. For the three major characters, Sonny, Duane, and Jacy, it is a painful experience. What was the tragic flaw (hamartia) in each of them that caused them to fail in their quest for happiness? Describe a scene in which the flaw becomes evident.

3. Charles Peavey, in a critical essay about the novel, stated, "It is through the medium of sex that the inhabitants of Thalia seek (and find) their identity" (181).

Briefly, using one male and one female character as examples, explain the meaning of the statement. (In other words, two characters used sex to establish themselves as a person. What were they before and after?) Use quotations where possible.

4. On page 191 the narrator comments: "They didn't question Bobby Logan because his father didn't want him to know what homosexuality was yet." What did McMurtry want the reader to perceive after reading this line? What tone is implied?

5. A mythological aspect of this novel is that each of the major characters embarks on a series of journeys in search of something. Cite one specific example and explain what they were searching for literally and figuratively.

6. On page 280, read from Ruth's line, "What am I doing apologizing to you?" to the end. What motivates Ruth to conclude with, "Never you mind?" Is the phrase believable? Why or why not?

QUESTIONS FOR GROUP DISCUSSION

1. What social, legal, or moral judgment(s) is McMurtry making about how we prepare young people for adulthood? Cite examples from either or both the text or the film.

2. Larry McMurtry has attained fame as an author in his stories about both the modern and past western United States. What elements of the novel or film show how the world has changed between the setting of the novel, its references to its past, and the influences of the time in which it was written?

3. From the perspective of most critics, both the novel and the film are presented as realistic. To what extent do you see the novel as a realistic representation of adolescents of the 1950s? Of today? Cite some specific scenes as examples for comparison.

4. Identify two or three contemporary films or novels that you might compare or contrast with these examples of coming of age. Discuss the comparisons with regard to mode of presentation and verisimilitude.

5. Focus on the characters Billy, Ruth, and Genevieve as they appeared in both the novel and film. Discuss to what advantage or disadvantage the screen actor had in portraying the character. Determine first the literary function of the character (what purpose they served in communicating the story) and then to what extent the actor fulfilled that purpose and by what specific means.

PART IV

MORALITY AND MAGIC

One of the oldest and so far most evasive human quest has been to find a perfect and universal concept of good and evil—one set of perfect values that everyone can accept and abide by. For the most part, the task, beginning far back in antiquity, has been a province of the various organized religions. Certainly we can all agree that religion has not been very successful. Religious sectarianism has created as many disputes leading to violent behavior as it has been able to solve differences. The "troubles" between Catholics and Protestants in Ireland, the conflict between Sikhs and Hindus in India, and the Middle East where Arabs and Jews have been fighting over land possession for three thousand years are but three ancient feuds that are still manifest. What creates much of the problem is that each religion bases its beliefs on a simple concept: each assumes it alone possesses the real truth. It becomes the truth when a vision of reality, that is, the real world of man and *mana* is revealed to them and them alone. Religion dictates that a true vision of reality is realized when we consciously perceive ourselves, both as an individual and as part of its particular abstract belief system, as coexisting within the natural world. However, one similarity between those religious cultures informs us that simply to acknowledge existence is not enough. *Mana* demands that we need to know why we exist. Once a purpose is established, as fully conscious beings, it becomes important to define the best mode for ensuring that existence will continue. From the beginning of recorded time, humanity has sought a code that will not only ensure human life continues, but will establish how an intelligent being ought to live. Contemporary life has come to place less emphasis on religious teaching and more on scientific humanism, which does not settle the conflict. It has, if anything, only expanded the conflict.

Immanuel Kant (1724–1804), considered the father of modern philosophy, theorized that we can know what is morally right by a form of intuition. Moral law does not depend on what we will or desire, but rather what we ought to desire. Kant labels this a *categorical imperative*, an innate sense of what is right and wrong and is genetically inherent in the mind of all humanity. In essence, this concept forms a base for Jung's collective unconscious and is manifest in all cultures as *mana*, the spiritual dimension. Existentialism is a modern antithesis of Kant's categorical imperative.

Since religion and philosophy have been somewhat unable to solve the problem, the door has been opened to science. A recent excursion into television by Stephen Hawking, entitled simply *Stephen Hawking's Universe*, opens with the interesting hypothesis, "If man could construct an equation that would identify the relationship between energy-time-matter, he would then understand how the universe began. We know such a relationship exists because we are here." While this might explain for the scientific world how we got here, it would add very little to the problems we have created since. What the equation could not give us is a guidebook by which to live. The equation cannot explain human emotion, morality, and the spiritual dimension we know as *mana*.

There is no question that morality is real; it is those principles most clearly defining how we should live. Morals or ethics are the human attempt to synthesize a metaphysically designed code with a natural need and to include within the establishment of that code a justification for an obedience to the code—a code that will establish whether those aspects of life not covered by legislative law are permissible, demanded, or forbidden. In order to determine and impose the code, it is necessary to engage human consciousness, particularly with regard to what really motivates humans to act.

Colin Falck, in *Myth, Truth, and Literature*, theorizes that the best place to find this reality is in literature:

Reason is our imagination employed to make the best conceptual sense that we can of the whole of reality; but there are also imaginative fictions which invest that reality with a local habitation and a name, and which link our phenomenal experience . . . directly to our vision of reality by means of symbolic or metaphorical relationships. (142)

Falck theorizes that literature in the form of myth was the original guidebook for ancient societies. As such, it is "literature [that] *inscribes* reality" (123). This idea carries over into today's culture. Modern literature, providing the same basic truths found in ancient myths, will increasingly replace religious writing as the purveyor of truth because cultures cannot agree on a single religious authority. "Beyond all ideological distortions and falsifications which may infect our work, poetry or literature remains the most reliable access to reality that we can have" (169). For our purposes, we add motion pictures to the list. Although the story originates as a written form, and therefore as literature, the majority of people exposed to its message will do so in a theater or on their home television rather than the written page.

As a test of Falck's thesis, in Part IV we examine selections that present very divergent views of reality as it exists in our world. Because morality and motivation are irrevocably linked, they pose a greater problem in a free society than in an authoritarian one. If, like ancient Rome, our nation goes into decline, it will be due to a failure from within to live up to those ethical and moral standards on which our free society is based. To place this idea into literary perspective, Part IV offers four visions of morality. Robert Penn Warren's *All the King's Men* and Jerzy Kosinski's *Being There* approach the problem of morals from the perspective of politics. Warren's novel is a vision of the world following World War II, and Konsinski's novel shows us what we have become in the aftermath of Vietnam and the cold war. In these novels, the spotlight shines on the politician—that man in a free society who is elected by the public to represent them in matters of government. Once in office, he or she gets to choose what laws to enact that will govern the rest of us. If morality is to be found in the motivations of humans, what better place to seek it than in those in a real position of power?

Although politics is an obvious location to observe morals in action, it is necessary to recognize that morality must exist everywhere if we are to survive. Two very diverse cultures and two very diverse authors, having in common only the fact that each uses a sporting event as their perspective, will demonstrate that morality is not limited to the great and the powerful. These stories span some sixty years. Ernest Hemingway wrote *The Sun Also Rises* in 1925, a novel in which he attempted to redefine the morality of a world that had lost its way in World War I. He culminated his search in a bullring in Pamplona, Spain. W. P. Kinsella, publishing *Shoeless Joe* in 1982, will take us to a farm in Iowa, where his protagonist will build a lighted baseball field in order to redeem not only the living but also the dead.

The Sun Also Rises was published in 1926, the film version came much later, in 1957. One aspect that seems intriguing about this selection is that the novel was written in the 1920s about the after-effects of World War I and the first film version was made ten years following World War II, neatly sandwiching Warren's *All the King's Men* in between. To look at the stories in tandem provides an example of how rapidly culture changes when it experiences terrible events. What is common is that both World War I and World War II had atrocities that damaged its participants physically and psychologically. How this difference plays out can be inferred from a semantic example concerning the psychologically damaged veteran. Following World War I, he was labeled "shell-shocked." During World War II, the label was changed to "battle fatigue." Later this century, the same illness was presented as the "Vietnam syndrome." We may soften the language, but the fact is that the psychological damage remains long after the physical damage has healed.

Beyond the personal damage imposed by the war on its veterans, their families, and the communities are the changes it imposes on our belief system resulting from the inhumanity we cannot ignore. The steady advance in military technology increases the horror of war in direct proportion to the softening of the language our history books use to describe it. Therefore, it is the novel, and not the history books, that most accurately communicates the real effect on the individuals most affected by its violence. Hemingway's novel is not merely an assessment that war is immoral. It transforms, "through the medium of style and tone, a kind of moral network that linked [his characters] together in a unified pattern of meaning" (Aldridge *ALG* 231). War can dim the spirit, but it cannot destroy it.

In order for readers to understand how literature plays a part in conveying reality, novels alter their focus to one of ordinary people. Out of this emerges a third type of hero. Hemingway, although this novel was written thirty-six years prior to Kesey's *Cuckoo's Nest* and fifty-six years prior to King's *Shawshank Redemption*, may be more representational of modern man than either of the later stories. In fact, many twentieth-century critics feel that Hemingway in his novels and short stories established a code by which all modern heroes and possibly all humans may be judged. *The Sun Also Rises* established Hemingway as an important author for two reasons. No other modern author, American or foreign, has had as great an influence on literary style than Hemingway. It might also be said that Hemingway has proved to be the exception to the rule in that although his style was the subject of hundreds of imitators, no one has been able to improve on the manner in which he structured his narratives, particularly his written dialogue. Hemingway firmly believed that the least amount of material possible to maintain the story and move it to a conclusion is the best form. As biographer Gene Phillips commented, "Much of the power of Hemingway's writing resides in what he leaves unsaid; that is, in his ability to imply much more meaning than he explicitly spells out on the printed page" (125).

The other reason lies in the subject matter about which he chose to write. As F. Scott Fitgerald is frequently labeled the chronicler of the Jazz Age, Hemingway is the recognized chronicler of the lost generation, a title coined by Gertrude Stein and given to the disillusioned young dropouts following World War I. It is Hemingway seeking to find meaning in an individual shattered by the aftermath of war. In his quest to find a meaning, Hemingway developed a set of values defining the *code hero*. The quest of Jake Barnes in *The Sun Also Rises* is the first in a long line of novels and stories culminating with *The Old Man and the Sea*, Hemingway's final and most complete model for the code hero.

To Hemingway, "All good books are alike in that they are truer than if they had really happened and after you are finished reading one you will feel that all that happened to you and afterwards it all belongs to you; the good and the bad, the ecstasy, the remorse and sorrow, the people and the places" (Baker 106). Falck would seem to be correct in his theory based on this opinion. Hemingway would seem to agree that literature possesses the insight to show us a direction. Hemingway, in creating the code hero, gives us one model to follow. Robert Penn Warren expands the perspective to its philosophical zenith. For Warren, it is not merely the individual who is lost, it is the entire culture.

To prove there is hope, the next selection examined takes us further back into time than any of the others. In today's technological world, we have a tendency to think or feel we are at the mercy of science and technology to give life a morality and a meaning. Science and technology are totally dependent on the truth of determinism, a basic law of science: every effect has a cause. If you mix the correct ingredients, you will get the expected outcome. This imposes a severe limitation on life and especially any attempt to imply a meaning beyond the physical. Claude Lévi-Strauss accepted the fact that there is a way humans may extend knowledge beyond science. Writing in *The Savage Mind* he states:

One can go further and think of the rigorous precision of magical thought and ritual practice as an extension of the unconscious apprehension of the *truth of determinism*; the mode in which scientific phenomena exist. In this view, the operations of determinism are divined and made use of in an all-embracing fashion before being known and properly applied, and magical rites and beliefs appear as so many expressions of an act of faith in a science yet to be born. (11)

"A science yet to be born" may well be a theme for W. P. Kinsella's *Shoeless Joe* (film version *Field of Dreams*). What we call magic has its origins in a time long before people began keeping records. Magic is a form of determinism: if I perform the correct ritual, a predicted event will follow. "If you build it, he will come." Kinsella's protagonist builds it, and, sure enough, he and many of his friends do come and inhabit the pages of this novel. Is it reality? Is it a truth? The concept leads us into a whole new framework of knowledge. Can everything in the universe be explained by a scientific equation?

The final selection, *Being There*, is a short novel by Jerzy Kosinski (1933–1991). After immigrating from Poland at the age of 24, Kosinski became an English teacher, a poet, a novelist, and a prize winning screenwriter. However, it was his experiences as a youth in occupied Poland during the war years and subsequent emigration that provided him with a unique view of the world and the United States. In *Being There*, he manages through subtle satire to point out many of the shortcomings he found in present day culture. While politics and government seem to be the focus, the subtle criticism of the electorate and its reliance on television for information cannot be overlooked. This simple story demonstrates how effectively the myth form works to convey meaning.

Roland Barthes, French lexicographer and sociologist, said it this way:

In passing from history to nature, myth acts economically: it abolishes the complexity of human acts, it gives them the simplicity of essences, it does away with all dialectics, with any going back beyond what is immediately visible, it organizes a world which is without contradictions because it is without depth, a world wide open and wallowing in the evident, it establishes a blissful clarity: things appear to mean something by themselves.

A perfect description of Kosinski's book.

A very interesting feature of these stories lies in the metaphoric device each author chooses to create his view of reality. For Hemingway, life's real meaning can be found by courageously facing one's mortality in a bullring. Kinsella finds his meaning on a baseball diamond scratched atop Mother Earth. The function of a setting is to provide the character an arena in which a meaning can be discovered for his individual life. Warren contends that reality is found not in space but at that moment when the individual recognizes his mortality. Kosinski's delightful story prefers to show us the negative, which hopefully will lead toward enlightenment. What connects these stories is how life's meaning can be truly found only within the individual. However, the manner in which one faces the challenge life presents—be it as a country lawyer, a matador, a farmer, or a gardener—will determine the meaning of a life. The true value of good literature is to show us a way to a moral reality.

Chapter 9

A "Good" Politician Is Hard
to Find

All the King's Men
by Robert Penn Warren

One will deal with various levels of romantic realism in *One Flew over the Cuckoo's Nest*, *The Color Purple*, and *The Shawshank Redemption*; discover some mildly depressing realism in Ernest Hemingway's *The Sun Also Rises*, and become really depressed by the satire found in *The Last Picture Show*. Although each of those novels provide: some degree of environmental influence, none approaches the depth to which a culture can completely dominate and alter the values and will of a mature character. *All the King's Men* by Robert Penn Warren takes us on a journey into the world of corrupt politics and the ends to which a politician will go to gain and administer power over others. It becomes a contest between the strength of one man's will and the rules by which the "game" is played. In the end, as protagonist Willie Stark confronts his own choices, he will seek redemption for allowing the environment to win.

In the previous novels and films explored, the protagonists are men and women who sought their own redemption in their involvement with others. The act of redemption is a need to purge evil from within one's being through a cleansing ritual form of rebirth. Andy Dufresne, Randle P. McMurphy, and Jake Barnes seek to purge their transgressions by giving to others. In this novel, the evil is not simply the act of committing a wrong due to ignorance or errors in judgment. For Willie Stark, evil goes much deeper as the details imply at every moment of choice, he knows precisely what is right and what is wrong and consciously chooses to perform one malevolent act after another. His transgressions violate the laws of God, nature, and society.

Evil may be defined on two levels. First is the abstract level, which may or may not exist as an actual extrinsic spiritual force. Either way, in every culture, it is a transgression of those moral values the culture has traditionally held we ought to live by. These values, such as love, honor, and respect for tradition may be derived from a religious or humanistic base, are open to interpretation, and vary a great deal by culture. A second definition of evil is applied on a concrete level when the moral or ethical value is codified into law. These are values supported by logic or science and are accepted by most civilized societies—pragmatically to ensure their continuance. These moral judgments deal with such societal problems as murder, theft, incest, and monogamy. A transgression of a law or a tradition will receive a label identifying the type and degree of the violation—for example, vice, venality, corruption, crime, malevolence, immorality, iniquity, sin, or abomination. These terms are symbols that our language provides to identify certain actions by individuals or groups that violate a moral or ethical principle we have codified by law or tradition.

A major philosophical question is inherent in this concept: Are there standards higher than those made by humans? Our culture, having its moral and ethical foundation in Puritanism, predicates many of its laws and mores on that religious base. Puritanism is founded on a dualistic concept that good and evil are forces existing in a spiritual domain and acting in conflict for the immortal soul of each person. In order for humans to deal with these forces, each person has a will—a capacity to choose what is done, how it is done, and, if guided by rational thought, why it is done. Humanism, expressed as moral relativism, tends to deny the influence of extrinsic or spiritual forces. For the humanist or existentialist, laws are an extension of nature and may be shaped by the entity that happens to possess power at the moment. In a purely democratic society, moral and ethical rules evolve into laws and mores based on what will benefit, as opposed to what brings harm in some form to the individual, society, or culture.

The effect of a belief in the presence of an actual force brings into conflict essence and existence. *Essence* freely translates as soul or, from an existential standpoint, the inner being, our unconscious self. *Existence* refers to the physical environment within which our essence exists. Generally, we are motivated to act in a manner we perceive will best enhance our existence. We can behave rationally, that is, make sensible choices based on a particular code or system of values, or we can act irrationally, in opposition to the rules and mores. In translating life into literature, tragedy occurs when a protagonist consciously makes an irrational choice due to a tragic flaw (hamartia) in his or her character and as a result fails in the completion of the quest. Tragedy, since the days of Aeschylus, Sophocles, and Euripides, has dominated good literature. This is a necessary attribute of literature, for without a belief in the existence of an evil force, tragedy cannot exist—nor will it be entertaining if redemption is not a possibility. It is the act of redemption that provides the reader a sense of hope, which gives his or her own life, be it in existence or essence, a reason to continue the journey.

Classical tragedy emerges from the belief that forces do exist, whatever the source. Without actual forces, human or superhuman, acting in conflict for human essence, redemption would not have any real meaning. Robert Penn Warren's *All the King's Men*, published in 1946 and filmed for the first time in 1949, places into classic literary form how these forces manifest themselves within a modern American quest for power. Warren goes beyond the presence of good and evil to include the influence of a third force, existential nihilism. There is a subtle omission of any specific moral code in the attitudes of both protagonists freeing them, in a sense, to act without restraint (*All the King's Man*, like *Cuckoo's Nest*, shares the role of protagonist between two characters). This adds to the complexity, for beyond the extrinsic forces of good and evil competing for the souls of Willie Stark and Jack Burden, a purely natural human force arises. It is a primeval reality, a power, or as Plato's friend Thrasymachus states in *The Republic*: "I proclaim that justice is nothing else than the interest of the stronger" (Book 1). In the struggle for power, as in war, the winner gets to set the rules. This story becomes more complex as Warren extends the conflict for power by contrasting values inherent in politics with those in religion and with those affecting social relationships. The conflict exists not only between individuals—Willie Stark and his political opponents—but also extends to philosophical conflicts between the ethics of politics and the values of religion and to social morality: family, friends, and associates.

It has also become obvious that a film director, having a much greater commercial responsibility, often shades a story to appeal to a much wider audience than that of the novel. For example, in the film version of *Shawshank*, the warden and captain of the guard are brought to justice, while in the novella, King chooses to ignore their transgressions. Robert Rossen, director of *King's Men*, chooses to omit the conflicts between the societal entities, concentrating entirely on the Willie Stark character. Robert Penn Warren, like French writer Albert Camus, is concerned with the effect that a devaluation of religious influence may have on other cultural entities. Where Camus uses physical isolation to separate his protagonist from the real world, Warren places Jack Burden and Willie Stark within a fast-moving political environment. Warren, as did Michael Ondaatje, sees life as motion. By continually interweaving the past and the present, Warren can include a search for individual meaning in Jack Burden's personal quest and simultaneously broaden the scope to examine how existential nihilism affects both the individual and southern culture. The result is a complex novel and a relatively simple film.

Robert Penn Warren was America's first poet laureate, being selected for that honor in 1944, two years prior to the publication of *All the King's Men*. From 1934 until 1942 he was a professor of English at Louisiana State University, which coincided with the rise and fall of Huey Long. During this same period he witnessed the rise of Adolf Hitler in Germany and Benito Mussolini in Italy (Warren spent the 1939–40 academic year on sabbatical in Italy), together providing a base for the plot and theme of this novel. His first creation of this story was as a poetic drama completed in 1942. Although Warren was a success as a poet, his play and first two novels were rejected for publication. Warren was thus personally familiar with success and failure. His academic career and his poetry were imminently successful while his early attempts at drama and narrative were summarily rejected. Understanding tragedy, having firsthand knowledge of the politics of demagoguery, and possessing a poetic soul gave Warren the depth to undertake such a monumental task in creating one of America's great tragic novels.

As we enter the tragic mode, we know the hero will fail. The mythological connections, however, are just as strong for stories of high tragedy as for comedy, in which the hero triumphs. This story is high tragedy. *All the King's Men* focuses on powerful men who administer, directly or indirectly, the law of the land. In dealing with powerful men competing for high political office, the situation presents an extremely complex form of myth. The tragic hero, Willie Stark, is a powerful individual involved in a quest for power and, in similar form to a heroic myth, is a controller of the action. Ironically, as a political candidate in a democracy, he must also acquiesce to forces capable of granting his success—the many facets of an electorate. What becomes ultimately important is what motivates a person to subject himself or herself to this paradoxical situation.

To facilitate a tragedy, the character must possess a sense of goodness, a metaphoric innocence. In its archetypal form, tragedy becomes a form of sacrifice. "Tragedy is a paradoxical combination of a fearful sense of rightness (the hero must fall) and a pitying sense of wrongness (it is too bad that he falls)" (Frye *AC* 214). Adam in the Garden of Eden must fall, for without his fall, the story will have no meaning. It is sad he falls, but it has to happen. As a metaphor, the reason Adam falls (Eve's supplying him with the forbidden fruit) is of less importance than the fact that he falls. We are not told why Adam takes the fruit, only, "The woman whom thou gavest to be with me, she gave me of the tree, and I did eat" (Gen. 3:12). In focusing the meaning on the fall, a first step in moving the story from a poetic metaphor, as in the story of Adam, to a tragedy is to include, as a major aspect of the hero's fall, the hamartia that caused the fall. For example, a hero may begin his quest with the noblest of intentions and become corrupted by the power or prestige of office. This type of hero is found in Greek tragedy in Oedipus whose tragic flaw (arrogance or hubris) caused his downfall. It is the oldest of Western tragedy: the noble leader who, due to his tragic flaw, fails in his quest and suffers horribly or dies as a result. Shakespeare's big four—Macbeth (ambition), Hamlet (vacillation), Lear (ego/hubris), and Othello (jealousy)—are all men possessing a basic goodness. But each man has a weakness that eventually will cause him to subvert his goodness and in essence sacrifice himself.

To qualify as tragedy, the flaw must be seen as a weakness and not an intrinsic evil nature. For tragedy to connect, the audience must feel a sense of pity—one of Aristotle's requirements for tragedy. Aristotle theorized that for tragedy to be effective, the audience must feel both pity and terror—a sorrow that the protagonist failed and a fear that if it could happen to Willie Stark, it might also happen to them. These feelings are assuaged cathartically when it is realized that the tragedy did not happen to them; therefore the audience feels cleansed. In other words, a reader or viewer must at some point be able to empathize or sympathize with the protagonist. Characters without some possibility of redemption are not attractive and certainly not entertaining. We can probably agree that it is not a tragedy when an evil character receives justice.

If one goes back in time to a point when early humans began to organize their religious beliefs, there was a dependency on magic—not magic as a performing art, but magic as a means by which humans saw relationships in objects within their environment. Sir James Frazer explores this phenomenon in *The Golden Bough*, an influential work in understanding the development of myth into religion. Most children are familiar with the admonition while walking on a sidewalk, "Step on a crack, break your mother's back." We know that a child who steps on a freeze strip in concrete will not affect his or her mother in any way, but we have this sense that there just might be a connection between the two, particularly if, after stepping on a crack, one's mother cuts her finger or sprains an ankle. We have within our culture many superstitions based on the principle of relationships between objects and behavior: good luck charms, mood rings, and incantations are examples. The next step is to accept the presence of a sorcerer who can make the connections occur or prevent an event from occurring. This is "sorcery [by a single practicioner] practiced for the benefit of the whole community" (Frazer 52). Today, we might call these "sorcerers" politicians. Frazer continues his description of the ancient sorcerer:

The profession accordingly draws into its ranks some of the ablest and most ambitious men of the tribe, because it holds out to them a prospect of honour, wealth, and power such as hardly any other career could offer. The acuter minds perceive how easily it is to dupe their weaker brother and to play on his superstition for their own advantage. Not that the sorcerer is always a knave and imposter; he is often sincerely convinced that he really possesses those wonderful powers which the credulity of his fellows ascribes to him . . . it is just these men who in virtue of their superior ability will generally come to the top and win for themselves positions of the highest dignity and the most commanding authority. (52)

The primitive sorcerer does not attain position by calling on an outside force but deals with the problems using what nature provides, such as collecting a lock of hair from the enemy and by magical act or word, "causing" the enemy to suffer pain or death.

Frazer thus provides a perfect description of Willie Stark, protagonist of *All the King's Men*. What today we label as political charisma is in reality the ability of the perpetrator, not by the use of magic wands or amulets, but voice and body to impose his or her will on the public by convincing them he or she, by the sheer power of being, has the means to solve problems and make life better. The only way the sorcerer can be defeated is when someone appears with stronger magic.

This magic becomes a source for more romantic forms of myth, the connection coming in the insinuation between man and man or nature of a spirit that could control the ultimate outcome, the ritual battle for a human soul. Instead of the sorcerer's being dependent on magic or the natural relationship between objects, a supernatural deity fills the gap between cause and effect and with whom the sorcerer establishes a working arrangement. The interposition of a deity moves the conflict beyond nature and into spirit, *mana*. The Judeo-Christian Bible presents several references for this spiritual conflict. One such reference comes from the Old Testament's Book of Job, where God and Satan gamble on the goodness of a wealthy landowner. Job is tested by God allowing the devil to take his wealth, his family, and finally his health, but Job remains faithful, and in the end God wins. All of Job's losses are restored, except for the dead family members. From the New Testament we learn a moral lesson regarding faith, "For what is man profited, if he shall gain the whole world, and lose his soul" (Matt. 16:26). The antithesis of this is portrayed in the story of Judas's betrayal. As he is named the betrayer, the Bible states, "Satan entered into him" (John 13:27), implying that an extrinsic demonic force possesses him. A recurrent and often used literary symbol is the 'thirty pieces of silver' Judas receives for his action. For the reader, this invokes the earthly presence of the forces of heaven and hell and makes the story romantic and is a direct attempt to codify the natural, human earthly experience, with the supernatural—the devil literally possessing the person. In all three of these stories, the line between good and evil is clearly defined. Morality follows biblical law. When necessary, that law is then enhanced by extrinsic forces stronger than human will.

One of the best-known literary examples of spiritual conflict for a human soul comes in the Faustian myth. In this myth, the devil (Mephistopheles) strikes a bargain with Faust in that the devil will allow Faust to gain power and riches in exchange for his immortal soul. This story has the attribute of combining the old magic with Christianity. Christians of the Middle Ages believed "magic could only be performed successfully with the aid of evil spirits" (Cavendish 270). The Faust legend—selling one's soul for immediate gain—has been repeated in many forms, even a Broadway musical, *Damn Yankees*, in which an elderly Washington, D.C., Senators fan sells his soul to the devil to become a young baseball star who will lead the Senators to defeat the Yankees.

As society becomes more complex and less emphasis is placed on the spiritual dimension, the line between what is moral and good and what is immoral and evil has become blurred. The mythical influence of the story remains with us, however, and we merely attempt to find a loophole, as did many of the Faustian clones through the years. One way to do this is to reinterpret the ancient myth. Andrew Lloyd Webber and Tim Rice in their stage and film version of their rock opera, *Jesus Christ Superstar*, question the evil in Judas by implying he is "Condemned for All Time" and therefore has no free choice. If the story is to be realistic, the character must be "sufficient to have stood . . . and free to fall" (Frye *AC* 211). Webber and Rice's play implies Judas was a scapegoat and therefore a human sacrifice necessary to further the purpose for which Jesus came, a form of deus ex machina. Modern adaptations are strongly influenced by existentialism, which tends to deliteralize philosophical and religious beliefs by placing the emphasis on human free will to choose between a culturally determined good and evil.

As protagonists become more representative of ordinary humans, the romantic nature of the literature shifts toward realism. This change occurs not only because of the alteration in the protagonist's relative position in life, but also due to emphasis on the will of the character to choose freely without regard to deistic influence. The hero of modern tragedy must also be "free to fall," even though it is not, or should not be, a contest between supernatural forces of good and evil but between secular forces of right and wrong. It is not his immortal soul that is in danger, but his relationship to the human forces in the ritual redemption. A person's measure depends to a great extent on the respect he or she warrants by family, friends, neighbors, and associates. For political protagonists, these forces would include the above in addition to the electorate, power brokers, constituencies, personal friends, and, most important, historians. When the hero becomes an ordinary person, the forces involved in the conflict tend toward the natural, instituted and created by human action.

When forces within the natural environment tend to exert undue influence or control over a character's motivations and choices, the story leans toward naturalism. Modern novels, focusing on the inner consciousness of the protagonist, tend to interweave realism and naturalism. For example, Mario Puzo's *The Godfather* was a poor Italian immigrant when a corrupt politician "forced" him into a life of crime. Once the environment provides the extrinsic motivation, a redemptive quality is provided for the protagonist. Puzo is then free to create a romantically realistic novel using a naturalistic act to provide an acceptable redemption for his protagonist. Don Coreleone is the epitome of an oxymoron—an honest criminal in whom we could see a goodness. We are told that the attempt on his life is because he opposes the inclusion of a pernicious evil—narcotics in his criminal operations. As a payback, he eliminates only those who had harmed him. The film's graphic ending demonstrates the lack of fear characters have in the loss of their soul. As the final scene shifts from the church where Michael Coreleone is acting as godfather to his sister's infant's baptism, his "soldiers" are systematically eliminating his criminal competition. His father has been avenged, and the audience accepts the action as retribution; no moral judgment is required. Michael's presence in the church suggests redemption. (Note that *Michael* is the name of a biblical archangel: "And there was war in heaven: Michael and his angels fought against the dragon" [Rev. 12:7–9].)

In this novel Warren elevates its literary quality to expand the base and increase the level of complexity by encompassing more than a single life or a small group. The story's setting is broadened to include an entire state. Whatever the form of government, it is impossible to exclude any of the inhabitants when determining leaders. In previous stories, we dealt with microcosms of a culture or society, a hospital, a small town, and a prison. Now we deal with a macrocosm. This does not mean the focus is not on a single protagonist. What it indicates is that the focus is broadened in such a way to make the antagonism more complex. As individual choices become more complicated by the inclusion of a multitude of natural forces, as opposed to supernatural forces, a determination of ethically or morally correct positions becomes much more difficult. This inclusion provides the opportunity for two journeys: an intellectual-philosophical quest to find a relationship between truth and fact and a more traditional physical quest seeking to understand what truly motivates someone to act irrationally, albeit immorally. Jack Burden discovers the meaning of his life in the lives of others (Cass Mastern, the scholarly attorney, Judge Irwin) and in the insights he receives in a darkened hotel room in California. The personal answer he seeks is not to be found in the outside world, but can be found only by looking inward. Warren provides his solution to the philosophical question in the death of Willy Stark and finally in the ruminations of the scholarly attorney.

Students frequently find reading this novel difficult. One reason is the philosophical depth to which Warren goes in interweaving conflicts between individuals and conflicts between the divergent groups that make up society. For example, one philosophical perspective emerges in the conflict between the ethical code accepted in politics and the moral code expected to be followed in social relationships. In America, there exist two value systems. One is the Judeo-Christian code, on which the early Puritans based their beliefs and is infused into the founding of America. This tradition advocates a real and a spiritual moral order, instituted by God through his holy word, the Bible. A second forum, emerging from the increasing influence of humanists, is labeled moral relativism and exists when a group or culture has the authority to establish its own rules based entirely on what is good for the culture. From the beginning of Jack Burden's quest to its very end, these two forces, as represented in the politics of Willie Stark and the religion of the Scholarly Attorney, compete for his judgment. To grasp Warren's profundity in presenting these two contrasting beliefs requires solid reading depth.

All the King's Men received a Pulitzer Prize (1947) and great critical acclaim. Several critics felt this novel was equal to *Huckleberry Finn, Moby Dick*, or *The Grapes of Wrath*. The film won Academy Awards for Best Picture, Best Actor (Broderick Crawford), and Best Supporting Actress (Mercedes McCambridge), with nominations for Best Supporting Actor (John Ireland), Best Director, and Best Screenplay. This novel and its film were written and produced prior to the advent of television. For novels and films demonstrating the influence of television on politics, read Jerzy Kosinski's *Being There*, a simple satire demonstrating how easily people can be fooled by what they see. For one with a little more realism, consider Carl Bernstein and Bob Woodward's *All the President's Men*, which details the investigation and resignation of President Richard Nixon. It was the televised Senate hearings more than the newspaper accounts that ultimately turned the public's perception of the Watergate scandal and forced the president to resign.

Prior to television, elections were primarily dependent on party politics and a well-oiled political machine. A candidate who was supported by the state, county, and local party organizations that held a voting majority could generally count on winning the election without much challenge. There are many real-life examples of this process. President Harry Truman received his start in politics as an obscure county judge in Jackson County, Missouri. He was selected as a potential success by the Pendergast machine, a notorious and powerful Kansas City political organization. Truman rose through the ranks to become a congressman, a senator, vice president, and on the death of Franklin D. Roosevelt, president of the United States (1945–52). It is also one of politics' great ironies that President Truman is uniformly respected as one of our most honest and forthright presidents.

The recurrent archetype present in *All the King's Men* paradoxically places Willie Stark in a position where he must choose the manner in which he will attain political success. Willie's political success came with a very high price. Just as in the Faustian myth it is possible to gain the world and lose one's soul, Willie Stark chooses to become the most powerful man in the state. By making this choice, he manages to lose not only his personal honor but his wife and son—the son to death and his wife to separation. An additional paradox emerges as to whether the effect Willie Stark has on the state and its voters is good or bad. One can say that voters in a democratic society get the government they deserve. By allowing themselves to be fooled by what they see and hear, they would seem to deserve what they get. Warren traces in detail how much Governor Stark did in improving the way of life for his average to poor constituency, the misbegotten of his state, even to the point that it ultimately cost him his life. Tragedy is truly "a paradoxical situation," a form of human sacrifice. The paradoxical circumstances identify Willie Stark as a true tragic hero. As Sartre describes, "Man makes himself; . . . he makes himself by the choice of morality, and he cannot but choose a morality" (Sartre 349). It is the existential paradox: One must choose because to refuse to choose is a choice. Stark chooses his path, but so do all the others in the novel. Is the electorate that chooses Willie to blame? Is Jack Burden the guilty party because he sets into motion the events that lead to Willie's death? Or is it Jack's mother, because she does not face the truth of Jack's parentage, who set it all into motion the day he is born? Where does anything begin or end? This becomes a major theme.

Critics of Warren continually make reference to Huey Long and cite the book as a biography. Long was a governor and U.S. senator from Louisiana during the late 1920s and early 1930s. His rise to power in the state was undoubtedly a source for the story of Willie Stark. Also, Long was assassinated on the steps of the Louisiana capitol in July 1935, which adds a bit of realism to Warren's story. However, Warren goes to great lengths to assure readers that this is not a biography and although there may be parallels in Long and Stark, there are also parallels with other political demagogues. It is not *what* the characters do that intrigues Warren; it is *why* they do it—their motivation.

Warren tends to portray his characters as products of their environment who have no desire to escape as did McMurphy, Sonny, and Dufresne. Willie Stark wants to dominate the environment, to remake it in his own image. It is his way or no way. And as Britisher Lord Acton predicted, "Power tends to corrupt; absolute power corrupts absolutely." If we assume this is true, what flaw in human consciousness causes this reaction? By making the political environment interact with the Machiavellian nature of his characters, this story appears on its surface to be naturalistic. Willie Stark is a moral individual until he loses an election to the political machine. At that point, he knows that if he wants to win, he not only has to play the game by their rules but has to be better at it than they are. We are made aware that Stark knows exactly what he is doing and, in fact, receives a perverse joy in destroying his competition before they can destroy him. It is not that the environment has changed him; it has merely set the tiger free by removing the element of restraint. We become aware throughout the novel that he has both the skill and the power to transcend a corrupt environment, but does not possess the will. There is too much pleasure in the way things now exist. Willie Stark loves walking the tightrope, being the decoy just long enough to lull the opposition into thinking they have won, only to open the trap door and smile as they fall through.

Warren is also making a case that corrupt politics breeds corruption. From the very beginning we know that Stark, like McMurphy, is at the mercy of life's ironies. Where the old machine uses corruption for personal gain, Stark will use corrupt methods in order to improve the lives of "hicks." He challenges the system on its own ground and by its own rules, knowing every moment that one false step and the "King will fall."

All the King's Men offers one reason for the failure of men to live up to our expectations. On his deathbed, Willie utters the magic word *If*. As a parallel, Jack Burden is faced with a moral choice when he encounters Sugar Boy in the library (420). "Suppose I could tell you who—" set up the assassination. Burden knows Sugar Boy will take full revenge. Burden makes a choice, to do the "right" thing. *If, suppose*, and *maybe* are all moments of choice. At that moment, Burden chooses his morality. *Why* Willie Stark does not make the "right" choices and live up to the traditional or relative standards we expect from our leaders is a major theme of the novel. It is a myth as old as the Garden of Eden and as modern as Marlowe's *Faust* and America's Richard Nixon. What causes an enlightened man to pursue a course in life that is harmful to himself and to his family? What inner consciousness causes Willie Stark to continue pushing the envelope until it explodes?

Dealing with that question is key in developing a theme for the story. Knowledge is not enough; one has to have the will to make the right choices for the right reason. Contrast this story with the serpent's temptation of Eve in the Garden of Eden. She knew she was not to eat of the forbidden fruit, yet she did. The serpent told Eve, "in the day ye eat thereof, then your eyes shall be opened, and ye shall be as gods, knowing good and evil" (Gen. 3:5). Do we blame the serpent/devil, or is Eve the guilty party, being motivated by a desire to "be as gods"? While Jewish tradition uses this as a myth to explain the presence of evil in the world, Warren offers the story of Willie as Eve and power as the fruit. Willie also becomes Dr. Faust the moment he realizes the political machine is using him to further its own ends. He can retire to the practice of law and lead a respectable life, or he can sell his soul and challenge the machine with his strength, demagoguery. Warren adds to the story a narrator who searches for an explanation of why Willie/Eve/Faust will dare to choose what they know is evil. It is on this point where the film deviates from the book. Jack Burden's personal quest is not a direct part of the film. There are moments when his narration is used as transition between events, but his direct participation in Stark's rise to power is kept much more outside of the action than the novel portrays him. In fact, Burden, played by John Ireland, like the Chief in *Cuckoo's Nest*, has his part in the film reduced to a supporting role, for which he was nominated for an Academy Award. It is in the novel, through Jack Burden, that we learn not only the background of Willie Stark and most important, what makes him tick, but we see through Burden's delving into the past how life is not being (existing) but is motion. "It was not any one event, which was important, but the flow, the texture of events, for meaning is never in the event, but in the motion through the event" (271). From this knowledge, we begin to understand the theme Warren is producing.

This story develops, perhaps more fully than any others examined in this book, the application of mythological criticism. The mode of this novel and film is realistic and therefore conforms to the season of autumn. It coalesces nature's cycle of life, birth, dormancy, redemption, and fall. In addition, the story conforms to Aristotle's theory that tragedy is brought about through human weakness—in this case, hubris. Willie Stark is a contemporary example of the archetypal tragic hero. His principles in the beginning of his quest are to do the right thing, but something within the culture causes or allows him to become purely Machiavellian. He possesses a true vision of good. It is his desire to provide the benefits of government to everyone in the state, which to this point has been limited to a chosen few. It is his methods, ironically freed by his environment, that prove to be his flaw. Willie Stark has a definite opinion regarding human nature—human nature is not perfect; every human has a weakness—and acts accordingly. "Man is conceived in sin and born in corruption and he passeth from the stink of the didie to the stench of the shroud. There is always something" (191). Stark's version of the Machiavellian code of a good outcome's justifying whatever means necessary is the law of the jungle in its most basic sense. The only way to survive is to succeed. Power determines success. This means taking full advantage of other's weaknesses.

In addition, the literary form of the quotation expresses its own irony. By paraphrasing the comment in biblical language, yet implying a more nihilistic influence, the overall effect is to secularize the religious content. According to Willie, man is born evil and will remain evil. Once he accepts this as a truth, he is free to use that information to further his own career.

A human being, as portrayed by Willie Stark, is reduced to a primeval reality. Paradoxically, it is the world in which he lives that both drives him and provides him with the means to succeed. Willie Stark's dying declaration, "If it hadn't happened, it might—have been different—even yet," implies "it" had been a free choice (400). We may not all agree on the meaning of each "it," but the *if* is one word to which we can all connect. "If," as Dennis Hopper tells us in Francis Ford Coppola's *Apocalypse Now*, "is the middle two letters of life." Joseph Conrad in *Heart of Darkness*, the source of Coppola's film, wrote, "Perhaps all the wisdom, and all truth, and all sincerity, are just compressed into the inappreciable moment of time in which we step over the threshold of the invisible" (120). "It is judgment that defeats us" (Kurtz in *Apocalypse Now*). Jack Burden, Willie Stark, Judge Irwin, Anne Stanton, and Adam Stanton freely choose their path. The irony comes from the fact that they cannot accurately predict or control the effect each choice will produce. It is the irony between the idea of life as motion or as being. A goal becomes the icon of motion. Underlying each judgment is the danger of unintended consequences that we can never accurately predict. Each act requires another act, demanding another act, until the goal is reached, which presents another goal. Once the motion is begun, it takes on a life of its own. The path or motion does not stop by withdrawal from the game. Ironically, one cannot withdraw by refusing to choose, for that is a choice.

For example, each character over and over has the same opportunity Willie Stark gave Byram White. White signs the undated resignation and is sent away. Willie reflects:

"I gave him every chance," the boss said glumly, "He didn't have to say what I told him to say. He didn't have to listen to me. He could have just walked out the door and kept on walking. He could have put a date on the resignation and handed it to me. He could have done a dozen things. But did he? Hell, no. Not Byram, and he just stands there and his eyes blink right quick like a dogs do when he leans up against your leg before you hit him, and by God, you have the feeling if you don't do it you won't be doing God's will. You do it because you are helping Byram fulfill his nature." (133)

The rationalization Willie makes is undoubtedly the same one Mephistopheles makes as he poses the question to Dr. Faust. If the man is stupid enough to exchange his eternal soul for "thirty pieces of silver," "you [Willie/Mephistopheles] have the feeling if you don't do it [take his soul] you won't be doing God's will." In that moment Willie feels sympathy for White, and possibly a reader may see a redeeming quality in Willie Stark. Each character acted in accordance with his personality. Could either have behaved differently? The real question is not whether the novel makes this point, but whether the film does.

Stark's dying comment (in both media), along with the denouement (only in the novel), expresses Burden's rejection of the "great twitch" theory and provides Warren's pattern for redemption. A driving force for Willie's dying confession and Burden's redemption is guilt. First comes a recognition that a wrong has been committed, which is then followed by contrition, which ultimately leads to a restructuring of life. Burden seeks redemption by providing a home for his destitute stepfather, marrying the defiled Anne, and returning to Burden's Landing to write the story of Cass Mastern, an ordinary man who places doing what is right above his personal comfort—in other words, redemption. The will is stronger than the environment only if one is able to see the truth beyond the facts. An interesting aspect comes at the end of the novel with the Scholarly Attorney's epiphany (437). As almost an afterthought, Warren incorporates a religious morality into Burden's (and the reader's) thinking. One critic, Robert Chambers, editor of *Twentieth Century Interpretations of All the King's Men,* labeled the final words the novel's "central meaning" (14).

Separateness is identity, and the only way for God to create, truly create, man was to make him separate from God himself, and to be separate from God is to be sinful. The creation of evil is therefore the index of God's glory and his power. That had to be so that the creation of good might be the index of man's glory and power. (437)

A person's true value is measured by the quantity *and* quality of his goodness. A separate but equal attribute is an ability to overcome evil. What Warren does not fully explain is exactly how one keeps score. It is up to each individual reader to determine by what method the final outcome is measured; however, Warren does seem to suggest it is found in human relationships rather than in material worth.

The story's title is a pun on the word *fall.* It is part of the rhyme, "Humpty Dumpty had a great fall and all the King's horses and all the King's men could not put Humpty Dumpty together again." It is drawn from the allusion of Eden, for Adam's transgression is known as the fall of man. Fall is a season where the animals hibernate and plants go dormant in order to survive the winter. And finally, it is a verb, "to descend by the force of gravity." All of the definitions and implications apply to Willie Stark.

QUESTIONS

In your responses, identify a specific reference by quotation or page number

1. John Donne, an English minister and poet stated, "No man is an island." This statement could be a theme for the novel. Briefly discuss how this statement might be thematically applied to Jack Burden, Willie Stark, Judge Irwin, and Cass Mastern.
2. On page 157, Jack Burden states, "I tried to discover the truth and not the facts." Explain what is different, at least in his mind, in the truth and the facts.
3. On page 400 (and in the film), Willie, on his death bed says to Jack, "It might have been different, Jack . . . You've got to believe that . . . if it hadn't happened,

it might—have been different—even yet." What do you think Willie means by *it?*

4. What does the theory of the great twitch explain in relation to the behavior of Jack Burden and Willie Stark? Does it cause us to feel sympathy for Stark? Explain your answer.

5. Eve, as part of the sentence given for her transgression, is told by God; "In sorrow thou shalt bring forth children" (Gen. 3:16). Willie Stark, on page 157 and again on page 191, tells Jack, "Man is conceived in sin and born in corruption and he passeth from the stink of the didie to the stench of the shroud. There is always something." What do these two statements have in common? What statement is Warren making about twentieth-century man?

QUESTIONS FOR GROUP ACTIVITY

Television has come to be a dominant player in every aspect of our lives, and perhaps the defining aspect in politics. However, with regard to the American sense of justice, freedom, morality, and truth, the story is as contemporary as it was in 1949. What seems to be occurring today is a growing acceptance of actions that in the 1940s and 1950s, had they been known, would have condemned a politician to defeat. From that standpoint, Warren's story could be taken as a warning against politicians who allow power to dominate their actions.

From a literary perspective, when we compare this narrative to the previous ones, it is important to recognize that the themes and the subjects with which they deal are growing extremely complex. The archetype of tragedy is sacrifice. We know Willie Stark is defeated in that he is executed/murdered because of his actions and beliefs. In previous stories, the enemy was clearly identified: McMurphy has Nurse Ratched; Andy Dufresne has the wardens, the guards, the sisters, and to some extent the prison system. For Willie Stark, the antagonist becomes even more complex. His struggle begins from something deep within his very being. Is it real spiritual forces representing God and the devil competing for his soul or is it simply a conflict between his unconscious and conscious mind? Is man bound to a code of ethics? If so, who or what decides on the code? If morality and ethics are truly relative does that mean the most powerful "sorcerer" gets to make the rules? What we are seeing is the progression of our myths to be back where we began—trying to explain the unknown by focusing on a known. In a modern global society, we continually attempt to superimpose a singular supernatural explanation, only to find great disagreement on who or what that explanation might be. Maybe we should recall Pogo's parody of Commodore Perry's 1812 line, "We have met the enemy and he is *US.*"

1. Focus on how the public is portrayed in both media. Is there any real difference in how Warren and Darabont view the populace? If so, what is it? How is it presented? If they are similar, what conclusions may be drawn?

2. Which of the two media more clearly depicts present-day morality? Begin by defining *present-day morality* and then imposing the definition on one of the episodes or scenes.

3. Has television improved or harmed politics based on the depiction in the novel and the film? Support your decision by comparing a present-day circumstance with what was presented by this film and novel.

4. Frye tells us that tragedies (autumn) are "myths of the fall, of death and sacrifice and of isolation of the hero" and satires (winter) are "myths of the triumphs of the powers of darkness, the return of chaos and the defeat of the hero" *(AC* 156). Apply these definitions to Willie Stark, Jack Burden, and previous tragic protagonists and explain why satire or comedy is more negative toward human culture than realism is.

5. Basing your analysis on the study of all the works so far, what conclusions may be reached about how our culture sees itself?

Chapter 10

Heaven Comes to Iowa

Shoeless Joe/Field of Dreams by W. P. Kinsella

In the opening scene of Shakespeare's play *Macbeth* (1606) three witches are hovering over a boiling pot. As the protagonist passes, the "weird sisters," as they are labeled, call out to Macbeth that he will be "King hereafter!" The rest of the play develops the manner in which this in fact did happen. Not to be outdone, Arthur Miller, in his 1953 play *The Crucible*, implies that the seventy-two men and women hanged for being witches in Puritan Massachusetts during the 1628 witch trials occurred because a slave named Tituba, along with several young ladies of Salem, sang, danced, and chanted around a boiling cauldron in an attempt to conjure up a dead baby. Even today, the practice of voodoo is a reality. Voodoo is a form of necromancy, "the conjuring of spirits of the dead for purposes of magically revealing the future or influencing the course of events." Is any of this real? If there is even the remotest possibility that it is real, why not a baseball field in the middle of an Iowa cornfield on which games are played by long-dead athletes?

The origins for this selection go one step further back into primeval mythology than either Shakespeare or Arthur Miller. It begins when the common belief of a culture is a direct relationship between nature and magic. Sir James Frazer, in his multivolume work *The Golden Bough*, stated:

Thus its [magic's] fundamental conception is identical with that of modern science; underlying the whole system is a faith, implicit but real and firm, in the order and uniformity of nature. The magician does not doubt that the same causes will always produce the same effects, that the performance of the proper ceremony, accompanied by the appropriate spell, will inevitably be attended by the desired result. (56)

Frazer theorizes that magic has a much closer relationship to science than it has to religion. Magic is a primeval explanation for naturally occurring events, before the advent of the formal laws of chemistry and biology. It is from this magical base, "If you build it, he will come," W. P. Kinsella evolves his story.

Kinsella, using the game of baseball as his constant, presents a story that interweaves fact and fantasy in order to develop its verismilitude. The novel was popular, particularly among sports fans. The film, playing to a more general audience, was a major success. Both media presented the fantasy in a believable form through the sincerity of the characters. In fantasy, a reader or a viewer must believe in a character's honesty if there is to be any expectation of verisimilitude. It goes beyond sympathy into empathy; the story must take in readers. The protagonist, Ray Kinsella, is created so open and honest that no matter what he does or how he does it, we believe.

W. P. Kinsella's principal literary device in accomplishing this believability is to have Ray (his namesake? alter-ego?) interact with real people in real places, such as J. D. Salinger, Thurman Munson, and Shoeless Joe Jackson, Cooperstown, Boston, Fenway Park, and many, many others. As readers or viewers, we are drawn into this fantasy and told that if we too will believe, we can actually see the fantasy. And whether it appears in our mind's eye from the novel or our eyesight when viewing the film, we *can* see the images. This provides a rather unique, but effective way to mesmerize us into believing it is real. (From this point, *Kinsella* refers to the author, and *Ray* refers to the protagonist).

This novel and film will probably never become classic, but the characters, in a less grandiose manner, are already a part of our popular culture. *Shoeless Joe* by W. P. Kinsella was published in 1982, and the film, *Field of Dreams* directed by Phil Alden Robinson, opened in 1989. The film received nominations for Best Picture, Best Original Score, and Best Screenplay from Another Source. This film was also nominated for a Hugo, an award given by the World SciFi Society.

This film is a form of scientific magic in which Kinsella is able to make a connection between man and nature and spirit using the game of baseball as his sorcery. It is the writer's art that makes it work. Just as in painting, an author chooses the mode by which to portray his archetype. For example, Jackson Pollock is known for his expressionistic paintings, created by dripping, pouring, and splashing paint on a canvas resting on the floor. For him, it was a way to bypass rational, programmed thought and rely entirely on his unconscious self to create what he considered a shared universal image. To connect with his paintings requires the viewer to participate imaginatively by allowing his or her imagination to connect with the painting, not with the artist. At the same time Pollock was producing surrealistic expressionism, painting's counterpart to Jung's collective unconscious, Georgia O'Keefe, an American master living and working in New Mexico, was creating modernistic paintings that may be defined as symbolic realism. Her natural subjects—desert flowers, sun-dried skeletal remnants, and landscapes—are easily recognizable individually, but when placed together conjure overlapping images evoking a spiritual response. Kinsella's art is somewhat similar to Pollock in that he sprinkles his canvas, a printed page, with splashes of fantasy, interweaving just enough bits and pieces of reality, similar to O'Keefe, to make the story believable and allegorical. Like Pollock's paintings, all it requires is for the audience to use their powers of imagination. (O'Keefe's art would compare with literature's ventures into the world of romantic realism we saw in *The Color Purple* or *One Flew over the Cuckoo's Nest*, relying on symbols for a metaphorical connection.) In order to understand a culture, one needs to look at all of the modes, seeking to find what each has to contribute.

Kinsella contributes a romantic comedy detailing one man's quest to find heaven on earth. His story conforms to Frye's "second phase of comedy, in its simplest form, a comedy in which the hero does not transform a humorous [uptight] society but simply escapes or runs away from it, leaving its structure as it was before" (*AC* 180). Ray does not change society; in fact, he does not even try. Ray is a quixotic-type character who chooses to create his own form of reality rather than challenge the world. Like Don Quixote, he sets out on a journey in which he will face windmills (his experiences in South Chicago), answer the grand inquisitor (J. D. Salinger), and finally overcome the Knight of the Mirrors (Annie's brother Mark and the bank) in order to fulfill his dream. Metaphorically, baseball is Ray's Dulcinea, for like Don Quixote, who is able to see virginal beauty in a whorish scullery maid, Ray sees eternity in a night baseball game played in a converted cornfield by ghosts from the past.

Although the film and novel were commercial successes, the film does not fully convey the content of the novel. The novel includes a journey or quest much longer and more complex than is present in the film. One interesting archetypal circumstance in the novel, omitted from the film, is Ray's identical twin, Richard. Ray is an idealist. As we are told in flashback episodes of Ray's childhood, he was unusually imaginative from the beginning. Richard, who is physically identical in every way, is a realist. The twins, which have many mythological references including their own astrological sign, Gemini, are reflective of the opposition of equals and generally recognized as being symbolic of the conscious and unconscious self. For example, Jung tells of an ancient myth of the Navajos in which there are, in the third cycle of creation, twins who were "united in their mother's womb" and "forced apart at birth.... In these two children, we see the two sides of man's nature. One of them, Flesh, is acquiescent, mild, and without initiative; the other, Stump is dynamic and rebellious" (*MS* 113). Their ultimate goal is to be reunited. Roman mythology has the story of Romulus and Remus, born of a mortal mother after having been raped by Mars, god of war, who are suckled by wolves, and grow to found the eternal city, Rome. What binds these stories from such divergent cultures is the figure of two striving to be one. In order to become one, they must first become three, as in Christianity, when the Father and Son become One with the inclusion of the Holy Ghost to become the Godhead. For the Kinsella twins, it is when Richard can finally see the players, specifically the incarnation of their father, that the three are reunited as one family (214).

A second form of magic leads the story to identify a kind of afterlife, a form of myth that exists within every civilized culture. There is an expectation that at some point in time, the individual, the culture, and the world will attain eternal paradise. In Christianity, it is called the "New Heaven," a prophecy describing the return to earth of Jesus Christ and a restoration of Eden. It is within the inheritance of this ancient myth that the theory of the seasons forms the strongest connection. Anthropologists generally agree that one of the first ideas of primitive people in caring for their dead must have come from their observance of the coming of spring. Each spring they would witness the regeneration in nature. Plants regenerate and animals emerge from a winter's hibernation. If it is true for the flora and fauna of the forest, surely it must be true for people, so in most cultures they "planted" the remains. The novel's denouement includes a burial scene in the outfield, along with an inference that eternity is a dream state from which, if the desire is strong enough, one can find a heaven on earth (211).

For a moment, consider that deism had not entered into the equation. Suppose that magic, as it appears in nature, is the unifying force for the as-yet-unexplained occurrences and events. Kinsella expresses this idea when Eddie Scissons asks Ray, "Do you believe in a hereafter?" (105). Ray responds, "Seems to me that's getting into religion, . . . I try never to discuss religion or politics—I don't have enough friends that I can afford to" (106). Later he comments, "The kind of people I absolutely cannot tolerate are those, like Annie's mother, who never let you forget they are religious" (148). Throughout the novel, Ray discounts religion as anything other than a factor causing differences. He chooses to place his beliefs in a more natural source, his affinity for Mother Earth. The voice he hears that begins his journey emanates not from heaven but from the cornfield. When he hears of the conglomerate's plans for his farm, he responds: "But you owe the land something. . . . It's not just a product. Not plastic or foam and bright paint imported from Taiwan or Korea, meant to be used once and discarded" (163). Earlier, in Part I, Ray firmly establishes his feelings by describing an act of mythical magic:

It was near noon on a gentle Sunday when I walked out to that garden. The soil was soft and my shoes disappeared as I plodded until I was near the center. There I knelt, the soil cool on my knees. . . . Suddenly I thrust my hands wrist-deep into the snuffy-black earth. The air was pure. All around me the clean smell of earth and water. Keeping my hands buried I stirred the earth with my fingers and I knew I loved Iowa as much as a man could love a piece of earth. (14)

At that moment, Ray is making contact with Mother Earth in a pure and primeval manner. "From the outer world the senses carry images to the mind, which do not become myth, however, until there transformed by fusion with accordant insights, awakened as imagination from the inner world of the body" (Campbell *IR* 31). When the love for the land (Iowa) fuses with Ray's inner consciousness, a totally believable consequence occurs, bringing with it a real world of the imagination.

There have been many novels and films expressing an idea describing the search for and/or journey toward paradise: *The Devil and Daniel Webster* by Stephen Vincent Benet (film 1941); *Lost Horizon* by James Hilton (films 1932 and 1973); *The Razor's Edge* by Somerset Maugham (films 1946 and 1984); Cervantes' *Don Quixote* (film, *Man of La Mancha* 1972); and even Charles Dickens's *A Christmas Carol*, to name but a few literary masterpieces on this subject. These novels, as do most other search-for-meaning quests, rely more on a religious journey. This novel places into perspective how humans thought and believed before the narrowing of belief to identify an intermediary supernatural being between earth and heaven or between the physical and the spiritual dimensions. Each person, using his or her own *mana*, can make a connection with the metaphysical world. As we learned, some people possess more *mana* than others. Ray is obviously such a person.

This story may be compared to "Rita Hayworth and the Shawshank Redemption," particularly in its archetype. Although the narratives share a common bond in focusing on one man's search for paradise, they differ in style and mode. Much of the novella is realistic. Its language, setting, and plot are told in a terse and no-nonsense style reminiscent of Hemingway. In fact, the short story, even at its end, follows a realistic style, while the film tends to create a more romantic view of paradise. Kinsella, on the other hand, has a tendency to have his character think and speak in a more poetic language, conveying a romantic tone from the beginning. For example, Ray and his twin brother, Richard, are watching the field as Ray comments:

Richard can't see the players on the field as we see them. As I realize this, I become aware that instead of feeling sorry for him, I am highly elated. I know without asking that all he is aware of is the deadly silent park sitting in the cornfield, illuminated by one stark bloom of lights on a single standard. Richard's eyes are blind to the magic. (167)

This would seem to be a very poetic comment, perhaps out of character for a farmer, but certainly indicative of Kinsella's style. This style enhances acceptance of Ray's visions. He speaks in the language of a visionary.

The novel opens with a disembodied voice uttering a line that has become a part of our folklore. "If you build it, he will come" (3). It is the stimulus that causes an Iowa farmer to build a lighted baseball diamond in the middle of his cornfield. For Kinsella, the game of baseball represents a microcosm of life. It is played in stages, nine innings; both sides get an equal chance at offense and defense; it is continuous from beginning to end, with no quarters or half-time break; and there are specific rules that must be observed. Additionally, baseball is the one sport where the rules and manner of play have changed the least of any other major sports activity. Except for better equipment and the unfortunate introduction of a designated hitter in the American League, baseball is played today much as it was a century ago.

Where Kinsella goes beyond the game is in his ability to combine reality and magic to the degree that it is difficult to determine just where the demarcation appears. Two words that continually appear in Kinsella's work are *magic* and *imagination*. These words act interdependently in each of the characters and their ability to see the images playing baseball. This novel's protagonist, like King's Andy Dufresne, defines his life by hope. Unlike Andy Dufresne, paradise to Ray is not to be found on a beach in Mexico. Paradise is not necessarily a place; it is a happening, an event where you can relive a time past and convert perceived wrongs into things right. All you need to do is listen carefully to the transcendental voices in your cornfield, build a lighted baseball diamond, travel halfway across the country, convince a reclusive, cynical author to join your fantasy, and return before the bank forecloses on your farm. Once you accomplish this test, you will be given the opportunity to redeem not only yourself, but a wrong imposed on a long-past sport's icon, Shoeless Joe Jackson, a major league baseball player who was banned for life for participation in a scheme to throw the 1919 World Series between the Chicago White Sox and the Cincinnati Red Stockings. (*Eight Men Out* by Eliot Asinof is a film/novel combination detailing this event.) Ray is motivated by his imagination to perform the magic. If you do not possess the imagination, you are unable to see the magic.

The emphasis on baseball is somewhat misleading. It is not really necessary to know anything about the game of baseball to enjoy this novel. The novel is about people whose lives happen to be connected by the game of baseball. There are no lengthy game descriptions. Lesley Choyce in an essay "Three Hits and a Miss," explained it this way: "W. P. Kinsella's

Shoeless Joe performed one of the rarest accomplishments in my reading history: it successfully sucked me into one man's private modern vision of ecstasy, and that vision wrapped itself like soft calf leather around the sport of baseball" (253). The "private view of ecstasy" to which Choyce refers, is, to continue the sports metaphor, becoming a Monday morning quarterback—that is, being able to replay Sunday's game (in Ray's case, a missing relationship between a father and a son; a chance at bat for a one-inning major leaguer; and redemption of a misguided and foolish baseball star from the past) and by correcting the mistakes, altering the outcome to be what you want rather than what you got. Daniel Okrent, in a *New York Times Book Review* sees the novel as a love story:

Mr. Kinsella is drunk on complementary elixirs, literature and baseball, and the cocktail he mixes of the two is a lyrical, seductive, and altogether winning concoction. It's a love story, really the love his characters have for the game becoming manifest in the trips they make through time and space and ether. (25 Jul. 82, p. 10)

There have been many stories in which time travel has been created that would allow a person to go back in time and make a course correction in his or her life. One type is *Back to the Future* in that Michael J. Fox is able to travel into the past and recreate his present, which is obvious fantasy. In *Shoeless Joe/Field of Dreams*, Kinsella and Kevin Costner bring the past into the present. By reversing the fantasy and qualifying those able to participate, they are able to envelop the viewer with a sense of verisimilitude. It is, in a sense, similar to the holy grail, which performs its miracles only for believers. Before you can "see," you have to believe. The film reduces the number of active participants, diminishing for the viewer the extent of the vision. In addition to the missing Richard, the Eddie Scissons story is omitted. Their inclusion in the novel provides for a much more complex story and increases the reader's sense of belief. A reader is given several more sprinkles of reality through real people and real situations. The effect on the film removes a great deal of its myth identity.

This does not mean the film misses Kinsella's point. The film attempts to make the point with fewer ingredients. Kevin Costner certainly portrays Ray with total honesty and commitment. He uses a technique of underplaying, walking in a narrow space between controlling the action and having the action control him. One specific example of the actor's art occurs on the ride back from Fenway Park. Ray mentions the writing on the scoreboard and Terrance Mann (played by James Earl Jones) denies having seen anything. Ray accepts without question Mann's honesty. There is no anger or resentment. He simply accepts the fact as presented and quietly presumes to go on to Minnesota alone. His quiet demeanor reflects a depth of character the audience respects and believes—in Pudovkin's language, "that process of setting up a profound linkage between the subjective personal element of the actor and objective element of the play" (246). Kevin Costner, by facial expression, body language, and voice, has totally linked himself with the objective element, the character as plot—a man operating on the belief that the voice, whatever its source, has a plan and all he has to do is follow it.

One serious loss, by omitting the character of Richard, is that the film also omits the carnival symbol. A carnival embodies, according to the novel, something "scummy and sickening," a place where "people pay to be disappointed" (175–176). Ray's visit to the carnival and Richard's way of life evoke a memory in the form of flashback to provide insight into the distance between the twins. For Richard, the carnival, with its broken and bent promises, represents the realist. In contrast, the people who attend a carnival go knowing they will be cheated. A carnival depends on the audience's gullibility and willingness to pay to be fooled, whether at a sideshow or a baseball throw. Because of this, Richard believes it is his responsibility to take money from anyone foolish enough to pay seventy-five cents to see pictures in a jar. Directly opposite is twin brother Ray, the dupe, who would pay the seventy-five cents, as exemplified by his searching for a "left-handed glass stretcher." Even when his rational mind tells him, "It began to dawn on me that I had been the butt of a joke," he could not bring himself to challenge it. Instead, he removes his mark of identity, "a bright green T-shirt," and hides in the back of the truck until his father and Richard return to go home (180). Even as a child, it was not reality that governed the life of Ray; it was his imagination, his unconscious mind overruling, or at least causing doubt in, his rational being. The fusion of "accordant insights, awakened as imagination from the inner world of the body." With that kind of imagination, it is much easier to accept his willingness to "build it" (3), to "go the distance" (79), and to "ease his pain" (27).

Also, by including Richard and the story of Eddie Scissons, the most important ingredient of redemption is invoked, making the story more appealing. Richard begins in blindness and through redemption is able to see. Eddie, whose adult life has been based on a lie, is able, through confession, to be forgiven, and because his love for baseball is so strong, he is allowed to join the heavenly players. In addition, the novel uses a respected and successful living American author, known for his reclusive and cynical nature, to become the fictional Ray's partner in making the fantasy a reality. The person Ray brings to Iowa in the novel is J. D. Salinger, author of *Catcher in the Rye*, a popular and realistic novel of the 1960s noted for its existential and pessimistic outlook on coming of age in America. For Salinger to become a believer is the ultimate miracle. If you can accept that, the rest is easy. The film chooses to create a fictional character, Terrance Mann, played by James Earl Jones, for this role. This creates a major change in the symbolism. Salinger's *Catcher in the Rye* symbolically refers to Ray and Richard's passage from adolescence to adulthood. The film, by converting the role to one of political protest, underscores Ray and Annie's willingness to rebel against the power structure (Mark and the bank). This, in a small way, compensates for Richard's omission.

When Mann gains redemption, we are led to believe it is because of his political past rather than his pessimistic attitude toward people. When J. D. Salinger receives redemption, those readers who vicariously shared the problems associated with Holden Caufield, the depressed protagonist of *Catcher in the Rye*, also share in the cleansing. It is writing that Ray describes as modern magic, especially a novel such as *Catcher in the Rye*, which affected and is continuing to affect young readers. By incorporating a living person, the novel establishes a contemporary reality not matched by the film. Robinson did attempt to identify the power of the written word in his public school board meeting and the humorous dialogue between Annie and the town purists. It certainly is Amy Madigan's big scene, which may have been the director's motivation for its inclusion. Other than providing a setting for Ray's second message from beyond, the scene has little to do with the plot.

What the two media have in common is the restoration of Eden to connect in a very special way to an audience. Leonard Maltin described the film as "a story of redemption and faith, in the tradition of the best Hollywood fantasies, with moments that are pure magic" (421). Redemption, faith, fantasy, magic: what more could you ask for in a myth? Roger Ebert stated in his review:

As *Field of Dreams* developed this fantasy, I found myself being willingly drawn into it. Movies are often so timid these days, so afraid to take flights of the imagination, that there is something grand and brave about a movie where a voice tells a farmer to build a baseball diamond so that Shoeless Joe Jackson can materialize out of the cornfield and hit a few fly balls. This is the kind of movie Frank Capra might have directed and James Stewart might have starred in—a movie about dreams. (254)

For it to fit into the mode of myth, there must be an element of truth. That truth may exist in the real-life result. For the film version, a farm was rented in Iowa and an actual baseball field constructed. Today, the field remains a tourist attraction. Just as in the film, people come to the farm and continue to buy tickets to sit in wooden stands and allow their imagination to wander. It is doubtful that everyone is able to see Shoeless Joe Jackson, but obviously they see something or would cease coming. The fact that they come underscores the existence of that fleeting *mana* in all of us.

QUESTIONS

In your responses, identify a specific reference by quotation or page number.

1. The novel's opening chapter might be entitled "Love." Discuss why, in your opinion, W. P. Kinsella chose to set this type of tone for this type of novel. What is the connection between love and magic? Identify one quotation or scene as your example.

2. In Chapter 2, Ray is told to "ease his pain" (page 27). Identify the bond Ray Kinsella finds that connects him to J. D. Salinger. In what manner does Salinger fit into the plot of this novel as a character and as a symbol?

3. Chapter 3 emerges with the phrase "go the distance" heard by Ray (page 79) and confirmed by Salinger (page 85). Our disembodied voice has now spoken three times, to be heard only by first one and now two. What literary devices does Kinsella use during the scene at the ballpark to make the phrase believable? Use quotations in your response.

4. Pages 174–180 relate Ray's visit to his twin brother Richard's carnival in Iowa City. Two particular symbols emerge to amplify why Ray is able to see the players and Richard does not: the "dozen glass containers" and "the left handed glass stretcher." How do the symbols, each representing a brother, connect to the reason(s) Richard cannot see the players and Ray, Annie, Jerry, and Karen can?

5. Select one quotation from the novel (from one sentence to a paragraph in length) that would function as a thematic summary of the novel, and briefly explain how the theme emerges from the diction in the quotation.

QUESTIONS FOR GROUP DISCUSSION

1. A motif for both the novel and film is how willingly the character of Ray Kinsella responds to signs. For example, in the film, Ray is twice rejected by Terrance Mann and starts to leave. He turns, noting that the door, when slammed, did not latch. This became a sign for him to return. Identify three other examples from the film and three from the novel. Discuss the relative effectiveness of visual and literary presentations. In each medium how did the author/director/actor convey the character's attribute?

2. Compare and contrast the characters of J. D. Salinger and Terrance Mann. Make a list of the attributes the novel reveals and those portrayed in the film. From a purely cultural standpoint, what is the effect Kinsella wanted in using the real author of *Catcher in the Rye* as a character? What is the effect Robinson wanted in his creation of a 1960s protest leader, Terrance Mann? Does the fact

that Salinger is white and Mann is black affect the overall theme of the novel? Why or why not?

3. A great deal of the film was shot outside and in vivid color. To what extent is this an influence in conveying the plot and theme?

Chapter 11

Finding Morality in a Bullring

The Sun Also Rises
by Ernest Hemingway

The words of the Preacher, the Son of David, King in Jerusalem.
Vanity of Vanity, saith the Preacher, vanity of vanities; all is vanity.
What profit hath a man of all his labour which he taketh under the
  sun?
One generation passeth away, and another generation cometh:
  but the earth abideth forever.
The sun also riseth, and the sun goeth down,
  and hasteth to the place where it arose. (Ecclesiastes 1:1–5)

The word *vanity*, at the time of the King James Version translation, meant "empty or emptied, hence without substance" (Partridge 757). This biblical quotation begins what many consider to be Ernest Hemingway's best novel, which also happened to be his first, *The Sun Also Rises*. Hemingway chose this title because his protagonist in the novel, Jake Barnes, is actively engaged in a search for a meaning for his life in a world seemingly empty and without substance. Barnes's search is a fictional quest, but because Barnes is certainly the author's alter-ego, it probes mythologically into an ancient and ongoing quest in which Ernest Hemingway seeks to find a true base for morality in an effort to acquire a meaning for his own life. Hemingway, like many other authors, uses his fiction to indemnify a personal quest.

From 2500 B.C.E. until the nineteenth century C.E., this search for good and evil existed primarily in connection with a religious belief. Most religions offer some type of a specific plan—for example, the Judeo-Christian Ten Commandments. The ultimate rise of scientific knowledge has, for some, broadened the search into philosophic areas—ethics, metaphysics, and teleology being the most common. However, the search for moral truth is not limited to philosophy and religion.

For nonbelievers and humanists, the search emerges out of atheism or agnosticism and tends toward an existentialist nihilism, some seeking to internalize morality into a "if it feels good, it must be good" sense of good and evil, right and wrong. More responsible nihilists, such as Nietzsche, Sartre, and Hemingway, strive to find a workable code that will both sustain humanity and provide a set of rules expressing how people ought to live.

This movement toward a more humanistic approach separates morality from its dependence on religion. It came about naturally. "The popular modern notion that religion and morality are separate phenomena is rooted in the Enlightenment of eighteenth-century Europe, the philosophical [humanistic] movement [being] characterized by aggressive rationalism, high-spirited skepticism, a love of learning, and a doggedness in thinking things through" (Panati 89). Western culture, particularly the intelligentsia, began to accept the idea that human rationality as expressed through the will exceeded the influence of any metaphysical force, if in fact such a force actually existed. Such diverse innovators as Sigmund Freud consistently argued, as did Marxist philosophy, that religion is actually a deterrent to an individual's accepting moral responsibility for his or her own judgment. Hemingway, who had been raised a Roman Catholic, began to move away from a reliance on religious beliefs to provide a foundation for morality. His brush with death during World War I had undoubtedly caused him to question his previously held beliefs. In fact, a comparative reading of Hemingway's writing during this period (*The Sun Also Rises* was completed in 1925), and his later works mirrors his gradual defection from religion as a realistic moral base. For example, near the end of the novel, Brett Ashley, commenting on her discontinuance of the affair with Romero, says to Jake:

"You know it makes one feel rather good deciding not to be a bitch."
"Yes."
"It's sort of what we have instead of God."
"Some people have God," I [Jake] said. "Quite a lot."
"He never worked very well with me."
"Should we have another martini?" (245)

Even at this early point in his career, Hemingway was having some difficulty placing reliance on a religious belief. From a 1933 short story, "A Clean Well-Lighted Place" Hemingway, some seven years after *The Sun*

Also Rises, expressed a greater disassociation in his attitude toward religion. His protagonist in this story is an old man who spends his evenings in a café drinking brandy. An older waiter feels great sympathy for the old man and rejects the idea that religion can fill the void left by aging. He responds by parodizing the Lord's Prayer: "Our nada who art in nada, nada be thy name . . . Hail nothing full of nothing, nothing is with thee." Hemingway is concluding that whatever exists to give a life meaning, it must be found within each person.

In place of a reliance on religious belief, since man had, in Hemingway's judgment, obviously been unable to live harmoniously with his own kind, what is needed is a realistic and believable code—not a set of imposed rules providing no margin for error but instead a simple code that will provide a set of guidelines showing how one ought to live. A man or woman who, within the confines of his or her life transcends the ordinary by choosing to live according to the code, becomes a hero. To Hemingway, the code that signifies a hero is simple. Leo Gurko, in a summary of Hemingway's major works, *Ernest Hemingway and the Pursuit of Heroism*, explains that these works "are not primarily studies of death or simply researches into the lost generation. . . . They are essentially portrayals of the hero, the man who by force of some extraordinary quality sets the standard for those around him" (55). Heroism is "to dare more than other men, to expose oneself to greater dangers, and therefore more greatly to risk the possibilities of defeat and death" (165). It is worth mentioning, that Hemingway's heroes are male. It is not just that he consistently treated women as less important, his interest was primarily directed toward the male as a result of his own experiences.

These feelings evolved in Hemingway in the years following his experiences as a Red Cross ambulance driver assigned to the Italian army in World War I. Possibly that experience, specifically the posttraumatic effects of a near-death experience following his wounding, was the turning point of his life. Although severely wounded, "he heaved the wounded soldier over his shoulders and began stumbling back to the rear." Upon arrival at the first-aid station, "the man was dead, and Hemingway, what with shock, exhaustion, and loss of blood, nearly so" (Gurko 11). This event shaped his life in trying to understand fully what motivated himself, at the tender age of nineteen, to behave in this manner. He understood, in retrospect, that what he did at that moment was not a result of some outside force, it came from deeply within, possibly resulting from something innate within all men. In contrast, what he found among the postwar social and literary culture, which became labeled a "lost generation," and from his observations as a correspondent for the *Toronto Star* was a sense of indifference among the citizens of postwar Europe. From this, he began to effect a personal search through his characters for attributes of the true hero—that person who can live a morally good life in a world in which there are no universal rules other than those nature imposes.

This archetype, a protagonist in a search for meaning, is a different direction from the two previous hero types. Andy Dufresne and R. P. McMurphy are courageous men who place their own lives in jeopardy for the sake of others—Dufresne in his quest to establish a library and provide a sense of hope for Red, and McMurphy in his willingness to "lay down his life for his brother." Jake Barnes's search is more universally defining. His search is to find the code that will lead to the good life.

To place this in a larger and mythical perspective, consider Homer's *Odyssey*. Odysseus, following the Trojan War, travels back to his beloved wife, Penelope. During the course of his journey, he has many great adventures, each designed to further his knowledge about the world and what kind of man he has become. It is when one seeks answers from within himself that a true meaning can be found. Julian Jaynes, in his book, *The Origin of Consciousness and the Breakdown of the Bicameral Mind*, sees Odysseus as the pivotal mythological figure who transcends total reliance on the fickle and self-serving gods of the Greek world to place more and more emphasis on the inner thoughts and motivations of the individual. *The Odyssey*, which Jaynes believes was written over a century by several authors, demonstrates the movement of Odysseus from god consciousness, a reliance on forces beyond human control, to adherence to an inner voice, a self-consciousness. This is shown as

consciousness and morality are a single development. For without gods, morality based on a consciousness of the consequences of action must tell men what to do. . . . [And, according to Solon, Greek poet 640–560 B.C.E.] it is now moral right that must be fitted together with might in government and which is the basis of law and lawful action. (286–87)

Without consciousness, there would be no need for morality. With consciousness and the ability to transcend nature, it becomes necessary to establish responsibility. If a man is not responsible to God, then to whom or what?

Odysseus becomes the myth model for Hemingway's code hero. *The Odyssey* is the story of a very courageous man who is trying to return to his home, but is forced to "expose himself [and his brave followers] to greater dangers," overcoming all obstacles and in so doing proving himself to be a man among men.

In an act of transference, Jake Barnes is not only a twentieth-century version of the wandering Odysseus, but also represents the author in seeking to find "his emotional and spiritual self" in a world that has "lost its purposiveness . . . since [being] abandoned by God" (Gurko 237). For Hemingway to attempt to derive a code presupposes the existence of some manner in which life should or ought to be lived. Hemingway states this position in a conversation between Jake and Bill Gorton, Jake's fishing companion and probably the most rational of the characters, concerning Mike Campbell. Gorton has just returned from a night of drinking and carousing with Mike, Brett, and Robert Cohn. He stops by Jake's room at the hotel:

"There was a fellow there [the Milano Palace] that had helped pay Brett and Mike out of Cannes, once. He was damned nasty."
"I know the story."
"I didn't. Nobody *ought* to have a right to say things about Mike."
"That's what makes it bad."
"They *oughtn't* to have any right. I wish to hell they didn't have any right." (my italics 204)

The use of the term *ought* implies a universal value—a value not necessarily ascribed to any specific authority other than how nature prescribes one human being should live among other human beings. There are certain behaviors a person should do simply because he or she *ought* to. Hemingway tosses in an interesting irony immediately following the above dialogue. As the chapter closes, Jake informs Bill that there was "a man killed outside the runway" during the running of the bulls. Bill's response was a simple, "Was there?" inferring that the insult to Mike, since he was a known entity, was much more evocative than the death of an anonymous citizen. This amplifies how one must be as aware of what is implied in the dialogue as what is actually said.

Hemingway was a member of the lost generation that remained in Europe following the war, generally congregating in Paris. Among the more prominent members with whom Hemingway came into contact at one time or another were Americans F. Scott Fitzgerald, Gertrude Stein, and poet Ezra Pound; Irish novelist James Joyce; and British writer and publisher Ford Madox Ford. What thematically emerges from Hemingway is a cross between European existentialism and an American idea of manifest destiny. Living in Paris at that time was like a modern version of Adam, out of the Garden, on his own, and requiring a form of personal heroism. The character does not exist within an existential vacuum. In a truly American way, he takes control of his life in accordance with a specific code of conduct derived not from a supernatural entity but emerging out of nature. Jake Barnes, the protagonist of *The Sun Also Rises*, is not yet the hero, but during the course of the novel, he does meet and admire the first in a long line of code heroes created by Hemingway, bullfighter Pedro Romero.

The novel, which interweaves Hemingway's actual experiences with his imagination, is set in Paris, later moving to several locales in Spain during the years immediately following World War I. Barnes is an American correspondent with an office in Paris. At the time the novel was being written, Hemingway was living in Paris as a correspondent for the *Toronto Star*. In 1925, Hemingway and a group of friends similar to the fictional characters of the novel visit Pamplona, Spain, for the Fiesta of San Fermin and the running of the bulls. Where Hemingway and Barnes part company most decisively is Barnes's war wound. As a result of an accident involving the ambulance he was driving, Barnes is rendered impotent, requiring him to look beyond the physical pleasures that command the attention of at least three of his traveling companions: Mike Campbell, Robert Cohn, and Lady Brett Ashley.

This deviation in the real life of the author and the fictional life of the protagonist is the one factor making his search more focused. Therefore, an understanding of the novel begins with this ultimate irony. "Jake's impotency is a metaphor for the spiritual condition of these emotionally exhausted, physically sterile individuals who, like himself, are awash in postwar disillusionment and unable to sustain any fruitful and lasting relationships" (Phillips 122). To be a young, reasonably successful American, living in Paris among the morally disenchanted "beautiful people" and unable to fulfill his normal desires, would be comparable to a child's spending his childhood with daily access to Toys 'R' Us yet unable to play with the merchandise. Stanley Edgar Hyman, in his book *Standards: A Chronicle of Books for Our Time*, sums up Barnes's condition: "In boldly choosing for his subject matter the love between an impotent man and a frigid promiscuous woman, Hemingway found a truly representative and deeply disturbing metaphor for the human condition" (30).

The human condition to which Stanley refers is a quest to find meaning and morality where none seems to exist. Barnes's every action and thought will connect either directly or indirectly to this frustrating circumstance. For example, while viewing the unloading of the bulls at Pamplona, there is a reference to the presence of "steers" in the corral to "keep them from fighting" (133). Readers cannot help but connect Barnes's war wound with the role he seems forced to play among his friends, for how he deals with friends' conflicts is a major part of the story. The effect on the novel is that while dealing with his individual quest, in order to be heroic, he must also point the way for his friends to find their meaning and as a metaphorical myth show how a reader may find his or her way.

Another major factor affecting the manner in which the novel is to be understood is the point of view. The narrator, Jake Barnes, is telling the story in retrospect and therefore knows the outcome from the beginning. The effect we as readers must recognize is the narrator's bias. The degree of subjectivity is most noticeable regarding the tone used to describe those of the group whom Jake dislikes and those to whom he gives approval. Robert Cohn from the very beginning is spoken about with disdain. The reader at that point does not know why, but as the novel continues, we learn it is a direct result of Robert's brief affair with Brett at San Sebastian prior to their arrival at Pamploma. The description of the frequent associations Cohn has with Barnes prior to the San Sebastian event certainly imply the two were rather close friends. On the other hand, regardless of Mike Campbell's drunken behavior, Barnes adheres to a certain acceptance and forgiveness, perhaps based on pity, but his attitude toward Mike is obviously in contrast to his feelings toward Robert, yet both have been Brett's lover.

While Jake Barnes is obviously the protagonist, the dominant character in the novel is the "damned good-looking" Lady Brett Ashley. It is through the character of Lady Brett that Hemingway makes a stated mythic connection. Mike Campbell tells the group that Robert Cohn has named her Circe: "He claims she turns men into swine" (144). As part of Jake Barnes's journey, he, like Odysseus, must encounter the sorceress Circe (Brett Ashley), a provocative female found in Homer's *Odyssey*. In Homer's story, one of the amazing adventures of Odysseus on his journey back to Penelope involves the beautiful sorceress. Odysseus, in order to restock his stores, anchors at the Island of Dawn, Circe's domain. His men go ashore to explore and are greeted most cordially and then wined and dined by the beautiful and seductive Circe. The lady has at her disposal a potion that turns men into pigs, literally. When Odysseus discovers the sorcery, he confers with his friend Hermes (Roman Mercury) and is made aware of an herb, moly, that counteracts the spell. Odysseus dines with Circe and, being immune to the sorcery, threatens to slay her, causing her to beg for his mercy. In exchange for her life, she must return his men to human form. His protection comes not from the direct intervention of a god but rather from nature. Circe, even in defeat, remains a seductress and, feigning submission, coaxes Odysseus to share her bed. During this interlude, Odysseus finds time to father three sons before returning to his wife. This sets up the final irony when one of the bastard sons, Telegonus, several years later becomes his father's killer during a sea battle. In Greek mythology, as in Hemingway's novel, the seductive power of a woman strikes man at his most vulnerable point. The ironic aspect is even stronger for Jake Barnes because his loss of sexual potency does not prevent the sorceress from working her magic.

Webster's defines *sorcery* as "the use of power gained from the assistance or control of evil spirits especially for divining: necromancy." In Ernest Hemingway's creation of Lady Brett Ashley, her powers of seduction are so great that they extend beyond personal contact. For example, during the fiesta, Jake, Brett, Mike, Bill, and Robert are sampling the wine and fun. In a crowded bar, they encounter a group of celebrants who "formed a circle around Brett and started to dance. They wore big wreaths of white garlics around their necks." We can assume the dancers were all male as they encouraged Bill and Jake to join their circle. When Brett attempts to join in, the men stop her, wanting her as the icon, the goddess to whom they are openly paying homage (155). The "wreaths of garlic," become the dancers' moly, symbols of protection from the spell the goddess could produce. This provides another aspect of the human paradox, an inherent pull of the evil sorceress while at the same time wearing an amulet to protect the dancers from it. Earlier the world possessed God to protect its inhabitants from the scourge of evil. Now, in the age of agnosticism, to what do we turn? Garlic? It was knowledge about the moly given to Odysseus that protected Odysseus from Circe. If Jake's war wound is not sufficient to protect him from this sexual sorceress, it would be doubtful a wreath of garlic would protect the dancers. Whether or not Hemingway is making a cruel joke or presenting the scene sympathetically is left up to the reader. In either case, the film omits the scene.

This is the point where the code must intervene. If morality and the good life, as defined by Hemingway, are to be attained, it is the code that ultimately will elevate humans. Pedro Romero, the true hero in this novel, is the only one to take all the evil the sorceress could give and not become a pig. He is the "man" who places Lady Brett into the position of choosing, causing her to withdraw, rather than himself to concede. Romero, the nineteen-year-old matador, whose occupation demands courage in the face of danger, forces Brett to choose honor over ecstasy. The future great matador has taken a terrific beating from the former boxer, Robert Cohn, and still maintains his composure, skill, and courage in the final corrida. In a second and probably more dangerous and career-threatening action, he takes Brett to Madrid with him. While there, he proposes to Brett, requesting her to become "womanly" by letting her hair grow long. At every step, Romero chooses to do the honorable thing, not because he has to but because it is the thing he ought to do. In keeping with the spirit of the moment, Brett, possibly for the first time in her adult life, "decides not to be a bitch" and does what she ought to do (245). Romero, we may assume, went on with his life, after paying the hotel bill for Brett, as a final touch of honor.

This brings us to the moral and mythical center of the novel, Pedro Romero's second corrida. (167–69). For Hemingway, Spanish bullfighting was not a sport—"It may be described as a spectacle, a ritual, a ceremony, a sacrifice, or an art, but never a sport" (Josephs 228). The *toreo* (bullfight) has all the ceremony of the mythical rites of animal sacrifice of ages past: the parade into the arena, the devout study by the *aficionados*, the art associated with the matador's work, and finally, the ceremonial killing of the bull with its awarding of a tail and ears for outstanding fights. The bull is as subject to honor as is the matador. It is singularly transfixing—the center of the ring where a solitary man waits for the bull, pitting his skill and daring against an animal who has been bred for the single purpose of goring him. The matador's task is to control the bull:

[With Romero] always it was straight and pure and natural in line. . . . Romero had the *old thing*, the holding of his purity of line through the maximum of exposure, while he dominated the bull by making him realize he was unattainable. (my italics, 168)

The Fiesta of San Fermin is a religious holiday. The corrida is the culmination of that holiday, which can be fulfilled only with the sacrifice. The fact that a human dies is tragic, but not of importance unless that person is the matador. The matador is the priest engaged in the rite of sacrifice. It is not a sacrifice in the traditional form, where an animal is simply killed, but a sacrifice in which the priest-matador must conquer the animal before it can be sacrificed. The period of time in which the corrida occurs is mythic, sacred, or eternal time (Josephs 231), a period where real time stands still and the congregation in attendance momentarily leaves their world behind.

An interesting story concerning the choice of an actor to play Pedro Romero occurred during preshooting. Director Henry King wanted a Spanish or Mexican bullfighter to play the role in order to use close-ups of the corrida. He made visits to both Spain and Mexico and found a young Mexican bullfighter he thought could play the role. Producer Darryl F. Zanuck felt he "looked like a waiter" and cast a young actor, Bob Evans, in the role. When both Zanuck and King realized that Evans was not right for the role, there was insufficient time for the young bullfighter to master the English language. Evans tried to appear Spanish, but is questionable. Part of the problem may be that he played opposite talented actors and looks weak by comparison (Phillips 132).

This novel is a character study, a travel guide, a lesson on fishing and bullfighting, and, certainly, a bar guide. To say everyone drinks is an understatement. Drinking plays a huge part in the development of the characters. The drinking certainly qualifies as a character attribute, however, one must also consider the drinking as a literary device. As each moves from drunkenness to sobriety, the reader sees beyond the surface as the alcohol lowers inhibitions and allows us to see the inner person. Robert Cohn shows no outward effect but becomes more obsessed; Mike Campbell grows wild and free, a comical drunk; Brett becomes more sensual, and Jake gets philosophical. What at first reading may seem to reflect an author fascinated with alcoholic beverages can, as the story develops, show how alcohol is used to break down the facade humans use to cover their real feelings. Jake Barnes, following an evening of drinking, sits alone in his room. Like most of the characters in the novel, he consumes large quantities of liquor without visible effect; however, as we learn, it does have a psychological effect. In Chapter 4, Jake reads a wedding announcement from an acquaintance, Aloysius Kirby, whose daughter, Katherine, is getting married. The wedding announcement triggers two responses: First, "Lady

Ashley. To hell with Brett. To hell with you, Lady Ashley" (30). A short time later, after several attempts to change the subject in his mind, Jake suddenly starts to cry while thinking about Brett (31). The chapter finishes with the line: "It is awfully easy to be hard-boiled about everything in the daytime, but at night it is another thing" (34). In other words, after an evening of drinking and socializing, it is difficult not to feel the hurt that life has dealt. The war has prevented Jake and Brett from consummating what each believes is their one true love. While Jake is absorbed with his daytime life, making a living doing a job he enjoys, he forgets the pain. At night, in the quiet of the evening, he is forced to confront that inner self, the one that tends to be set free by alcohol, and his life takes on a different perspective. Alcohol fits into Hemingway's irony as it has the capacity to act as both stimulant and depressant.

There are many critics who feel Hemingway's novel is depressing because everything ends badly. On the other hand, there are always those who are able to find something beneficial in whatever they encounter. This novel in at least one way is a triumph. Jake Barnes has been dealt a severe blow. It would be relatively easy for him to be "lost." However, he does not withdraw and subject himself to self-pity. Jake in his own way is dealing with the life he has been given with style and grace. He is not immune from mistakes, nor does he seek to be excused from them. He is able to see in Pedro Romero the ingredients it takes to become a great bullfighter. Bullfighting, as a metaphor for life, is not a contest where there are winners and losers. It is a ritual in which each matador, using his or her skills, is pitted against the natural skills and instincts of the bull. Neither participant is judged on survival alone. They are judged on how well each faces death in the arena. Life's meaning, then, is not to be judged on the basis of wins and losses, but in how well one faces the many crises each will encounter throughout life. This is the reality Jake accepts when he responds to Lady Brett's final admonition: "Oh Jake, . . . we could have had such a damned good time together." Jake replies with great simplicity: "Yes, . . . Isn't it pretty to think so" (247). The use of the word *pretty* implies both a sense of reality and abstraction as in fantasy. The word can be associated with beauty, a purely abstract concept, or it can be applied to something directly pleasing to one's senses. In this case, it is obvious that Hemingway meant both. Jake realizes and accepts it might have been a "good time," while at the same time recognizes that it is only a thought, never to be realized.

The film, like the novel, met with mixed reviews. Present-day critics of Hemingway films would generally agree this was certainly not one of the best translations of a Hemingway literary work. Most generally accept either of the versions of *A Farewell to Arms* as the best. Hemingway never saw a film version he approved of and had some sarcastic comments to make about all of them. However, his criticism seemed to be more focused on the medium than on the actual screenplay. Gene Phillips commented:

he consistently chose to dismiss virtually every film made from his work with a derogatory quip—whether he had seen all of it or not—one suspects that he somehow felt required to knock almost any movie adaptation of his work in order to preserve his literary status. It was unnecessary for him to do this, however, since his literary reputation and that of his work was not affected one way or another by any film made from his fiction. (131)

This film version certainly had the elite of Hollywood in its cast. Tyrone Power, Ava Gardner, Errol Flynn, Mel Ferrer, and Eddie Albert were among the most respected and popular actors of the time.

There are some interesting differences that require discussion. One is the different attitude of the novel and film with regard to religion—for example, there is a scene where Brett goes into the church to pray. In the novel version Jake joins her as she kneels silently, then, "After a little I felt Brett stiffen beside me, and saw she was looking straight ahead. 'Come on,' she whispered throatily. 'Let's get out of here. Makes me damned nervous.'" Later she comments that praying "never did me any good," repeating the comment moments later (208). By repeating the statement, a reader may interpret she is either uncertain or her conclusion is more certain. In the film version, Brett goes into the church and kneels alone dressed in a light blue dress with a small round hat that might convey a halo, especially with the soft light coming from above and behind giving her a nunlike appearance. Jake enters the church later and waits for her near the entrance. As she leaves, Jake asks, "What did you pray for?" "I prayed for him," was her reply as they continued down the street. She then asks Jake to "look after him." Jake replies, "Lucky I'm here to look after your wounded." There is no expression of negativity toward religion. In fact, "Twentieth Century-Fox suggested to theater managers that they ask local clergymen to preach sermons on the famous Ecclesiastes text from which Hemingway took his title" (Lawrence 142). It is doubtful that if the film had followed the language of the novel, the clergy would have approved of Brett's dialogue and would not have been interested in promoting the film, but probably would have condemned it. Although Jake admits, "I'm pretty religious," his actions seem to deny any active pursuit of that belief. When Brett says, "He [God] never worked well with me," Jake's reply is, "Should we have another martini?" (245).

Another major difference is in the attitude expressed by Jake toward the Jewishness of Robert Cohn. For example the word *Jew* or *Jewish* is never mentioned in the film. For *Jewish*, the screenwriters substituted the word *intellectual*; therefore instead of Robert Cohn's offending people because of his "Jewish superiority," it became "intellectual superiority." Another missing piece was Brett's grand entrance into the dance club with a group of homosexuals. The novel uses this to enhance the irony of Jake's sexual dysfunction and Brett's sexual excesses. The gentlemen accompanying Brett can only be glimpsed as the camera moves quickly away to other shots. This possibly can be attributed to the fact the film was made in 1956, when Hollywood was still operating under a moral code.

There is no doubt that during his long and very successful career, Hemingway continually tested and revised his code. He did this through his writing and through his experiences, such as big game hunting and fishing. It has been said by many people who knew Hemingway that if he found you interesting, at some point in time you would become a character in a novel or short story. With this close connection to life, taking his characters and conflicts from personal experience, Hemingway touched reality perhaps more closely than any other author. Yet for a large number of people, both critics and readers, there seems to be something missing. For most, Hemingway's work is either loved or hated. There is no doubt that Hemingway provided a good forum in which to test Falck's hypothesis: "The defining objective of literature continues to be realism; its function is to express what it truly feels like to be alive" (cf. 17). It is a combination of style and substance that makes this possible. The simplicity of style combined with a quest for a fundamental code gets us close to reality. As we discovered in McMurtry and Walker, it is not the complexities of life that should confuse us; it is in understanding the importance of love and honor in our daily lives that affords us meaning. Hemingway, writing a generation before either McMurtry or Walker, established the direction. Less, when attempting to find a meaning in an individual life, may in fact be closer to the truth.

QUESTIONS

In your responses, identify a specific reference by quotation or page number.

1. Consider the hypothesis of Colin Falck explained in the introduction to Chapter 7. Identify and evaluate two aspects you feel Hemingway may be suggesting are examples of reality reflecting a fundamental truth about human nature.

2. Briefly review the dialogue between Jake and Georgette (pages 15–20) and explain how this encounter connects to other conversations in the novel. In your response, identify specific lines of dialogue that suggest your response.

3. Pedro Romero becomes for Hemingway the model for his code hero. Identify five lines from the novel that make the reader aware of a specific attribute Romero possesses that Hemingway considers heroic.

4. Omitting Pedro Romero, there are four major male characters in the novel: Jake Barnes, Robert Cohn, Mike Campbell, and Bill Gorton. Place them below Romero in accordance with their own degree of heroism, first with the character closest to Romero. Identify specific incidents in the novel to support your ranking.

5. On the final page of the novel, between Brett's final line and Jake's response, there is a brief description of the setting. What, in your opinion, did Hemingway have in mind by placing this between the dialogue?

QUESTION FOR GROUP DISCUSSION

1. Identify a minimum of five possible reasons the film failed to capture the essence of the novel and why the film might have failed at the box office.

Chapter 12

Politics and the Public

Being There by Jerzy Kosinski

This 115-page novel was published in 1971, prior to the resignation of President Nixon, but certainly after the impact television had on the 1960 as well as subsequent presidential elections. As *All the King's Men* reflects the nature of politics prior to television, *Being There* gives us a glimpse of the role television may play in the selection of political leadership. The power structure of the old boys' network so active in *King's Men* is still in place, in that power brokers are still present and calling the shots. It is just that television provides for them a new outlet that might be more powerful than they. Kosinski makes no attempt at realism. This novel is pure satire from beginning to end, which may, in fact, make it all the more frightening. John W. Aldridge in *Saturday Review* writes:

Kosinski's vision is primarily philosophical. He is interested not in making a satirical indictment of modern society—although satire is an abrasive secondary feature of his point of view—nor in attempting to explore in the French manner the various possible ways of dramatizing individual consciousness. He is concerned rather with understanding the nature and meaning of the human condition, the relation quite simply of human values to the terms of existence in an essentially amoral and surely anarchistic universe. (*SR* 25)

Kosinski ventures into the ontological base of humanity in an attempt to find the true nature of his being. What he seems to find there does not elevate humans to any noticeable degree.

    This story is told by an anonymous narrator who possesses complete omniscience. What is especially well done is how this omniscient voice uses innuendo and inflection to reveal his most cogent thoughts. Nothing seems to come to us directly or in any great detail. This is a story of a semire-tarded middle-aged man who, having been sheltered from the outside world his entire life, is suddenly thrust into a world without any firsthand knowl-edge about it or any basic survival skills. His only contact has been the radio and then television for perhaps the past ten years. Although the dates for the story are vague, references would indicate it is probably during the Vietnam War and the cold war with the Soviet Union. The man's name is "Chance." Although his origins are kept intentionally vague, it is made very clear that he has been raised by a wealthy man and upon reaching working age was provided employment as a gardener in exchange for his room and board. During his entire lifetime, Chance, like Adam, has been confined to the garden, which in Chance's case is surrounded by a very high ivy-covered wall. His basic needs have been the responsibility of a housekeeper, narrowing his life to eating, sleeping, gardening, and watching television. It is important to understand that for all practical purposes this has been sufficient. Chance is perfectly happy and content with his sheltered life.

It is with the garden and its trees we will find the strongest connection to ancient myth. A brief comparison between the story of Adam and the Garden of Eden, and the famous Bodhi tree under which Buddha is said to have discovered nirvana provides the substance: Adam, like Chance, is being severed forever from the garden as at Eden's gate stood "a flaming sword which turned every way to keep the way of the tree of life" separated from man forever (Gen. 3:24). In Chance's case, it is not a flaming sword but a lawyer who informs him, "This house will be closed tomorrow at noon. At that time, both doors and the gate to the garden will be locked" (20). In contrast, Buddha, while sitting beneath the tree was given the Eightfold Path that people must follow in order to reach nirvana, a oneness with the universe. The tree in this case becomes a symbol for nirvana, drawing people to it. Kosinski draws from both myths, giving his story a broad foundation in spiritual truth. Chance, like Adam, is cast from the garden; however, like Buddha, he immediately sets out to find the garden (tree), which will again bring him to paradise.

The story opens with the death of the old man and Chance's confron-tation with the estate's lawyer. There is nothing in the will to continue his support and no employment record. This opens the satiric tone on a subtle note. Someone who does not possess some form of documentation—a birth certificate, driver's license, or social security card—obviously does not exist. One other subtle line that may account for Chance's origin occurs when we are told by the subjective observer that the old man's finely tailored clothing "fit [Chance] very well" and he has free access to the wardrobe. This may imply that Chance is more than a foundling; perhaps he was directly related to the old man but hidden because of the status of his birth, or his intellectual level, or both. Kosinski maintains this subtlety of tone throughout the novel, requiring the reader, as with Hemingway, to be aware of what is not being said as much as what is. Because there is no employment record and no will to extend care for him, Chance is forced to exit his beloved garden.

He packs a suitcase with the richly tailored clothing and journeys out into the world. An act bordering on deus ex machina occurs; as he is passing between two parked cars, the limousine in front backs up preparatory to leaving the parking space. Chance is trapped between the cars and screams in pain. The chauffeur and occupant of the limousine, a Mrs. EE (Elizabeth *Eve*) Rand, are distraught, and offer to take Chance to their home and have their private physician care for him. Because Chance has no doctor of his own, he is totally acquiescent to their requests. He is moved into the Rand home and placed in a guestroom, treated by their doctor, and told to rest for a few days and he will be fine. Having nowhere else to go, he accepts their offer, especially since he can have a TV by his bed.

The remaining part of the novel engages the imagination of the reader as this semiretarded, illiterate gardener is misunderstood by his new benefactors and labeled a very private, well-educated businessman who for some reason has abandoned his former life. His name now is "Chauncey Gardiner," a misinterpretation of "Chance the Gardner" that EE hears when Chance says his name. This encounter brings to the light another subtle aspect of human nature so open to Kosinski's satire: how we so frequently hear what we want to hear or expect to hear and miss the real meaning. Fate continues to intervene when the president of the United States happens to pay a personal visit to Mr. Benjamin Rand at the precise moment Chance has recovered sufficiently to join in a brief meeting. The president and Mr. Rand are discussing how the problem of a depressed economy might be approached in an upcoming speech. Chauncey, speaking of his garden, is heard as a profound thinker. He remarks, "In a garden, growth has its season. There are spring and summer, but there are also fall and winter. And then spring and summer again. As long as the roots are not severed, all is well and all will be well." The president and Ben Rand are struck by the simplicity of the metaphor for the economic situation plaguing the country; the president uses the line in his next speech and credits Chauncey. Suddenly, this illiterate gardener is national news. This man who forms his behavior in every situation on what he has seen characters do on television is now identified as an adviser to the president of the United States.

The story expands to include a somewhat unexpected cultural pattern as Chauncey, at a United Nations gathering, meets and in his silence captivates the Russian and French ambassadors. His "cool" demeanor, appearance, and poetic gardening metaphors make him a newsmaker. The reader surely expects someone to recognize Chauncey for what he is, but in the herd mentality the writer obviously is satirizing, everyone listens intently and then marvels at Chauncey's "uncanny ability of reducing complex matters to the simplest of human terms" (88).

The novel concludes with the Russian KGB and the American FBI trying desperately to research Chauncey's background and failing, and the ambassador and the president rationalizing this failure. The novel ends with a group of political power brokers plotting who will be the president's running mate in the next election. When Gardiner's name is mentioned, the final and perhaps greatest irony is broached: Would the lack of background information harm his chances? One answers, "The damn trouble was that they [the other candidates] all had background, too much background! A man's past cripples him: his background turns into a swamp and invites scrutiny!" (116).

The film presents this short novel in a strangely abbreviated form and, in true Hollywood tradition, includes several scenes not found in the novel. Several of the film's scenes generate comedy while providing character delineation. Immediately after Chance exits his beloved garden, he encounters a small group of young black males. Upon asking directions, a young man inquires if he has been sent by Rafael. This becomes a running joke throughout the film and provides even more comedy at the end. While the credits are running, we are treated to several outtakes of Peter Sellers's difficulty in dealing with the line while awaiting his X-ray. This would effectively kill any possible postviewing audience contemplation about a theme. Another example of Hollywood overkill occurs during the final scene of the film and takes away much of the satire created in the novel. Perhaps the director felt the novel's ending was too close to reality and required a fantasy finish to assure audiences the story is satire, or perhaps the ending is director Hal Ashby's attempt to underscore the messianic myth.

Among Hollywood directors, Hal Ashby has a proven record in dealing with the offbeat story. His credits include *The Landlord* (1970, from a novel by Kristin Hunter) about a young, rich, white man who buys a tenement building in the black section of Brooklyn and then gets personally involved with tenants. In 1974, he brought to the screen *Harold and Maude*, relating the love connection between an adolescent boy and a much older woman. The screenplay is filled with many eccentric characters. It would seem Ashby is highly suited to telling this type of story.

In addition, Jerzy Kosinski was the screenwriter and was nominated by the Writers Guild of America for Best Adapted Screenplay. Melvyn Douglas won the Best Supporting Actor award and Peter Sellers was nominated for Best Actor. Both received Golden Globe awards for their performances. This obvious critical success did not carry over at the box office. Commercially, the picture did not attract audiences, perhaps because the satire left audiences too self-conscious. It may have been that because the film was released following the death of Peter Sellers, audiences did not feel comfortable laughing. There may be other explanations too.

QUESTIONS

In your responses, identify a specific reference by quotation or page number.

1. Assess the level of deus ex machina in the novel. What incidents seem to require divine intervention to develop a degree of verisimilitude? Does this harm the overall meaning of the story?
2. The story is obviously a satire. Even though the story is seemingly simple, there are many complex aspects of our culture being satirized. Identify three human cultural weaknesses.
3. There are several direct parallels between this story and the creation story in Genesis. Identify a minimum of three beyond the garden allusion.
4. How is the theme of the story enhanced by the use of allusion?
5. According to Frye, satire is a product of winter and therefore negative and depressing. What makes satire, and therefore this story, depressing?

QUESTIONS FOR GROUP DISCUSSION

1. Roger Ebert comments that the film "begins with a cockamamie notion, it's basically one joke told for two hours." What is the joke to which Ebert refers? Identify at least three different modes of presentation, and discuss if the retelling is successful.
2. The purpose of satire is to point out weaknesses in human activity and in institutions. Select three scenes that appear in both media and discuss the techniques and/or devices each uses to present them. Which medium seems to use the devices available more effectively? Be sure you identify what human frailty or institutional weakness is being satirized.
3. What is Kosinski's message? Does the film convey the same message? Why or Why not?

PART V
CLOSURE

When we began, our objective was to perform as amateur critics of both contemporary novel and film. Our mode of criticism was to treat those novels and films as modern mythology, representing Western culture since the mid-twentieth century. As a perspective, we have imposed one form of critical assessment—a formula using a natural base from which contemporary literature forms a relationship with other literature covering other times and places.

One very important aspect is becoming aware that art, whether visual or conceptual, is always in motion. Even when we look at one representation, it is not only reflective of the time in which it is produced, but has a connection to both past and present forms through its mode and archetype. Archetypal criticism has its share of critics. Among other forms and theories of criticism are the purely formalist, which focuses on the literal structure and form (plot, characters, conflict, etc.) of the written text, and the psychological, which may stem from a Freudian or Jungian base, or may try to get into the mind of the author, analyzing the relationship between his or her biographical experiences and the action and characters within the novel and later the film. In historical analysis, the novel or film is placed within a context of history and evaluated on the basis of its verisimilitude or lack of it. A dominant theory among modern literary scholars is structuralism, which is based on its semiology in both literature and film. As the name implies, it separates the media into composite structures. "At its simplest, it claims that the nature of every element in any given situation has no significance by itself, and in fact is determined by its relationship to all the other elements involved in that situation" (Hawkes 18). This form of criticism would seem to be more viable as film criticism than its application to literature. However, whatever the media, any criticism will focus on form or content, or both.

The fact that criticism had become so complex is one reason Frye developed his archetypal-mythological approach, an attempt to place the idea that art/literature has a common base and can be best understood as a continuum. Claude Lévi-Strauss, a noted French anthropologist, in *The Savage Mind* stated, "Mythical thought for its part is imprisoned in the events and experiences that never tires of ordering and re-ordering in its search to find them a meaning. But it also acts as a liberator by its protest against the idea that anything can be meaningless with which science at first resigned itself to a compromise" (22). Literature in its modern form attempts to bridge the gap between the physical world in all its complexities and the superconscious world we label as spiritual. Unlike the laws of science, literature, particularly in the form of archetypal myth, is not bound by any rules except the capacity of the human mind to conceptualize—to create a story that will fit into the human world as it might exist at a distinct moment in time and place. It also needs to be noted that science in its own way has softened the outlook toward "laws" and established theoretical forms in physics and mathematics, its own compromise.

This format provides the same basic approach that humans have been using to understand the full meaning of their lives since recorded history and probably before that. We know there is a way to connect the physical and the abstract or spiritual world. It may be through religion, but it is not dependent on religion. Many of the greatest authors profess to being atheists but still manage to reach out with a spiritual connection. We may label it morality or ethics, or teleology, or *mana*. Whatever the label, this inner consciousness provides a connection with a reality beyond our physical being.

A student who looks at the body of literature and film produced within the past fifty years of the twentieth century will find representatives of every mode, from romantic fantasy to surrealism, and everything in between. It happens this way because an author, for whatever personal or experiential reason, selects a particular part of nature's cycle as a canvas on which he or she will present his or her version of one of life's many journeys. This provides a literary portrait that allows a student to understand better the fullness and diversity of his or her culture—what was believed, revered, celebrated, feared, and hoped for with regard to birth, initiation, redemption, death, and rebirth. The mode—fantasy, romance, realism, irony, or satire—is the framework within which the writer expresses his or her impressions of the quest. It is in the focus on rebirth and restoration, which requires a sense of romantic idealism or fantasy, that we will encounter what most people accept as a meaning or purpose in life.

From the narratives of *Shawshank, Cuckoo's Nest,* and *Shane* we recognize the importance of having a heroic model that, in their quest for
salvation or redemption, places principle above material value. In today's
world, we encounter many so-called heroes from sports or entertainment
whose values are subject to public scandal. In politics, one party or candidate wants to portray his or her opponent with some fatal flaw that will
cause the public to look on the candidate with disfavor, not realizing they
may be showing their own flaw in the portrayal. In economics, our heroes
are those who end up with the most property or power.

It seems, paradoxically, that we can find real heroes only in fiction, which
tells us about ordinary humans who perform extraordinary acts. Hopefully,
these stories tell us about ourselves. In our contemporary society, although
we still enjoy the idea of the knight on the white horse who slays the dragon
and makes the world safe, we have come to know, as Leon Uris describes
in his novel *Exodus* about the holocaust survivors fighting for the establishment of Israel, that the real hero or messiah is within each of us. This
certainly is confirmed by Alice Walker and Larry McMurtry.

From Alice Walker, Michael Ondaatje, and Larry McMurtry we discover
that the road an adolescent must travel prior to becoming an adult is full
of potholes, even a few canyons. Alice Walker compares one black girl's
journey in the American South to one in Africa. Larry McMurtry makes
his reader aware of how much the loss of our pioneer spirit has cost modern
teenagers. In each case, the characters are no longer seeking a savior but
discover, as Celie did in *The Color Purple*, that whatever we gain, we must
go after it "in the old fashioned way, we must earn it." We begin to understand the relation we as individuals have to the environment. The characters in both stories have lost something. What they, and by implication
we, have lost is the moral and ethical base from which, regardless of the
difficulties that base may impose, we collectively and individually receive
an identity; and with that identity comes meaning. The young Olinka girl
chooses to undergo the terrible pain and disfigurement of her initiation even
though she does not have to and is going to leave the continent. It is important to her to follow the tradition of her people. The act establishes her
connection to her family, clan, culture, and most of all, who she is in
relation to the physical world. Tashi may be the wife of Adam, but she is
also an Olinka. It is through one's identity that a connection is made with
nature. However, Walker seems to make very clear that although Tashi is
Olinka, Adam is American and their children will have the right to choose
between cultures. They would not be bound to the old ways unless they
choose them. Each person is an individual, and at the same moment, a
husband, wife, or child, a member of society, which is part of a culture,
which coexists with all other life on the planet. Each family becomes its
own unit within the culture with the right to choose its path. In the end,
Alice Walker wants us to know, the characters in *The Color Purple* are no

longer culturally bound by their ancestral past; as residents of a new world, they may choose to establish their own individuality in a new and free culture. Michael Ondaatje confirms the new culture is a global one. We are, in essence, one humanity.

For all the characters of *The Last Picture Show*, identity remains elusive. We can hope that as Sonny ages, he will become more like Sam the Lion. At some point, Sonny may recognize that Sam was the only person in Thalia, Texas, who seemed to know who he was and did not try to be anything else. Maybe Sonny will too. Do not expect to find out if Sonny makes it if you choose to watch the film sequel, *Texasville*. What you will see is what is lost when the original mythological base is subverted in order to cater to popular culture. This too may explain why a sequel is frequently disappointing.

How does one find identity and meaning in such a secular world? Albert Camus attempted to answer the question in his novel *The Stranger* (French film version available). The novel ends with Meurssault, his protagonist and a convicted murderer, awaiting execution in a small cell with one east-facing window through which he could, by standing on tiptoe, see the horizon. French custom at the time prevented the accused from knowing the date of his execution; he knew only that he would be executed at sunrise. Therefore, if he was still in his cell when, gazing hopefully through his tiny window he could see the sun rise, he knew he would live another day. Camus came to the conclusion that just having something to look forward to—in this case, a new day dawning—gives a life meaning. He rejected the pessimism of nihilistic existentialism and found that just being alive can give purpose. W. P. Kinsella produced that same feeling in his novel when he included the cynical and pessimistic J. D. Salinger as a major character. You can visualize his cynicism slowly dropping away as he strides optimistically into the corn field with the ballplayers. He now has something important to look toward.

Jake Barnes is not that fortunate. What gives Jake's life meaning arises out of how he, and he alone, chooses to live it. He can whine at the misfortune fate and the war have imposed on him. Or he can face this misfortune as an opportunity to show, regardless of the obstacles that he may encounter, he will do what he ought to do. He can face life as Pedro Romero faces the bull in the ring: with courage and determination. Life is not simply to be lived; it is to be engaged, challenged, and if possible controlled. What cannot be controlled must be accepted as part of the challenge. One is reminded of the film *Moonstruck*, starring Cher and Nicholas Cage, which has a poignant scene near the end of the film involving the characters playing Cher's parents. Olympia Dukakis, Cher's mother in the film, is talking to a man (John Mahoney) she had met in a restaurant. While dining, the man had been involved in a rather noisy separation scene with a younger woman. After receiving the contents of the young lady's wine glass in his face, he joined Dukakis, who was dining alone. As they talked, she asks him why older men seek liaisons with younger women. After a moment's evasion, he responds, "nerves." She counters with, "maybe it's because they fear death." Later that evening, Cher's fiancé, played by Danny Aiello, confirms her thinking that fearing death causes men to seek relationships with more than one woman. Seconds later, her husband (Vincent Gardenia) is returning home from a date with a younger woman. Looking him in the eye, she tells him, "Cosmo, I don't care what you do, you are going to die, just like everybody else." He replies simply, "Thank you, Rose." This, in a contemporary and somewhat humorous fashion, presents the conflict. Jake Barnes, because of his impotence, cannot attain immortality. Even if by some miraculous means he might regain his lost sexual potency, he would still have to face death, the ultimate challenge. As dramatized by the escapades of Brett and Robert, sex does not give life meaning. In fact, it would seem that Hemingway is implying that sex is a weakness that, if allowed to dominate one's life, can destroy the ability to live as one ought to.

Each of us seeks to find a way to prove we are alive and that there is a meaning to our life. For R. P. McMurphy, it was a subconscious need to accept responsibility for someone other than himself. We live life and simultaneously watch ourselves live it, knowing that the only possible outcome is death. There is no other moment when man is closest to nature than when he recognizes his mortality. This is the element of truth that underpins all myth. Novelists do not deal with the subject of death directly but life metaphorically. Remember that in the definition of *plot*, there must be a causality. Death cannot be a meaning to life, for it is its antithesis— an absence of life. Life's meaning is to be found in living. The more deeply the meaning exists within the structure of the story, the stronger the connection is between the character and the reader, the closer to reality becomes its archetypal/mythological theme.

Another way we might look upon the meaning is as *mana*—that part of our being that seeks to connect our physical and spiritual consciousness. For Alice Walker, the connection came with an identity. For Hemingway, it is courage. For King, it is found in hope. For Ondaatje and McMurtry, it is, in following the admonition of Shakespeare, to know thyself. And for Warren and Kosinski, meaning comes with knowing you are living your life as you ought to live it. The more complex the natural world becomes, the more difficult it is for us to apprehend conceptually our own reality and share our reality with those we love. Each of the stories establishes a bond between characters founded on love. There were two people in Thalia who cared for Sonny: Sam the Lion and Ruth. As the audience exits, it leaves with the image of Ruth and Sonny together. McMurphy's love was great enough for him to sacrifice himself for his "brothers." Andy Dufresne gave Red hope and Red gave Andy the skills necessary to survive, forming a life-long bond. Jack Barnes decided the only way he could give his life meaning was to share his love of nature and bullfighting with his friends. Celie and Mr. _____ (Albert) found they had much to share once equality was established. As Albert puts it, "But when you talk about love I don't have to guess. I have love and I have been love. And I thank God he let me gain understanding enough to know love can't be halted just cause some peoples moan and groan" (237). Jack Burden learns that "history is blind, but man is not" (436). The individual has the choice of how to live life.

Finally, W. P. Kinsella included the deep love Ray had for Annie, Karen, and the land. Each myth is infused with a unifying love. This may be what these authors are attempting to convey to us. In order for us to establish who we are, we have to create a space and then fill it. And once we establish our own identity we have to fill in our missing parts by sharing our life with others. Is life lived extrinsically or intrinsically, or both? Americans are very aware of themselves as individuals. At the moment we are aware of our individuality, we are also an American, resident of a city and state, member of a church or social organization, brother, sister, father, mother, friend, husband, wife, employee, and so on. When we read or view these stories—stories of heroism, loss of innocence, quests for meaning—we can connect and, like people of the past, find in those stories a guide toward a better understanding of life's trials, conventions, rituals, and celebrations.

W. P. Kinsella's metaphor for life, the game of baseball, can bring all our stories together. As we look back at all of the stories we have studied, we can see in each of them the essence of a game. In life, as in baseball, we win a few, lose a few, and have a few rained out. There are rules— some set by the game and some by nature. Our laws, traditions, and mores are a form of rule book, and we can use only the physical and mental attributes that nature and genetics give us. How we physically and mentally approach the game, to what degree, and at what intensity we compete in many ways determines how much fun we have. Each of us possesses a will, a right to choose. The only thing we cannot do is refuse to play. Each of the characters we observed by reading or viewing provided a twentieth-century example of what part of the game the author thought was important and what was not, what part we could control and what part we had to accept, and finally, a way to see what Horton saw "the who" that exists within us—that mysterious part of our being that "fulfills an indispensable function: it expresses, enhances, and codifies belief; it safeguards morality; it vouches for the efficiency of ritual and contains practical rules for the guidance of man"(Malinowski 101), past, present, and future.

Midterm Perspective

Will these novels and films be read or viewed by Americans of the twenty-fifth century? Only time determines what lasts into future generations. Two classics that are universally recognized are *Huckleberry Finn*, published in 1895, and *The Grapes of Wrath*, published in 1936. It is interesting to debate what makes these classic, while other stories, written before and after and presenting many of the same ideas, are so quickly forgotten. It is also interesting to note that both of these novels continue to be read and studied in academia *and* popular culture. Of the motion pictures made from these two literary masterpieces, only *The Grapes of Wrath* became a classic film. Why not one of the many film versions of *Huckleberry Finn*? An explanation may be explained that the surrealistic film version of *The Grapes of Wrath* is able to retain the metaphorical truths of the narrative while because of the romantic nature of *Huckleberry Finn*, a director is unable to project the coming-of-age archetype from which Mark Twain derives his story.

Perhaps a better example would be 1953's *From Here to Eternity*. The novel was popular for a short time during the 1950s, probably because the story's setting is a military post in Hawaii immediately preceding the Japanese attack on Pearl Harbor. There are several reasons the novel quickly lost its appeal, the main one being that it is overly written. One chapter, for example, spends six or seven pages describing the interior of a cabin near the post where a crap game is going to be held. The minute details go far beyond that necessary to convey the setting. The film, on the other hand, one of Hollywood's best, winning Academy Awards for Best Picture, Director (Fred Zinnemann), Cinematography, Supporting Actor, and Supporting Actress—Frank Sinatra for his portrayal of the tragic Maggio and Donna Reed for her portrayal of a prostitute. All of the elements of film came together, making this movie a memorable one.

First and foremost, we must recognize that literature appeals to a somewhat limited audience of readers, while motion pictures appeal to the masses. That does not imply a film made from a novel is required to alter the essence of the story in any way. The more natural the appeal, the more the audience, reader or viewer, will connect with the story. The final test comes in the storyteller's ability to present the story in such a way that it will coalesce our conscious mind with our collective unconscious.

The bond becomes the connection between the abstract—what is being signified—and the objective reality—the signifier. This connection, according to such diverse personalities as psychologist Carl Jung, mythologist Joseph Campbell, and literary critic Northrop Frye, emanates from a deeply embedded awareness of our cultural beginnings and innate responses to natural phenomena, which are part of our genetic nature. We began our study with romantic-realism as portrayed by modern-style heroes segueing into isolation reflective of winter. Whether satire, tragedy, romance, or comedy, in each theme there must appear an essence of truth.

In *One Flew over the Cuckoo's Nest*, Randle P. McMurphy, a modern swashbuckler and minor criminal, is placed in a mental institution for psychiatric evaluation and becomes a savior to the psychologically challenged inmates. Andy Dufresne, a nondescript Walter Mitty type, is unjustly sent to a maximum security prison and in his manipulation of the system ultimately escapes, to become a legend. A romantic hero such as Robin Hood or Sir Galahad will be protected by divine intervention, while the modern hero must be totally dependent on his own skills. He may be, as in Kesey's novel, symbolically connected to a known messiah and therefore caused to make the ultimate sacrifice. Or he may, like the heroes of the Old West, or perhaps easterners like Andy and Red, ride off into the sunset of a Pacific beach. Readers, in accordance with their own predisposition, connect to both of these. "The nearer the romance is to myth, the more attributes of divinity will cling to the hero and the more the enemy will take on demonic mythical qualities" (Frye *AC* 187). What Frye identifies as attributes of divinity we label as fate, or luck, or deus ex machina; all tend to give the story a romantic twist. In any form, the narrative enters our minds as a familiar theme. The myth, the recurrent narrative, establishes in a significant manner its archetype. The myth is the story; the archetype, its meaning. Dufresne and McMurphy are both modern, realistic characters and receive direct symbolic references to connect the real with the abstract, the objective reality with the spiritual. There is never a doubt in the mind of the reader or the viewer about the outcome. We know the characters ultimately will triumph, yet we are drawn into the conflict to see how they accomplish it. McMurphy, as a contemporary hero, is allowed to die, for this underscores this character as messiah and literarily amplifies the story's theme. It is in the death that the triumph occurs. We do not have to concern ourselves with whether McMurphy might be left to wander the halls in a lobotomized stupor and used by Nurse Ratched to frighten the patients into total subordination. In his death, as in Dufresne's escape, each man becomes a legend, to be remembered in the exaggerated tales that will be passed down from one patient or inmate to another, growing in stature the more the tales are told. What we do know from the novel is the patients are now free to live their lives on the outside and the inmates have a source of hope. Andy Dufresne, we are led to believe, finds his paradise on a beach in southern Mexico and is ultimately joined by the rejuvenated Red. Both King and Kesey included details identifying their protagonists as legends, connecting both directly to mythical status and ensuring their lives will have an eternal effect.

A somewhat different archetype is created by Alice Walker. In *The Color Purple*, Celie, a fourteen-year-old black girl, is raped by her stepfather, forced to give up two babies resulting from the rape, and then bartered into an abusive marriage. In spite of, or perhaps, because of, these adversities, Celie grows into a remarkable and successful businesswoman. The myth of innocence triumphing over evil continues through the ages. It identifies the good and evil within the culture presenting the images.

The plot or mode of all three stories can trace their literary origins back to Greek myths, the heroic stories of the Bible, and Celtic legends equally as old. These narratives can be told in a thousand different settings, but the relationship between the reader or viewer and the idea remains the same. What identifies the difference is how the creative techniques of the media set them apart from all the other versions. The more familiar the story is, the more creative the storyteller must be. The same literary devices are available to all writers and generally the same film techniques to all directors. We look to the one that attracts us in some new or different manner.

As a midterm exam, you are asked to perform the following: Write an essay in which you compare and contrast **one** combination of film and novel not studied in class. The combination may be taken from the list in Appendix C or, with teacher approval, a combination not on the list. The essay should respond to one of the following prompts:

1. Select a novel that evoked a strong response. Once you have selected the novel, evaluate to what degree the film was able to convey the aspect(s) of the novel that evoked the response. The premise is that it is one or more elements of the novel that, through the manipulation and skill of the author, is able to make a connection between the reader and the fundamental mythological/archetypal truth. That truth originates somewhere in an ancient version, but it is the present-day counterpart that causes your response. Did the film, through its individual elements, improve the level of communication, or did it fail? Compare and contrast the media presentations using the stated premise as a base for your thesis.

2. You may choose to respond from a purely critical perspective. Looking at all the combinations, perhaps there is one you feel, due to its theme or *mana* identity, will remain a part of our culture, attaining a classic status. Will both versions become classic, as did *The Grapes of Wrath*, or is one obviously classic material in its field while the other medium lacks something? With this choice, you will focus on one presentational form as the strong reason, with the other form acting as a supplement. Be sure your support is taken from the material in Chapter 2.

An approach can be made from one or more perspectives: (a) Your response was stimulated by the story's relevance in contemporary society; (b) a more personal connection, the narrative may relate closely to a similar experience(s); (c) if you are a serious academic student, how the narrative connects to aspects of psychology, sociology, anthropology, philosophy, whatever else is your particular area of interest. Whatever the approach, the foundation of your support should be derived using the elements identified in Chapter 2. In each area of support, one form will ultimately be more effective in expressing its truth. A conclusion should be made as to the superior form and be explained using principles of logic.

Form requirements for the essay:

1. A minimum of 500 words (not fewer than two or more than four pages).

2. Typed and double-spaced using 12-point type.

3. If outside sources are used, follow MLA parenthetical form for referencing, including an accurate and properly recorded list of works cited on the final page. Works cited, if identified in context, will not require a separate page. (optional)

4. Title page should include your name, instructor's name, class with section number and date due. See the syllabus for due date.

Appendix B

Research Project

Complete a documented essay comparing and contrasting a myth, a related novel, and a motion picture based on the novel. Subjects may be selected from the approved list. A novel-film combination not on the the list may be chosen *only with the instructor's approval*. The known myth will be included within the essay in similar manner to the text material. The novel-film combinations included in the text are not available for this assignment. One aspect for consideration should be the quality of the novel *and* the film. Quality is determined by the novel and film's reception as expressed through criticism, media awards, and commercial success.

ESSAY REQUIREMENTS

1. Follow MLA or APA form for both heading and referencing. The paper must conform to one style. All deviations will be subject to point deductions.
   A. Parenthetical documentation with a Works Cited page
   B. 1–1.25-inch margins, double-spaced; heading and title on page 1
2. A minimum of three literary and three film criticisms. Copies of annotated reviews and criticisms should be attached to the final paper. Use hilight pen for annotations; include marginal notes or comments.
3. The paper should be 750 to 1,000 words (three pages minimum, five maximum).
4. Essays due:

AREAS FOR RESEARCH

For the novel, search the Online Public Access Catalog (OPAC) by using the title as the subject (*s=title*). Check both the library catalog and the magazine and journal databases. A second search should be in the book reference section: *Literary Criticism*. Search both the author and title indexes for locations (volume and page numbers of criticisms).

For the film, search the OPAC. For the novel, use the film title as the subject; however, you should also search *s=motion picture, criticism*. Check for dates and specific genres to determine if the time or subject area is the focus of criticism. This may require looking for the full data. To verify a criticism will require locating the book and checking its index.

For students with access to the Internet, many novel and film reviews and criticisms are available. Use titles, author names, directors, and film collections as keywords to begin searches. Also, many newspapers and magazines have web pages allowing access to contents.

A quick search should be made of *The Reader's Guide*; volumes reflect a year's magazine and journal articles. Select the year's volume in which the motion picture debuted and look under "Motion Pictures." Reviews and criticisms for films are listed alphabetically. Magazines available in the library are marked in the front of the volume.

Thesis choices should follow one of these: *The novel or film* . . .

1. Was more/less effective in communicating the author's theme.
2. Created a greater influence or emotional impact.
3. Became a classic while the other is practically forgotten.
4. Amplified the author's theme to such an extent some facet of the culture changed.
5. Was imminently more successful than its counterpart. (Commercially or critically).
6. Evoked an idea or concept that was different than any of the above.

Although the focus of the essay is to be on content, each subject chosen must be connected to an ancient myth or truth. For essay purposes, you may consider Bible stories as myths. Use the text material as a model for your analysis and for interweaving myth, film, and novel. The text should not be modeled in length, only in the form of content and the interweaving of ancient myth with a contemporary presentation. Use any myth identified in the text. If you have difficulty in making a connection to a myth, discuss it with a classmate or the teacher.

Appendix C

Reading and Film List

Not all listed novels are still in print; however, they should be available through a library or possibly in a used book store. Film availability will depend on individual store or library inventory. Films labeled C are in color; if no C is present, the film is black and white. TVM denotes the film was made for television.

A Farewell to Arms by Ernest Hemingway
    Film: d. Frank Borzage 1932 78 min.
           d. Charles Vidor 1957 C/152 min.

The Accidental Tourist by Anne Tyler
    Film: d. Lawrence Kasdan 1988 C/121 min. (PG)

Advise and Consent by Allen Drury
    Film: d. Otto Preminger 1962 139 min.

All the King's Men by Robert Penn Warren
    Film: d. Robert Rossen 1949 109 min.

Amistad by David Pesci
    Film: d. Steven Spielberg 1997 C/232 min.

Animal Farm by George Orwell
    Film: animated, d. John Halas 1955/British C/75 min

Being There by Jerzy Kosinski
    Film: d. Hal Ashby 1979 C/130 min. (PG)

The Best Years of Our Lives by McKinley Kantor
    Film: d. William Wyler 1946 172 min.

The Big Sleep by Raymond Chandler
    Films: d. Howard Hawks 1946 114 min.
        d. Michael Winner, British 1978 C/100 min. (R)

Billy Budd by Herman Melville
    Film: U.S./British d. Peter Ustinov 1962 119 min.

The Blackboard Jungle by Evan Hunter
    Film: d. Richard Brooks 1955 101 min.

Bram Stoker's Dracula, novel *Dracula* by Bram Stoker
    Films: d. Dan Curtis 1973 C/100 min. TVM
        d. Francis Ford Coppola 1992 C/123 min. (R)

Bridges of Madison County by Robert James Waller
    Film: d. Clint Eastwood 1995 C/135 (PG-13)

The Caine Mutiny by Herman Wouk
    Film: d. Edward Dmytryk 1954 C/125 min.

Captain Newman, M.D. by Leo Rosten
    Film: d. David Miller 1963 C/126 min.

The Chase by Horton Foote
    Film: d. Arthur Penn 1966 C/135

The Chosen by Chaim Potok
    Film: d. Jeremy Paul Kagan 1981 C/108 min. (PG)

The Color Purple by Alice Walker
    Film: d. Steven Spielberg 1985 C/152 min. (PG-13)

Compulsion by Meyer Levin
    Film: d. Richard Fleisher 1959 B/W 103 min.

Contact by Carl Sagan
    Film: d. Robert Zemeckis 1997 C/150 min. (PG)

Cool Hand Luke by J. Pearce
    Film: d. Stuart Rosenberg 1967 C/126 min.

"The Dead" short story by James Joyce
    Film: d. John Huston 1987 C/83 (PG)

The Devil and Daniel Webster by Stephen Vincent Benet
    Film: d. William Dieterle 1941 85 min.

Dr. Jekyll and Mr. Hyde by Robert Louis Stevenson
    Film: d. Rouben Mamoulian 1932 97 min.
        d. Victor Fleming 1941 114 min.

The Duellists from "The Duel" by Joseph Conrad
    Film: d. Ridley Scott 1977/British C/101 min. (PG)

Dune by Frank Herbert
    Film: d. David Lynch 1984 C/140 min. (PG-13)

East of Eden by John Steinbeck
    Film: d. Elia Kazan 1955 C/115

The Education of Little Tree by Forrest (Asa) Carter
    Film: d. Richard Friedenberg 1998 C/117 (PG)

Elmer Gantry by Sinclair Lewis
    Film: d. Richard Brooks 1960 C/145 min.

Female Perversions by Dr. Louise J. Kaplan (non-fiction)
    Film: d. Susan Streitfield 1997 C/119 min. (R)

Field of Dreams novel: *Shoeless Joe* by W. P. Kinsella
    Film: d. Phil Alden Robinson 1989 106 min. (PG)

From Here to Eternity by James Jones
    Film: d. Fred Zinnemann 1953 118 min.

Giant by Edna Ferber
    Film: d. George Stevens 1956 C/201 min.

Goodbye Mr. Chips by James Hilton
    Films: d. Sam Wood 1939 U.S./British 114 min.
           d. Herbert Ross 1969 C/151 (G)

The Graduate by Charles Webb
    Film: d. Mike Nichols 1967 C/105 min. (R)

Grapes of Wrath by John Steinbeck
    Film: d. John Ford 1940 129 min.

Great Expectations by Charles Dickens
    Films: d. Stuart Walker 1934 C/100 min.
           d. David Lean 1946 British 118 min.
           d. Joseph Hardy 1974 U.S./British C/103 TVM
           d. Alfonso Cuaron 1998 C/122 min. (R)

The Great Santini (The Ace) by Pat Conroy
    Film: d. Lewis John Carlino 1979 C/116 min. (PG)

The Haunting from "The Haunting of Hill House" by Shirley Jackson
    Film: d. Robert Wise 1963 112 min.

Horseman Pass By/Hud by Larry McMurtry
    Film: d. Martin Ritt 1963 112 min.

Howard's End by E. M. Forster
    Film: d. James Ivory 1992 British C/140 min. (PG)

The Hunchback of Notre Dame by Victor Hugo
    Film: d. Michael Tuchner 1982 C150 min. TVM
          d. William Dieterle 1939 115 min.

I Am a Fugitive from a Chain Gang by Robert E. Burns (autobiography)
    Film: d. Mervyn LeRoy 1932 93 min.

I Never Promised You a Rose Garden by Hannah Green (autobiographical)
    Film: d. Anthony Page 1977 C/96 min. (R)

Intruder in the Dust by William Faulkner
    Film: d. Clarence Brown 1949 87 min.

In Cold Blood by Truman Capote
    Film: d. Richard Brooks 1967 134 min.

Jane Eyre by Charlotte Brontë
    Films: d. Christy Cabanne 1934 67 min.
            d. Robert Stevenson 1944 96 min.

Jurassic Park by Michael Crichton 1990
    Film: d. Steven Spielberg 1993 126 min. (PG-13)

Kiss of the Spider Woman by Manuel Puig
    d. Hector Babenco U.S./Brazilian 1985 C-B/W 119 min. (R)

The Last Picture Show by Larry McMurtry
    Film: d. Peter Bogdanovich 1971 118 min. (R)

Lolita by Vladimir Nabokov
    Film: d. Stanley Kubrick 1962 152 min.
            d. Adrian Lyne 1998 C/130 min. (R)

Lonely Are the Brave / Brave Cowboy by Edward Abbey
    Film: d. David Miller 1962 107 min.

Lords of Discipline by Pat Conroy
    Film: d. Franc Roddam 1983 C/102 min. (R)

Madame Bovary by Gustave Flaubert
    Film: d. Vincente Minelli 1949 115 min.

The Maltese Falcon short story by Dashiell Hammett
    Films: d. Roy Del Ruth 1931 80 min.
            d. John Huston 1941 100 min.

The Manchurian Candidate by Richard Condon
    Film: d. John Frankenheimer 1962 126 min.

M*A*S*H by Robert Hooker (Robert Hornberger)
    Film: d. Robert Altman 1970 C/116 min. (PG & R)

Masque of the Red Death, from a short story by Edgar Allan Poe
    Films: d. Roger Corman 1964 C/86 min.
            d. Larry Brand 1989 C/83 min. (R)

Midnight Cowboy by James Leo Herlihy
    Film: d. John Schlesinger 1969 C/113 min. (R)

Misery by Stephen King
    Film: d. Rob Reiner 1990 C/107 min. (R)

Mosquito Coast by Paul Theroux
    Film: d. Peter Weir 1986 C/117 min. (PG)

Mother Night by Kurt Vonnegut
    Film: d. Keith Gordon 1996 C/113 min. (R)

1984 by George Orwell
    Film: d. Michael Anderson 1956 British 91 min. (R)

Nineteen Eighty-Four
    Film: d. Michael Radford 1984 British C/115 min. (R)

Nobody's Fool by Richard Russo
    Film: d. Robert Benton 1994 C/110 min. (R)

Oliver Twist by Charles Dickens
    Films: d. David Lean 1948 British 105 min.
           d. Clive Donner 1982 TVM C/100 min.
           d. Carol Reed 1968 British C/153 min. *Oliver!* (Musical) (G)

One Flew Over the Cookoo's Nest by Ken Kesey 1962
    Film: d. Milos Forman 1975 C/133 min. (R)

The Ox-Bow Incident by Walter Van Tilburg Clark
    Film: d. William A. Wellman 1943 73 min.

A Portrait of the Artist as a Young Man by James Joyce
    Film: d. Joseph Strick 1979 C/98 min.

Postcards from the Edge by Carrie Fisher
    Film: d. Mike Nichols 1990 C/101 min. (R)

Primary Colors by anonymous
    Film: d. Mike Nichols 1997 C/135 min. (R)

The Razor's Edge by Somerset Maugham
    Films: d. Edmond Goulding 1946 146 min.
           d. John Byrum 1984 C/128 min. (PG-13)

Red River from a *Saturday Evening Post* story by Borden Chase
    Film: d. Howard Hawks 1948 133 min.

Red Sky at Morning by Richard Bradford
    Film: d. James Goldstone 1970 C/112 min. (PG)

"Rita Hayworth and the Shawshank Redemption" *Different Seasons* by Stephen King
    Film: *Shawshank Redemption* d. Frank Durabont 1994 C/142 (R)

A River Runs through It by Norman MacLean
    Film: d. Robert Redford 1992 C/123 min. (PG)

Schindler's List/Schlinder's Ark by Thomas Kenealy
    Film: d. Steven Spielberg 1993 C-B/W 195 min (R)

Seize the Day by Saul Bellow
    Film: d. Fielder Cook 1986 C/93 min. (PG)

Seven Years in Tibet autobiographical novel by Heinrich Harrer
    Film: d. Jean-Jacques Annaud 1997 C/131 min. (PG-13)

Shane by Jack Schaefer 1949
    Film: d. George Stevens 1953 C/118 min.

Ship of Fools by Katherine Anne Porter
    Film: d. Stanley Kramer 1965 149 min.

The Shootist by Glendon Swarthout
    Film: d. Don Siegel 1976 C/99 min. (PG)

Silence of the Lambs by Thomas Harris
    Film: d. Jonathan Demme 1991 C/118 min. (R)

Smooth Talk/"Where Are You Going?—Where Have You Been?" by Joyce Carol Oates
    Film: d. Joyce Chopra 1985 C/92 min. (PG-13)

The Snake Pit by Mary Jane Ward
  Film: d. Anatole Litvak 1948 108 min.

They Shoot Horses, Don't They? by Horace McCoy
  Film: d. Sydney Pollack 1969 C/121 min. (M/PG)

Tortilla Flat by John Steinbeck
  Film: d. Victor Fleming 1942 105 min.

Total Recall by Phillip K. Dick
  Film: d. Paul Verhoeven 1990 C/109 min (R)

Touch by Elmore Leonard
  Film: d. Paul Schrader 1997 C/97 min. (R)

20,000 Leagues Under the Sea by Jules Verne
  Film: d. Richard Fleiscer 1954 C/127 min.

The Verdict by Barry Reed
  Film: d. Sidney Lumet 1982 C/129. (R)

Wag the Dog novel: *American Hero* by Larry Beinhart
  Film: d. Barry Levinson 1998 C/98 min. (R)

The Wings of the Dove by Henry James
  Film: d. Lain Softley 1997 C/103 min. (R)

The World According to Garp by John Irving
  Film: d. George Roy Hill 1982 C/136 min. (R)

Wuthering Heights by Emily Brontë
  Film: d. William Wyler 1939 103 min.
        d. Robert Fuest 1970 C/105 min (G)

Works Cited

Aldridge, John W. "The Fabrication of a Culture Hero." *Saturday Review*. 24 Apr 71. Rpt. *Contemporary Literary Criticism*. 25:231.

———. "The Young Writer in America: 1945–1951." *After the Lost Generation*. New York: McGraw-Hill, 1951

"A review of *The Last Picture Show*." *Kirkus Reviews*. Sept. 1966.

Arieti, Silvano. *Creativity, the Magic Synthesis*. New York: Basic Books, 1976.

Atchity, Kenneth. *Los Angeles Times Book Review*. 27 Aug 82.

Bachofen, J. J. *Myth, Religion, and Mother Right: Selected Writings of J. J. Bachofen*. Ralph Manhein, trans. Princeton, N.J.: Princeton University Press, 1967.

Baker, Carlos. *The Writer as Artist*. Princeton: Princeton University Press, 1952.

Barthes, Roland. *Mythologies*. Trans. by Annette Lavers. New York: Hill and Wang, 1995.

Bierlein, J. F. *Parallel Myths*. New York: Ballantine Books, 1994.

Blake, Richard A. *America*. 28 Dec. 96.

Bluestone, George. *Novels into Film*. Berkeley: University of California Press, 1966.

Bonnefoy, Yves. *Mythologies*. Chicago: University of Chicago Press, 1991.

Brockway, Robert W. *Myth from the Ice Age to Mickey Mouse*. Albany: State University of New York Press, 1993.

Cahill, Thomas. *How the Irish Saved Civilization*. New York: Anchor Books, 1995.

Calder, Jenni. *There Must Be a Lone Ranger*. New York: Taplinger, 1975.

Campbell, Joseph. *Masks: Occidental*. New York: Viking Press, 1964.

———. *Masks: Creative*. New York: Viking Press, 1968.

———. *The Mythic Image*. New York: MJF Books, 1974.

———. *The Hero with a Thousand Faces*. Princeton, N.J.: Princeton University Press, 1968.

———. *The Inner Reaches of Outer Space*. New York: Harper & Row. 1986.

Camus, Albert. "The Myth of Sisyphus." Trans. by Justin O'Brien. New York: Knopf, 1955.

Cassier, Ernst. *An Essay on Man.* Cambridge: Cambridge University Press, 1944.

Cavendish, Richard, ed. *Legends of the World.* New York: Barnes and Noble, 1989.

Chambers, Robert H., ed. *Twentieth Century Interpretations of All the King's Men.* Englewood Cliffs, N.J.: Prentice Hall, 1977.

Cheuse, Alan. "Horror Writer's Holiday." *New York Times Book Review.* 29 Aug. 1982.

Choyce, Lesley. "Three Hits and a Miss." *Books in Canada.* Nov. 1984.

Clark, Walter Van Tilburg. *The Ox-Bow Incident.* New York: Signet Classic, 1940.

Conrad, Joseph. *Heart of Darkness: Norton Critical Edition.* Robert Kimbrough, ed. New York: W. W. Norton Company, 1969.

Connolly, Cressida. "A Time to Love and a Time to Die." *The Spectator.* 5 Sept. 1992.

Cozic, Charles P., ed. *American Values.* San Diego: Greenhaven Press, 1995

Eagleton, Terry. *Literary Theory.* Minneapolis: University of Minnesota Press, 1983.

Ebert, Roger. *Roger Ebert's Movie Yearbook 1996.* Kansas City, Mo.: Andrews McMeel, 1996.

Eliot, Alexander. *The Universal Myths.* New York: Meridian, 1976.

Emerson, Ralph Waldo. "Boston Transcendentalism." *American Literature,* vol. 2. Barrows Educational Series by Darrel Abel. Woodbury, N.Y., 1963.

Falck, Colin. *Myth, Truth, and Literature.* Cambridge: University of Cambridge Press, 1995.

Folsom, James K. *The American Western Novel.* New Haven, Conn.: College and University Press, 1966.

Frazer, Sir James George. *The Golden Bough.* New York: Collier Books, 1922.

Frye, Northrop. *Anatomy of Criticism.* Princeton, NJ: Princeton University Press, 1971.

————. "The Archetypes of Literature." *Myth and Method.* James E. Miller, ed. Lincoln: University of Nebraska Press, 1980.

Goodwyn, Larry. *The Frontier Myth and Southwestern Literature.* American Libraries 2:4 (April, 1971).

Graves, Robert. *Parallel Myths by J. F. Bierlein.* New York: Ballantine Books, 1994.

Guerin, Wilfred, et al. *A Handbook of Critical Approaches to Literature.* 3rd ed. New York: Oxford University Press, 1992.

Gurko, Leo. *Ernest Hemingway and the Pursuit of Heroism.* New York: Thomas Crowell Company, 1968.

Hawkes, Terence. *Structuralism and Semiotics.* Berkeley: University of California Press, 1977.

Hemingway, Ernest. *The Sun Also Rises.* New York: Charles Scribner & Sons, 1926.

Holman, C. Hugh. *A Handbook to Literature.* 3rd ed. New York: The Odyssey Press, 1972.

Hotz, Robert Lee. *The Arizona Republic.* 29 Oct. 1997.

Hyman, Stanley Edgar. "The Best of Hemingway." *Standards: A Chronicle of Books for Our Time.* New York: Horizon Press, 1966.

Jaffe, Aniela. "Symbolism in the Visual Arts." *Man and His Symbols* by Carl G. Jung. New York: Doubleday, 1964.

Jaynes, Julian. *The Origin of Consciousness and the Breakdown of the Bicameral Mind.* Boston: Houghton Mifflin, 1976, 1990.

Josephs, Allen. "Hemingway's Spanish Sensibility." *The Cambridge Companion to Ernest Hemingway.* Ed. Scott Donaldson. New York: Cambridge University Press, 1996. 221–242.

Jung, Carl G. *Man and His Symbols.* New York: Doubleday, 1964.

———. *The Essential Jung.* Anthony Storr, ed. New York: MJF Books, 1983.

Kesey, Ken. *One Flew over the Cuckoo's Nest.* New York: Signet Books, 1962.

King, Stephen. *Different Seasons.* "Rita Hayworth and the Shawshank Redemption." New York: Signet Books, 1983.

Kinsella, W. P. *Shoeless Joe.* New York: Ballantine Books, 1982.

Kirk, G. S. *Myth.* Berkeley: University of California Press, 1970.

Kosinski, Jerzy. *Being There.* New York: Bantam Books, 1972.

Landess, Thomas. *Larry McMurtry.* Austin, Texas: Steck-Vaughn Co., 1969.

Lane, Anthony. "Swept Away." *The New Yorker.* 25 Nov. 1996.

Lawrence, Frank. *Hemingway and the Movies.* Jackson: University of Miss. Press, 1981.

Levi-Strauss, Claude. *The Savage Mind.* Chicago: University of Chicago Press, 1966.

———. *Structural Anthropology.* London: Penguin Books, 1972.

Malinowski, Bronislaw. *Magic, Science, and Religion.* New York: Anchor Books, 1954.

Maltin, Leonard et al. *1996 Movie and Video Guide.* New York: Signet, 1996.

McMurtry, Larry. *The Last Picture Show.* New York: Simon and Schuster, 1966.

Medved, Michael. *Hollywood vs. America.* New York: Harper Perennial, 1993.

Monaco, James. *American Film Now.* New York: Oxford University Press, 1979.

———. *How to Read a Film.* New York: Oxford University Press, 1981.

Nietzche, Friedrich. "Live Dangerously." *Existentialism from Dostoevsky to Sartre.* Walter Kaufman, ed. New York: New American Library, 1975.

Okrent, Daniel. "Shoeless Joe." *New York Times Book Review.* 25 July 1982.

Ondaatje, Michael. *The English Patient.* New York: Vintage Books, 1992.

Ornstein, Robert. *The Right Mind.* New York: Harcourt Brace & Co., 1997.

Panati, Charles. *Sacred Origins of Profound Things.* New York: Penguin Books, 1996.

Parker-Smith, Bettye J. "Alice Walker's Women." *Black Women Writers*, Mari Evans, ed. New York: Anchor Press/Doubleday, 1984.

Partridge, Eric. *Origins.* New York: Greenwich House, 1983.

Peavey, Charles D. "Coming of Age in Texas: The Novels of Larry McMurtry." *Western American Literature.* Fall, 1969.

Phillips, Gene D. *Hemingway and Film.* New York: Frederich Unger Publishing Co., 1980.

Plato. "The Republic, Book I." *Social and Political Philosophy.* John Somerville and Ronald E. Santoni, eds. Garden City, N.Y.: Anchor Books, 1963.

Pudovkin, V. I. *Film Technique and Film Acting.* Ivor Montagu, trans. and ed. New York: Grove Press, 1958.

Puhvel, Jaan. *Comparative Mythology*. Baltimore: Johns Hopkins University Press, 1987.

Rutherford, Ward. *Celtic Mythology*. New York: Sterling Publishing Co. Inc., 1990.

Sartre, Jean-Paul. *Being and Nothingness*. Trans. and intro. by Hazel E. Barnes. New York: Citadel Press, 1964.

————. "Existentialism is a Humanism." *Existentialism from Dostoevsky to Sartre*. Walter Kaufman, trans. and ed. New York: New American Library, 1975.

Schaefer, Jack. *Shane*. Boston: Houghton Mifflin, 1964.

Schatz, Thomas. *Hollywood Genres*. Philadelphia: Temple University Press, 1981.

Schein, Harry. "The Olympian Cowboy." *The American Scholar*. Summer 1955.

Segal, Robert A. *Joseph Campbell: An Introduction*. New York: Penguin Books, 1990.

Simon, Hohn. "The Hungarian Patient." *National Review*. 31 Dec. 1996.

Smith, Huston. *The Religions of Man*. New York: Harper & Row, 1958, 1965,

Spice, Nicholas. "Ways of Being a Man." *London Review of Books*. 24 Sept. 1992.

Steinem, Gloria. "Do You Know This Woman." *Ms.*, June 1982.

Stout, Janis P. "Journey as a Metaphor for Cultural Loss in the Novels of Larry McMurtry." *Western American Literature*. Fall, 1969.

Thoreau, Henry David. "Civil Disobedience." *Social and Political Philosophy*. John Somerville and Ronald E. Santoni, eds. Garden City, N.Y.: Anchor Books, 1963.

Toynbee, Arnold. *Myth from the Ice Age to Mickey Mouse* by Robert W. Brockway. Albany: State University of New York Press, 1993.

Tyler, Parker. *Magic and Myth of the Movies*. New York: H. Holt, 1947.

Walker, Alice. *The Color Purple*. New York: Washington Square Press, 1982.

————. "In the Closet of the Soul" *Ms.*, Nov. 1986.

"Walker, Alice." *Contemporary Literary Criticism*. Daniel Marowski and Roger Maty, eds. Vol. 46:422. Detroit, Mich.: Gale Research, 1988.

Weston, Jessie. *From Ritual to Romance*. Garden City, N.Y.: Doubleday Anchor Books, 1957.

Wheelwright, Philip. "Notes on Mythopoeia." *Myth and Literature*. John B Vickery, ed. Lincoln, Nebraska: University of Nebraska Press, 1966.

Index

About the Author

WILLIAM K. FERRELL is a Professor in the English department at Glendale Community College in Arizona.

ISBN 0-275-96757-3

9 780275 967574

HARDCOVER BAR CODE

90000>

EAN